Uncommon Calling

UNCOMMON CALLING

A Gay Man's Struggle to Serve the Church

Chris Glaser

HarperSanFrancisco

A Division of HarperCollins*Publishers*

Library of Congress Cataloging-in-Publication Data

Glaser, Chris.
    Uncommon calling.

    1. Glaser, Chris.   2. Presbyterians—United States—
Biography.   3. Gays—United States—Biography.
4. Homosexuality—Religious aspects—Christianity.
5. Church work with gays.   I. Title.
BX9225.G54A3   1988   285′.137′0924[B]   87-46207
ISBN 0-06-0633122-8 (pbk.)

91 92 MPC 10 9 8 7 6 5 4

To gays and lesbians
who struggle to keep faith

CONTENTS

Foreword by Virginia Ramey Mollenkott   ix

Introduction by John Boswell   xvii

Preface   xxi

1. Growing Up Christian and Gay   1
   (Baltimore, June 1976 and Los Angeles, 1950–
   1970)

2. Exploring Social Justice and Sexuality   14
   (Los Angeles, 1970–1972)

3. Reconciling Homosexuality and Christianity   31
   (Los Angeles, Summer and Fall 1972)

4. Coming Out to My Family   47
   (Los Angeles, November 1972)

5. Letting Go: Sacrifice and Liberation   61
   (Los Angeles, December 1972–August 1973)

6. Spirituality and Ministry   71
   (New Haven, Fall 1973)

7. Coming Out at Seminary   85
   (New Haven, Winter–Spring 1974)

8. Coming Out to the Church   101
   (Los Angeles, Summer 1974)

9. Experiencing Homophobia   110
   (New Haven, Fall 1974–Spring 1975)

10. Beginning a Ministry with Gays   121
    (Philadelphia, Fall 1975–Spring 1976)

11. Becoming a Gay Rights Advocate within the
    Church   139
    (Baltimore, Philadelphia, and West Hollywood,
    Summer 1976)

12. The Task Force to Study Homosexuality   150
    (October 1976–February 1978)

13. The Task Force Recommendations and the
    Conservative Backlash   166
    (Summer 1977–Spring 1978)

14. The Presbyterian General Assembly   189
    (San Diego, May 1978)

Epilogue   207
   (West Hollywood, October 1987)

FOREWORD

My predominant impression of Chris Glaser is of a man who incarnates prophetic patience: prophetic in that he persists in trying to awaken the church from its slumber of stupendous ignorance; patience in that he never seems to lose his temper.

Consider, for example, the 1985 Presbyterian General Assembly in Indianapolis. I was there to address the luncheon of Presbyterians for Lesbian and Gay Concerns (PLGC). It was the first time that I had overtly claimed my lesbianism before an audience other than the Governing Board of the National Council of Churches of Christ. After the luncheon, several members of PLGC were to meet with several leaders of the "healing ministries" within the Presbyterian Church, with "healing" defined as turning gay people into nongay or sexually nonfunctioning people. In the hope that my presence might be helpful, I went along to the meeting as part of the PLGC contingent.

I felt stunned when the most powerful member of the "healing" contingent showed up wearing an enormous button that proclaimed the advice, "Don't hassle." I tried to imagine myself as a leader of a white middle-class political organization meeting with some hungry and homeless people who wanted to protest the insensitivity of my organization to their needs. What an insult it would be for me to wear a button telling them not to hassle me! I imagined myself as a corporate executive meeting with a group of underpaid workers whom I had just fired in order to move my lucrative plant to a place where labor would be even cheaper—and thought about the impact of wearing a button telling them they really shouldn't hassle me. I imagined myself a hospital administrator meeting with a group of people with AIDS to explain why my hospital would not provide them with medical care, and the implications of my wearing a "Don't hassle" button to that meeting.

Here was a white heterosexual seminary professor meeting with gay Christian women and men, denying our testimonies of God's presence within us, telling us we need to be healed of our very identity—and at the same time advising *us* not to hassle *him!* I became so angry at his cool "Joe College" demeanor that I was unable to speak calmly. And when "Joe College" accused me of bitterness, it was Chris Glaser who quietly, patiently explained that whereas the man with the button was approaching things from the privileged perspective of the normative group, our whole *lives* were on the line. Therefore a humorously pleasant and objective demeanor was considerably harder for us to maintain!

I left that meeting discouraged at my own rage and full of admiration for Chris Glaser's impeccable self-control and sweet reason. Perhaps my anger was as important as his conciliatory persuasiveness. But even when I fail to manifest it, I am a great admirer of prophetic patience.

In *Uncommon Calling*, Chris Glaser tells us where he gets both the courage to prophesy and the apparently tireless patience: from a disciplined prayer life. But I confess that I was relieved to learn from this book that at times even Chris Glaser uses a less irenic approach: when a "high-steepled" pastor who had just voted against the ordination of qualified gay people asked Chris not to take it personally, Chris refused the proferred handshake that would have had the effect of legitimizing that unjust act.

In 1978 Letha Scanzoni and I collaborated in writing a book called *Is the Homosexual My Neighbor? Another Christian View.* Ever since, I have been busy trying to build bridges between the church and the gay community. During all those years of lay ministry, at first from within the closet (a daily crucifixion) and now from outside the closet (an alarming yet empowering resurrection), I have become increasingly aware of the energy generated by uniting authentic spirituality with authentic sexuality. Like faith without works (or works without faith), the one is dead without the other. As Chris says, in contemporary American society it is often easier to discuss sexuality than spirituality: "to share honestly one's faith and one's doubts is a far more intimate activity than sharing one's sexual orientation." Yet Chris has persisted in bringing not only his sexuality but also his spirituality and his call to ministry out of the closet. And along every step of the way, each has provided meaning to the other. Chris's life thus forms a first-rate role model for people of faith, gay or non-gay: "We need to teach [our sexuality and spirituality] to dance together in complementarity, inspiring and fulfilling each other as lovers rather than pushing one another away. Spirituality should not be a wallflower at the disco on Saturday night any more than sexuality and sensuality should be wallflowers in worship on Sunday morning."

I know a great many gay women and men who are ordained pastors and priests working from within hideously constrictive closets. Silence about their sexual identity and denial of the full nature of their closest relationship is the price they pay for the ministry to which they feel called. Although the church is willing to utilize gay or lesbian labor as long as the laborer pretends to be either heterosexual or celibate, to date most churches will not confer ordination on people of Chris Glaser's integrity, people whose public and private life are equally open, honest, and sincere. It is not really their gayness the church rejects: it is the integration of gay sexuality with spirituality and ministry that the church finds objectionable.

Thus the church's stance forces some people into sexual bulimia, splurging in irresponsible sex and then purging in equally irresponsible piety. Many others are forced into the pretense that exacts a terrific toll from their ability to be warm and relaxed, even in private. But although gay clergy lose a lot, the church loses even more. It loses the power that openness would bestow upon gay clergy. It loses potential clergy like Chris Glaser who will not purchase ordination at the expense of the closet. And it loses the full experience of God's grace that can only be felt by extending that grace to everyone.

Having looked at the closet door from both sides, I am

aware that the matter is quite complex. On the one hand, I fully agree with Chris that instead of repenting of their orientation, perhaps gay women and men most need to repent of their closets. Ultimately, the church will grant justice to gay people only when the issue has been sufficiently personalized by the faces of thousands of gay Christians who openly thank God for the good gift of their sexuality. On the other hand, as a feminist I am also aware that gay people, like feminist people, are living in an alien or occupied territory called patriarchy. To the degree that we speak and act out of our conviction of human equality in God's image, we are subversive of the patriarchal status quo. Like the French underground during Nazi occupation, we cannot openly announce our subversive intentions without endangering our lives and our efforts. Like the Egyptian midwives who lied to their Pharaoh in order to spare the lives of Hebrew baby boys (Exodus 1:15–21), sometimes very honest people living within unjust systems are forced to lie in order to preserve their opportunity to serve humankind in the capacity to which they feel called. Subversion, posing, and lying are always dangerous to our souls; but sometimes, alas, they are necessary. Furthermore, total disclosure has never been a moral imperative. Each of us must learn to be sensitive to the guidance of God's Spirit within the deep center of our beings. And each of us must be prepared to pay the price of acting upon that guidance.

At any rate, thank God for Chris Glaser, who has found a ministry after all, despite church people's ignorant and prejudiced attitudes. If *Uncommon Calling* is read with even half the love and care Chris put into writing it, the book will result in miracles of healing grace.

Virginia Ramey Mollenkott
Hewitt, New Jersey

INTRODUCTION

Finding oneself in conflict with the church is a hallowed Christian tradition. Suffragettes, abolitionists, pilgrims, Protestant reformers, St. Joan of Arc, St. Francis, early monastics—almost every major reformer in Christian history was condemned and opposed by other Christians for beliefs or lifestyles or both. This might have been anticipated: the founder of the religion also encountered opposition and hostility from the authorities of his day, and he explicitly warned his followers that they would not endear themselves to the establishment—religious or secular—by pursuing his teachings.

Although Christianity began as a radical alternative to existing social and religious structures, its very success eventually transformed it into the establishment itself, and then it was as often part of the problem as it was the solution. From as early as the fourth century A.D. Christians were confusing Christian society with the Christian religion, and assuming that the rules about behavior they learned from family, friends, teachers, laws, public discourse, and so forth, must be Christianity, because the people who taught them were Christians and part of a Christian state. "In order to be moral," Augustine wrote in *The Good of Marriage,* "an act must not violate nature, custom, or law," forgetting perhaps that Jesus had frequently violated all three.

In fact, the majority of the customs and laws of Western Christian societies have not been Christian in any meaningful sense. Many statutes and customs that would seem to be derived from "Christian morality," such as those prohibiting marriage with close relatives and determining the date and mode of celebrating Christmas, are derived from explicitly pagan traditions. Confusing such human constructs with religious principles is precisely the mistake Jesus warned his disciples against when he criticized the Pharisees. Although they were devoted to God's revelation, the Pharisees consistently elevated their cultural habits to the status of religious truth or failed to see any underlying truth that might override literal understandings of scripture or traditions.

We could all learn from Jesus' message to the Pharisees. We are all Pharisees at times, and Jesus called us all to strive to become outsiders in regard to the religious establishment, challenging it to understand morality and Christian hope at a deeper level, to separate God's message from our cultural context, to focus on the essential rather than the external in formulating a godly society.

Nowhere have the conflicts between the religious establishment and Christian reformers been more acute in the second half of the twentieth century than in the case of gay people. As early as the 1950s Quakers were comparing homosexuality to left-handedness as something irrelevant to Christian morality and important only because of cultural prejudice. But many Christian bodies are still wrangling acrimoniously over the acceptance of gay people as clergy or even as members of the church.

Other minorities have fought oppression by Christian society: Jews, black people, women. In each of these cases the establishment used religious claims to justify inequality or injustice and the churches were often among the last organizations to respond to reform. Schools in the South, for example, were integrated before most churches; women have much greater access to civil office in most of this country than to ecclesiastical positions. When we now look back we find it incredible, for the most part, that scripture or Christian teaching was used to defend such inequities, but these efforts were not simply the cynical manipulations of malicious people: they were often the result of sincere confusion of social patterns with the Christian message. The conflation occured in both directions: since black people occupied an inferior place in Christian society, it seemed a "Christian" tenet that blacks were inferior, though there is no such Christian teaching. Since Paul said that women were to keep quiet in church and remain subordinate to men in the household, they obviously should occupy an inferior position in civil structures as well, although this did not follow logically even from the most literal understanding of the Pauline utterances. It is only hindsight that enables us to separate an underlying social prejudice from the fragments of religious tradition used to make it presentable.

Fragments of this sort are still used to buttress arguments against acceptance of gay people. There were objections in the early Church to homosexual acts (though not to gay people), but they were a small part of an elaborate program of moral asceticism, the other portions of which— prohibitions of remarriage after the death of a spouse, of lending at interest, of going to the theater, of intercourse during Lent or menstruation—have been discarded or reinterpreted by most Christian denominations or are simply ignored.

There are fragments in the Bible that can justify as "Christian" hostility to gay people, just as there are biblical passages used to oppose equal rights for black people or women or to oppress Jews. Many Christians with no wish to oppress anyone are naturally concerned about the meaning of such passages, but personal concern about the morality of certain acts is different from social oppression or discrimination. It is striking that Christian society, which cavalierly resists even token observance of many biblical injunctions(e.g., Matt. 5:28, 27, 40, 42; 23:9, 1 Cor. 5:11, to mention but a few) should make a fetish of rigorously enforcing the most literal and restrictive interpretation of a few biblical fragments possibly regarding homosexuality with the force of civil law. Divorce was opposed by Christ himself in three of the Gospels and unanimously opposed by theologians for the first seventeen hundred years of Christian history; yet the status of the divorced and remarried hardly begins to provoke the passion, bitterness, and hostility inspired by the subject of homosexuality, about which Jesus made no comment at all and which was a minor point of Christian ethics during most of Christian history.

The difference clearly results from the social prejudice against gay people so pervasive in this culture (as it is in some others, including non-Christian societies such as China and the Soviet Union). It is difficult for many people to separate moral ambiguities from personal misgivings of this sort, and many Christians mistake one for the other or conflate both. Violence against gay people in Christian societies, for example, is scarcely ever related to homosexual activity (which is not normally observable), but rather to the suspicion that the victim is a gay *person,* occasioned by his or her dress or manner. In some cases Christian leaders appear to pander deliberately to such prejudices as a means of maintaining or inspiring support for a general program of more conservative moral order. Almost no prominent churchmen of any denomination, for example, publicly campaign to bring divorce laws into conformity with strictly literal interpretations of scripture or tradition, but many lobby for laws restricting the rights of gay people. The reason for this is clearly a conscious or unconscious recognition that the latter will evoke visceral support from the general population while the former will not: hardly a sound doctrinal basis for establishing priorities.

Even within churches, although a distinction is sometimes made between "practicing" and "nonpracticing" homosexuals, the uneasiness, hostility, and discomfort focus much more on the person of the homosexual than on behavior actually under his or her control. The oft-invoked word "avowed" is evidence of this: "avowal" is merely honesty about who one is, not the performance of an act that may or may not violate an ethical code. Honesty and openness are admired in this society in all contexts other than sexuality, where a social taboo overrides other values. Clearly the "homosexual activity" most disturbing to many modern Christians is *being* a homosexual, something not condemned in scripture or Christian theology.

Since nearly all experts now regard homosexuality as an involuntary aspect of character fixed at birth or in early childhood, an exegesis that suggested gay people were condemned simply for *being* gay would be morally indefensible and would ultimately undermine the moral authority of the exegete rather than strengthen a case against homosexuality.

Although it took most of a century, the claim by Southern segregationists that blackness was the curse of Ham eventually inspired more disrespect for its white supporters than for the black people they hoped to keep in servitude. It is worth remembering, however, that many of those who argued for it at the time doubtless believed that they derived their views from the Bible rather than from social prejudice.

The origins of such hostilities toward distinctive social minorities are complex and not clearly understood. Nor is it clear how best to combat them. Correcting the false assumptions underlying them is an important but limited approach. In this book, Chris paraphrases a favorite saying of mine: you can't use reason to argue someone out of a position he didn't get into by reason. Precisely because it is, at rock bottom, a visceral feeling rather than a rational position, antigay hostility both inside and outside the Christian church can not be overcome simply by appeal to history, theology, or logic.

There are, on the other hand, ways to communicate and enlighten not dependent on mere information that can overcome deeply embedded prejudices better than argument. A life can be an argument; being can be a reason. An idea can be embodied in a person, and in human form it may break down barriers and soften hardness of heart that words could not.

This is, at least in part, what John the Evangelist means when he refers to Christ as *logos*. Although translators often render it as "word," it is much more than that. It is Greek for "reason" and "argument": our word "logic" comes from it. Christ was God's unanswerable "argument." His people had hardened their hearts against his spoken reasons, the arguments propounded—in *words*—for centuries by the prophets and sages. So he sent an argument in the form of a human being, a life, a person. The argument became flesh and blood: so real that no one could refute or ignore it.

"If anyone says, 'I love God,' and hates his brother, he is a liar; for he who does not love his brother whom he has seen, cannot love God whom he has not seen" (1 John 4:20). God found it necessary, finally, to send his son to become a flesh-and-blood brother to humans, so they would at last "see" him and be able to love him concretely. It is hard to love something too alien, too "other," and recognizing this, God made himself less "other" to help humans love him. It is easier to hate someone, by contrast, when one makes them as "other" as possible, by denying or ignoring the human elements that would form the basis of empathy, understanding, and affection. Stereotypes emphasize the particular "otherness" of some group of people and obscure the much greater area of common humanity the labeled share with the labelers. Sensitive people discover as they grow, however, that most of the "others" they feared, condemned, or hated as invisible abstractions—Communists, Jews, Catholics, "niggers" or "faggots"—turn out to be much less alien in the flesh when they can actually be seen. How likely is it, John asks us, that someone who could *not* recognize and love the humanity he shares with another person could truly love the divine, so much more different from him?

One of the beauties of Chris Glaser's story and life is that by choosing to be open and honest about his feelings he transforms "homosexual" from an alien, despisable abstraction into a real, flesh-and-blood brother to other Christians. They can see him, as they can not see an abstraction: see that he is one of them—a struggling, loving Christian human being, with the graces and flaws and glories and failings of a fallen and redeemed people. It is much harder for most people to remain hostile to and unmoved by a living brother than it is to rail against an abstraction. This is not only John's message in his epistle, but the whole message, in many ways, of the New Testament. God had to become one of us for us to see him. By remaining within the church as a gay man, Chris and others like him make gay people part of the Christian community in a way they were not before. Though rejected, they remain cornerstones, following in the footsteps of Christ.

The chance to meet our abstractions as real human beings is a gift, and also a test. The fair-minded person, confronted with a living person who challenges traditional labels and categories, reconsiders the labels. The bigot reconsiders the person. In Chris's story there are bigots of this sort, but there are more people struggling to understand more deeply, to see with more light, to follow the trail of truth even when it means stepping outside protective walls and opening closed doors.

Chris and other gay Christians are *logoi* in this sense, arguments incarnated in persons, like all the outsiders who have remained loyal to the church in the face of its hostility, and who thereby made their commitment, their lives, their beings an unanswerable, living statement of faithfulness and love. It is hard for them, and hard for their fellow Christians. Christianity is only easy when it is not taken seriously. For the Pharisees the answers are simple; for the followers of Christ they are not. They must struggle endlessly with new challenges and difficult questions. The followers who do so are themselves the answers.

John Boswell
New Haven, Connecticut

PREFACE

I offer my story because I believe it may serve as an example for those attempting to understand the experience of gay and lesbian Christians seeking to integrate faith and sexuality in the context of a church which does not yet respect our attempts at such integrity.

Through God's grace, I've had the opportunity to play a unique role in the church's struggle with the full participation of lesbians and gays in the church. I've lobbied the policy-making governing bodies of the Presbyterian Church, served on its Task Force to Study Homosexuality, provided sources of information for many denominations to help educate them about lesbian and gay issues within the church, and have developed ministries within the lesbian and gay community. These experiences make "my" story more than mine: it becomes the story of the church grappling faithfully with issues of inclusiveness, ministry, and ordination, particularly as these issues relate to lesbians and gays.

My experiences have also given me the bittersweet opportunity of hearing the stories of thousands of gay and lesbian Christians and of their families and friends. While incapable of remembering the details of every person's story, the feelings of each are stored in my gut and my heart. Out of my gut I want to scream out their pain, their hurt, their anger. Out of my heart I want to sing of their courage, their compassion, their love. This book is that shout and that song; may such a shout and song bring down the Jericho walls of the church's heart. My uncommon calling throughout my ministry has been to bring down the walls of hostility that unnecessarily divide us.

Without God's love, grace and peace embodied in those closest to me, I could never have written this book. I give thanks to God for my partner in life, George Lynch, for my

parents, Wayne and Mildred Glaser, and for other members
of my family. I am similarly indebted to three communities
of faith: the West Hollywood Presbyterian Church, particularly its Lazarus Project, the United University Church of Los
Angeles, and the Order of the Holy Cross, whose Mt. Calvary
Retreat House in Santa Barbara provided occasional sanctuary for prayer, reflection, and writing.

I thank three friends who, themselves writers, offered significant suggestions as well as encouragement: Pat Hoffman,
Henri Nouwen, and Scott Rogo. I am grateful to Jan Johnson
and Lyla White of Harper & Row, who both believed in this
book, and I am deeply appreciative of Yvonne Keller's gracious way of working with me and editing the manuscript.
Thanks also to Linda Brubaker who, through copy editing,
helped me communicate more easily with the reader.

I thank God for the "church within the church": gay and
lesbian Christians, our parents and families, our supporters
and friends and advocates. Collectively, they serve as a profile
in grace.

Chris Glaser
West Hollywood, California

Except for people I've mentioned by both first and last names, all names and identifying details have been changed.

Chapter 1

GROWING UP CHRISTIAN AND GAY

BALTIMORE
JUNE 1976

It was my first General Assembly of the Presbyterian Church. When the nearly seven hundred delegates gathered in the convention hall, sitting in rows at long, white–covered tables, they resembled a smaller version of a national political convention. And it *was* a political convention of sorts, replete with issues, lobbyists, resource persons, and hundreds of observers, including the media. But the issue that seemed to dominate both the mind of this Assembly and my heart was homosexuality. This annual gathering of elected commissioners had been asked for guidance on the ordination of "avowed, practicing homosexuals." New York City Presbytery and other regional governing units either already had, or anticipated having, such candidates for ordination as clergy, and had requested advice from our highest governing body. Someone noted a historical irony: fifty years before, when the Presbyterian Assembly had last met in Baltimore, the delegates hotly debated the ordination of tobacco-using clergy!

Now, as one of those "avowed, practicing homosexuals" seeking ordination, I monitored the General Assembly committee assigned the task of bringing a solution to the floor of the full Assembly. The forty people on the committee appeared a little fatigued after two days of hearing testimony and debating the issue. I had been one of those who testified, rather hesitantly, before this intimidating body. It brought back memories of being required to give my "Christian testimony" before the entire student body of my fundamentalist junior high school: painfully shy to begin with, then uncoached and unprepared, I had hemmed and hawed until laughed offstage. Just as I had earlier found it difficult and frightening to share my Christian faith in words, I felt awkward and nervous briefly explaining my faith experience as a gay Christian to this committee. Having come to this Assembly intending only to observe, the mantle of lobbyist fit awkwardly on my shoulders. I would rather have sailed with Jonah to Tarshish.

I watched the chairperson of the committee put his glasses down on the table in front of him, stretch, and rub his eyes made tired from the brightness of the overhead lighting. In the charged atmosphere of the committee room, the discussion now focused on what constituted a homosexual act. To make a point, the chairperson rose to his feet, inviting another committee member to stand. Without warning, the chairperson hugged the man. With his characteristically quizzical smile, the chairperson then turned to the other committee members and questioned, "Now, was that a homosexual act?" The object of the embrace, still flustered with surprise, caustically quipped back, "Not for *me*, it wasn't!" Laughter broke down walls and dissipated tension.

LOS ANGELES
1950–1970

When I had my first homosexual fantasies at the age of seven, I never would have imagined myself sitting in a room full of Christians discussing them! Reared in the Baptist church, I felt discussion of any form of sexuality was taboo. When I accidentally discovered masturbation, I immediately assumed anything so pleasurable having to do with "that part" of my body must be sinful. Great anxiety followed my first ejaculation upon reaching puberty, because I believed I had broken it and was being punished for my repeated sins. Though I once overheard my parents privately agree on the importance of their sexual relationship, it wasn't until high school that I figured out why they occasionally closed their bedroom door at night.

Unfortunately, children generally discover their sexuality long before anybody tells them it's God gift and therefore good. We grow up feeling bad about our sexual urges and our bodies because this early silence speaks louder than the subsequent words of assurance. A child assumes that what can't be talked about must be bad. Expression of sexual feelings among children and adolescents is usually met with parental anger or anxiety, because of parental protectionism and because of adults' own negative feelings about sexuality. All those children then grow up feeling bad about their sexuality and their bodies and become adults with similar attitudes. There are people who wouldn't favor the ordination of a *sexual* person, let alone a homosexual one!

A precocious child, I went forward at an altar call and was baptized at the age of six, which is as close as one can get to infant baptism in the Baptist church. Needless to say, my theology was unsophisticated. When asked the single question requiring a simple, affirmative answer at baptism, "Do you believe in the Father, Son, and Holy Ghost?", I did not respond, perhaps out of my painful shyness, perhaps because I didn't know. As the awkward silence became a low tittering in the now amused congregation, the minister explained that in our earlier conversations it was clear to him I did believe, and then immersed me in the cold tank of water in which we stood. What baptism meant to me was that I would be with God, with Jesus, and with my family and friends always. As such, it was an act of permanent reconciliation and belonging. I was now a member of the family of Christ. The years to follow would teach me more and more what that means.

In these early years I wrote my first story, simply the recording of a remembered dream. Years later, the parable-like nature of the dream cast it in a far more significant light vis-à-vis my life experience. In the dream-turned-story, a castle perched on cliffs overlooked a vast kingdom of villages and rolling farmlands. The king sponsored a vegetable-growing contest in which the prize would be half his kingdom and his daughter in marriage. Myself a peasant, I entered the contest and found my opponent to be a mean, ugly ogre. Both of us tilled the soil and built shade to protect the earth from the sun's burning glare. But when it came time to plant seeds, I didn't have any. My opponent did, and proceeded to plant them. I decided to plant my shoes, at which the ogre laughed mockingly, as did all the others observing the contest, reminiscent of the congregation laughing at my baptism. But lo and behold, my shoes took root and began growing all kinds of vegetables, and I won the contest!

For years the silliness of planting my shoes shrouded its significance, until, as an adult, preparing a sermon on the scriptures for Passion Sunday (which initiates Holy Week), I more fully understood. I recalled childhood nightmares that I had had regarding my shoes: I would dream I'd forgotten to put on my shoes before going to school, or I'd be in a public place and suddenly realize my feet were naked. My shoes served as a symbol of security as well as the covering of my nakedness. The planting of my shoes meant giving up my security and exposing my nakedness or vulnerability. It was an exercise in risk-taking, and an exercise that had paid off handsomely. After all, it led to a fruitful harvest and winning the contest.

Faced with scriptures regarding Jesus' own willingness to "plant his shoes," to give up security, to become vulnerable in passionate pursuit of a noble cause, I recognized that, to the extent I had done the same, I had experienced resurrection to new life possibilities. Jesus, of course, did more than plant his shoes: he "planted" himself, everything he was, and up grew a transformed Christ, winner of the contest with death, evil, and the tempter, ruler of God's realm, betrothed to God's "daughter" the Church.

It would not be until seminary that I would discover that in the Old Testament, uncovering the feet serves as a euphemism for sexual expression. It would take me twenty years to uncover my feet in that regard. Until then a part of me would have to remain hidden.

With the exception of sexuality, my family felt free to express feelings and ideas, probably contributing to my own freedom of self-expression. From anger to affection, politics to religion, everything got expressed or discussed. As I grew up, I began to think this abnormal; surely the more placid picture of family life presented in *Ozzie and Harriet* was the way things should be. But, having since met many who grew up in a Nelson-like home, I've learned the toll such suppression can take. I've also discovered that I experienced more demonstrations of parental love than most. My father and mother were experienced parents, since I was preceded in the family nine years by my sister and four years by my brother. Certainly my parents were more relaxed with me, although they still maintained discipline. I feared my father's switch, but enjoyed wrestling with him and my brother in play. I delighted in nesting in Mom's lap in her big chair, but avoided doing anything which would earn her stern look, a punishment often more powerful than a paddle.

My father spent more time with me in my early years than he had been able to spend with my sister and brother, since his army days in training and then in Japan had taken him away from the family. There are family stories of him rocking me for hours while I steadfastly refused to go to sleep. After a certain age, though, the subtle message was communicated that physical intimacy was not permissible between us, since we were both male. I'm not sure of the immediate origin of this message, whether peers or parents, but its ultimate origin certainly was our American society. I could always hug Mother, even sit on her lap, but the unspoken ban on hugging between my father and me was not overcome until I left for Europe after college, when Dad surprised me with a powerful bearhug in saying goodbye.

Even before puberty required this ban on same gender physical contact to express affection, I yearned for the intimacy with other boys that television suggested was to happen between a man and a woman. I had crushes on Sugarfoot and Bronco (characters in two then-current television series), and my feelings for the hero in the film *Johnny Tremain* was not patriotic camaraderie as I supposed, but powerfully sexual. The absence from television of males feeling what I felt for males gave me the impression that my feelings were wrong, and, because they had to do with the undiscussable sexual realm, *terribly* so. The print media available to me was not much more helpful. Though *Boy's Life* and Hardy Boys' books gave me an enticing sense of close male friendships, Ann Landers' columns labeled my desire for greater intimacy with males "homosexual" and recommended psychiatric treatment to change.

Religious taboos and psychiatric explanations led me to conclude my feelings were both sin and sickness. One might think of these as mutually exclusive categories, since one requires personal accountability while the other does not, but, when psychiatry began, most of those undesirable behaviors that religion labeled sin, the psychiatric profession unquestionably relabeled sickness.

Condemned already by religion and psychiatry, I was too afraid to seek the counsel of either minister or psychiatrist. So God became both minister and psychiatrist, as I had long walks and talks with God which often lasted over an hour. As with my family, it seemed appropriate to discuss anything with God, but in contrast to my family, "anything" meant also the realm of sexuality. I prayed to God for what I inferred from society was necessary to become heterosexual: I prayed for forgiveness, for change, for maturation—that I would "grow out of" my homosexuality. I began worrying about the efficacy of my baptism, since I had failed to answer "yes" to the question of belief. I heard other Christians' testimonies of miraculous conversion experiences, the "born again" phenomenon, and feared I was not "saved" because becoming a Christian for me had been far less dramatic. "Maybe that's why I'm homosexual," I would think. So, I accepted Jesus over and over again in my prayers, on my knees, after thinking "unacceptable" thoughts, sometimes as often as several times a day. I believed once I was "really" Christian, these thoughts would disappear. But they never did.

While church and society failed to recognize or value homosexual feelings, both nonetheless helped assuage my fear that I would never be understood. To this day, my greatest fear is of being misunderstood. Once I was spanked in

Sunday school for retrieving some crayons thrown out a window by another child. I thought I was doing good, but an adult determined otherwise, and I was punished without my story being heard. I believe a carefully guarded secret is that *most* of us grow up feeling misunderstood, a feeling that does not dissipate with adulthood. And so it is reflected in our religion, our literature, and our art.

My feeling of being misunderstood is, I believe, the reason I became so fascinated with the biblical story of Joseph and his brothers. To the delight of my teacher, I chose to rewrite the story as a fourth-grade project, complete with drawings. Although Joseph was a favorite child, his family took offense at his dreams. His brothers rejected him, selling him into slavery. He was later falsely accused by Pharoah's wife. Yet he forgave his family in the end and cried when reunited with them. Misunderstood, rejected, unjustly accused, yet forgiving as he was rejoined with those he loved, Joseph served as paradigm for my experience. I think this is what drew me to him and inspired me to retell his story in my own words.

Later, in early adolescence, *To Kill a Mockingbird,* both book and film, had a profound effect on me. The prejudice depicted in the story which destroyed black Tom Robinson and might have destroyed "queer" Boo Radley, was a pernicious form of misunderstanding. Though Boo Radley was "queer" in the "not-quite-right" sense, he served as a shadowy and somewhat closeted figure which paralleled the shadowy and closeted part of myself: unacceptable according to society's standards, but capable of being heroic and loving, as Boo ultimately proved to be. And when the protagonist, Scout, finally reached out for Boo's hand and befriended him, as Boo had so wanted her to do, I felt as if Scout were reaching out for my hand and welcoming me as her friend. I believe other readers may have felt much the same: we recognized unconsciously that Scout was reaching out to the part within each of us which is misunderstood. Experiencing this personal identification in the midst of a story about racial injustice drew me into the similarities between my experience and that of blacks in this country, transforming my ignorant conservatism into an understanding advocacy for black civil rights. As I felt misunderstood, particularly because of my atypical sexual orientation, I myself became more understanding of those who also suffered from prejudice.

Painfully aware of that aspect of myself that I believed no one would understand, I experienced for the first time in early adolescence antigay fear and hatred in the guise of Christian concern. My first inkling of it came as I left home one Saturday morning for a youth group outing to Disneyland. My mother warned me not to go into any restrooms with the Sunday school superintendent, a volunteer advisor who was organizing the trip. I then understood the nature of the phone call which my mother had received earlier that morning. Some well-intentioned gossip was warning parents, spreading a rumor I would later learn found its origin in the pastor's study. At that realization, my stomach turned somersaults; I felt as if I were suddenly falling, for I knew my mother's cautions also had to do with me, though she was unaware of it.

The advisor did not go with us, and I had one of the worst days of my life, even at the "Magic Kingdom." When the adult chaperons were absent, some of us young people spoke of what was happening. No one could actually say the word "homosexual," and, though everyone agreed it wasn't good (some said "disgusting" and "nauseating"), several said the news didn't matter to them. This kind man who had revitalized the church's Sunday school programs still had our love and support.

Somehow the pastor had learned that this youth worker had been turned down as a scoutmaster in another region of the country because of suspicions of homosexuality. *Why* the pastor had sought this information and then related it to the governing board of the congregation was unclear, since—at the time the information came to light—no incident had occurred to breach trust in him. In fact, everything pointed to his trustworthiness, although we knew the pastor did not get along with the man. When the pastor offered the volunteer the option of seeing a psychiatrist, the latter agreed only if the pastor would accompany him. In the early sixties, this was remarkably insightful on the part of the youth worker, for he recognized that what later would be called "homophobia" needed healing too.

Vitally important to me was witnessing my own parents' sympathetic response to the man whose sexuality was in question. He visited our home several times during this period and found a supportive, caring environment. He confessed to my father that he was indeed homosexual, but believed it to be wrong and chose not to practice it.

Despite efforts on his behalf, the man was forced to resign his unpaid duties and leave our church. Yet the pastor would not leave it at that. With Saul-like zeal, he pursued him to other churches he attempted to join and exposed his homosexuality. Even though I believed my own feelings were sinful, I could readily recognize injustice perpetrated in the name of Christ. I began a fictionalized book about my experience in the church in which the most carefully written chapter described this incident. In my account, however, the narrator played an active role defending the accused man, finally asking him if he was homosexual. "Does it matter?" the youth worker replied, "Should it matter?"

One Sunday evening following the incident, the pastor's sexually active daughter expressed interest in necking with me in the church's chapel. When I declined, she cruelly shouted, so others might hear, "You're a fag. Chris is a fag!" I feigned amusement to cover embarrassment, fear, and hurt, laughingly denying the accusation, as I was to deny myself multitudinous times in the years to come.

Later, a high school buddy persuaded me to drive with him to look at all the "freaks" on Sunset Strip, a portion of Sunset Boulevard near Hollywood, that had become a hangout for the "flower children" of the sixties. I sensed some of these were homosexual, and my stomach turned at the sight of them. A dream at this time proved revealing: walking down a dark city street, an effeminate male homosexual suddenly approached me from behind, and tapped suggestively on my shoulder. I ran from him screaming in sheer terror. I hardly needed a gestalt therapist to understand that the homosexual tapping on my shoulder was none other than a part of myself, seeking recognition. The terror I felt came from the thought of accepting that part.

I believed that if God wanted to change my sexual feelings, they would be changed. Gradually I came to believe God wanted me this way, that somehow the suffering caused by having sexual feelings of which I could never speak, let alone express and fulfill, would shape me into a better person. Greek heroes had their tragic flaws; the apostle Paul had his "thorn in the flesh." If Jesus could bear a cross for me, I certainly could handle unfulfilled sexual desire. I would have a need for intimacy that could never be fulfilled and would have to be kept secret until I died and received my reward in heaven. To cover the absolute pain of this experience, I jokingly call this my "Christian martyr" period. It was a martyrdom all right, but not of Christianity. "Martyr" literally means "witness," and my suffering was more a witness to the evil of homophobia inflicted on children and teenagers than it was of true Christianity.

If I felt myself somewhat the victim with respect to my unacceptable sexuality, I felt more than adequate in other areas of my life. I earned high marks in school, achieved a degree of recognition and popularity, and led my Baptist Youth Fellowship group by developing creative programs. Outwardly I had many friends; inwardly I was lonely, wondering if those friends would still love me if they knew who I was deep inside. Outwardly I was perceived as asexual or shyly heterosexual; inwardly I had crushes on other boys. As heterosexual friends expressed hopes of love and marriage, I assumed I would never have marriage with someone I loved. The only available role models for male homosexuals at that time were stereotypes: a limp-wristed, ineffectual man; a vicious child-molester; a sick, sad, and lonely "boy in the band." I thought I was the only "normal" homosexual. Some days I feigned illness, stayed home from school, and simply cried, lonely and depressed. The only friend on whom I could depend, the only friend who knew my terrible secret and yet had not deserted me, was God. This resulted in a heightened awareness of God's presence in my life and a deepening spirituality. At the same time, it led to my desire to convert my sadness into joy, something I intuited as God's wish for me.

An experience of God's grace suggested the possibility of such conversion. Eyes of faith helped me recognize divine graciousness in a visit with relatives in Texas one summer. There was no particular event or flash of insight. I simply felt welcomed by my uncle and cousins into a circle of love and acceptance that required neither conformity nor achievement. They were so relaxed and good-humored with one another and with me that I felt at peace. Perhaps it had grown from their suffering together the long illness and death of my aunt, their wife and mother, a few years earlier.

Feeling myself nearly a stranger, they nonetheless invited me into this circle of love, and I was transformed. It served as a kind of incarnation of Paul Tillich's famous "You Are Accepted" sermon, in which that great twentieth-century theologian preached God's acceptance and love of each of us. This experience of love became a paradigm for me of authentic love. And, mystically, their love and acceptance empowered me. I saw the way they were and knew that was the way I wanted to be. I inwardly evaluated who I was and decided: "Either you can continue as a shy introvert and fail to enjoy and achieve all you might, or you can risk everything as an extrovert and enjoy and achieve all you can. Either you can feel sorry for yourself for what you are not, or you can use everything that you are to be what you can be."

More than a decade later a neurolinguistic therapist friend led me in an anchoring exercise in which he asked me to remember a time, an experience, when I felt most fulfilled, most at peace with myself and the world. I recalled a scene from the first day of school following the summer of the Texas visit. When asked to give three characteristics of the scene, I said, activity, letting myself go, and not caring what other people thought. The exercise revealed to me I was most happy and fulfilled when active, when I let myself go, trusting my own sense of direction, and when I did not let fears of failure or judgment in others' eyes keep me from attempting something.

Initially this newfound sense of self and independence fueled my enthusiasm and involvement in the church. But by my junior year of high school I felt restless in my Baptist church, not because of my sexual orientation, but because of its narrowness, its failure to address adequately social issues, its distrust of knowledge and current discoveries. Two black women visited our all-white suburban church in North Hollywood in the early sixties. I overheard a conversation between two members during coffee hour after worship. One said about the black women, "I bet they came to try this integratin' stuff! But we showed 'em they were welcome, even if they are Negroes!" The Vietnam War was troubling the nation; the church's response was to resolve that it would *not* give sanctuary to draft resisters. A former pastor, a popular man, had gone on to attend seminary; when he subsequently served again as an interim pastor, many parishioners felt theological and biblical education had taken away his "fire."

I left the Baptist church at the beginning of my senior year of high school. I had worked very hard in Baptist Youth Fellowship, but it seemed as if those of us who were young had been frustrated by the untimely death of one pastor and disheartened by the homophobic actions of the one who followed. To me and to others, there was an air of hopelessness about the church. It had begun to feel like a dry desert rather than an oasis on the way to the promised land.

Leaving the church is relatively easy for young people. Perhaps church represents now questioned or rejected parental or adult authority and values. Or perhaps it doesn't capture the young person's creative imagination, or it fails to live up to youthful hopes and dreams. None of these reasons, however, explained my decision to leave. The church would forever be my family, but I needed to find a denomination in which I could fulfill my ministry, as Paul charged young Timothy. I did not feel I could do that in the Baptist church.

I felt called to the ministry as early as junior high school, when I experienced deep hurt for those who did not belong to the family of Christ, and I wanted desperately for them to be "saved." My understanding of ministry shifted in high school when I found both peers and adults confiding in me their problems, something for which my own "problem" equipped me in terms of sensitivity. The word *compassion* comes from root words meaning "to suffer with"; I suffered with others, had compassion, because of my own suffering. Long before Henri Nouwen was to influence me, I ministered as what he described a "wounded healer." A similar suffering with those who hurt meant *politically* championing the oppressed as well. I began a two-year search for a denomination in which I believed I could fulfill such ministry.

I had almost given up hope when, in my first year of college, some friends told me of a liberal church they had visited, which they believed I'd value. On the first Sunday of the new decade, 1970, I entered the First Presbyterian Church of Van Nuys, California. Within three months, I became a member. I had found home.

Chapter 2

EXPLORING SOCIAL JUSTICE AND SEXUALITY

LOS ANGELES
1970–1972

What intrigued me the first Sunday I visited Van Nuys Presbyterian was that the young student minister, Jim Nicholie, gave a sermon describing the last decade of the civil rights movement. Having never heard such a thing from a pulpit before, I was pleased and delighted, although I assumed his sermon was an exception. When the regular minister stood to preach the following Sunday, I thought, "Oh no, here it comes!", expecting less progressive views. But I found him to be more radical than the student minister! Dr. James King Morse became a role model for me: his carefully written sermons indicated a deeply-rooted spirituality that blossomed in an eloquently expressed concern for social justice. I began to realize that this church could support my fledgling political and religious reformation.

The previous fall, my first semester in college, I had taken my first comparative religions course, offered by the newly organized Department of Religious Studies at California State University, Northridge. The course was taught by a Methodist minister by the name of Dr. Thomas Love, an appropriate name because he was both a doubting Thomas and a loving man, combining intellectual skepticism with genuine love for religion and for his students. But the course left me deeply troubled. After class I'd sit under a tree I nicknamed my *axis mundi,* or "center of the world" (an allusion to Mircea Eliade's *The Sacred and the Profane),* and reflect on the cause of my depression. For the first time, I was hearing discourse that assumed the equal validity of other faiths, and I was learning biblical scholarship. Both seemed to call into question everything I'd been taught in my Baptist church and Christian day school. How could Christian faith have value if it wasn't the only true religion? How could the Bible be authoritative if one didn't accept it literally, word for word? At that tender age of rash judgments, passionate feelings, and increasing insecurity, many young people view these questions in an either-or light, casting about for sure anchorage in a growing sea of possibilities. Either Christianity is the only true religion, or it's of no value. Either the Bible should be taken literally, or it has no authority.

Eventually I realized the source of my depression after class: I *believed* the new information. I believed in the equal validity of different religions. I believed in the necessity of biblical scholarship. And though tempted to make an either-or choice, I believed that the answer was both-and. Yes, other religions had spiritual truths to offer, and so did Christianity. Yes, biblical scholarship helped reveal the spiritual truths of the Bible that were still authoritative in my life. Reared in a fundamentalist, literalist tradition, to hold such liberal views meant endangering my soul, risking the peril of eternal damnation. And yet I felt God leading me, even pulling me toward this unexpected perspective.

Another crucial point along this pilgrimage toward God's future occurred shortly after joining the Presbyterian church. At at gathering for young adults, married and single, I learned the church was planning a sex education course for its young people. Jim Nicholie invited me to help teach the course, remarking, "You'd be good at that!" I blushed, reminded of my own sexual desires and believing myself too naive about sexuality to be of much help. I had never had much sex education myself, and certainly never in the context of church! Though overjoyed at being included, I was also depressed, partly because I found Jim attractive and would have liked to please him by helping with the course, and partly because I wanted to please him in more intimate ways. But the broader context of my depression revolved around the thought of *any* discussion of sexuality in the context of church. Discussion of such a subject itself felt wrong, sinful. I felt the fires of hell licking at my soul. At home I sat and thought late into the night. If I risked discussing sexuality in the context of faith, I might also risk finding that my own feelings demanded expression. Sexuality was for me and is for the church a Pandora's box. And yet, at a cerebral level, I recognized that God created sexuality.

A similar crisis of conscience had struck Mark Twain's Huckleberry Finn. He had helped Jim, the runaway slave, to escape with him down the Mississippi River. But his conscience caught up with him: he remembered Sunday School had taught him that it was wrong to help a slave escape. He knew hellfire now endangered his soul. So, halfway through their adventures together, Huck composed a letter to Jim's owner, informing her where he was. He completed it and immediately felt much better, but then he began thinking about the time Jim saved his life and the time Jim took care of him when he was sick. Huck looked again at the letter, announced "All right, I'll go to hell!", and ripped it up.

That describes my own conclusion that night. I felt myself moving into dangerous, unexplored new territory. Risking God's judgment, I decided I had to do what I believed was right. I concluded that sexuality did belong in the context of faith. If that's what it meant in part to be Presbyterian and Christian, I'd risk hell. I never again let the fear of hell paralyze the movement of the Spirit. Perhaps this is what is meant by willingness to be damned for the glory of God.

I allowed sexuality to be a part of my faith picture, but I did not accept homosexuality. I still wanted to be what everyone expected in that regard: heterosexual, or at least the appearance of such. Besides, I had more important distractions. In college I worked on a double major of English and Religious Studies. The appeal to the senses and earthiness of the Romantic Age poets opened me to a deepened awareness of the sensual nature of God's creation. A Religious Studies course tracing "neopagan" themes in contemporary literature introduced me to Camus and Kazantzakis, and the risk-taking, life-living and faith-leaping Zorba became a second messiah, and *Zorba the Greek* a second bible. Fascinated by theology, I particularly found process thought, which viewed God and the world in a growth process, answered many of my questions, validated my own experience of the world, and served as an intellectual scaffolding for my more intuitive faith of the heart. Process thought's placing of beauty as the most encompassing good appealed to my spiritual and aesthetic sensibilities. I discovered the creation and my body as a part of it, initially expressed in letting my hair grow long, growing a beard and mustache, and wearing the colorful clothes then popular.

I became an experience gatherer. I enjoyed a wonderful sensual and sexual relationship with a woman I loved, celebrated nature, drank wine socially, smoked marijuana, and experimented a little with psychedelic drugs. I stopped smoking grass and experimenting with psychedelics later, when I recognized it was a form of suicidal escape for me, a way of forgetting my "queerness" and suppressing my true sexual needs. In this discovery of my body, the kid who always got a "C" in physical education took an ambitious body conditioning course of weightlifting and long-distance running and earned an "A"! And I finally accepted my curly red hair. I had grown it long and brushed it as straight as I could manage, in a vain attempt to bring it into conformity with what I believed attractive. A hair stylist advised me to cut it short and let it curl. I did, and interestingly enough this short and curly look became a popular style in later years, causing me to wonder why I had ever wanted it to be different.

Overall, college was an awakening to beauty. What scarred this awakening was the United States' involvement in the war in Vietnam. I had considered myself a pacifist, until Dr. Love, in a course on Christian ethics, demonstrated that my pacifism was not absolute by employing a hypothetical example: "A crazed maniac is slitting the throats of children at one end of a long hallway," he began gruesomely. "You appear at the other end of the hallway. You have a gun and you are an excellent marksman. The maniac is about to slit the throat of yet another child. What would you do?" Without hesitation, though it meant the end of my idealized pacifism, I replied,

"I'd shoot him." (Since then I have been verbally "shooting down" homophobic individuals who, psychologically or spiritually, have been wounding gay children, often unaware and unnoticed.)

Though not an absolute pacifist, I nonetheless opposed the United States' participation in Vietnam's civil war by writing, speaking, striking, and demonstrating against it. Beyond its affront to my sense of justice, I had personal reasons for bringing our involvement in the war to an end: young men my age, some of whom were friends, were being killed or permanently damaged. One friend returned haunted by memories of friends blown to bits; three others returned with drug dependencies; another suffered a mental breakdown in military training. As for me, I could no more imagine myself killing Vietnamese than I could imagine myself molesting children. Given a student deferment for college, I hadn't decided whether to escape to Canada or go to prison if I were called up when the first draft lottery was held. For once, I was glad not to "win": I drew number 243. Since I had little chance of being drafted with so high a number, the draft board reclassified me I-A. After waiting just three months to the end of the year without being drafted, I was released of any worry. The day I realized I was free, I literally danced in the rain! But I felt more keenly the responsibility of fighting against the war. There was now no taint of special pleading.

Of course the church became an arena for expressing opposition to the war. First Presbyterian Church of Van Nuys had experienced political turmoil long before I'd arrived. One elder had circulated a petition against the pastor, Dr. Morse, claiming he was a "communist." I was told the congregation was so divided on political issues that the conservatives sat on the right side of the sanctuary and the liberals on the left! My political assertiveness and bohemian style of dress once moved one woman to telephone a warning to many church members: "Better come to this congregational meeting, or the hippie will take over the church!"

Certainly some youthful arrogance fired my antiwar spirit. But, aware of that, I chose not to use either my youth or my chutzpah as an excuse to do nothing, though some used either as an excuse not to listen to whatever truths I may have spoken. Often frustrated, there came a time when I questioned the church's value as an agent for social reformation and justice and stopped attending for nearly two months. Two events brought me back.

The first was seeing Paddy Chayefsky's film, *Hospital*. In the film an urban hospital was plagued by inefficiency, labor disputes, and demonstrations against its needed expansion into a slum community. At the same time, the central character, a doctor, plans suicide, after undergoing a divorce, the breakup of his family, and vocational chaos. But he is interrupted by the appearance of a beautiful young woman, with whom he falls in love, who encourages him to come join her in practicing medicine in a far more idyllic setting. In this modern parable, the hospital serves as a kind of "Everyinstitution," and the doctor as a kind of Everyman. As the institution seems to be crumbling, its healing work devalued, this Everyman looks as if he is going to escape with the woman to a more peaceful and satisfying medical practice in a distant rural area. But, at the last possible moment, he turns back from this chance of a lifetime and returns to the hospital, explaining simply, "Somebody's got to be responsible."

The film's effect on me was profound. I had witnessed so many of my own generation "copping out" for personal pleasure rather than struggle with the "establishment." The film reinforced my desire to be responsible in the shaping of the institution of which I was part, the church. If, like the hospital in the film, the church inadequately used its powers to heal, was exploited and abused by selfish or evil forces, and was misunderstood by the community, I wanted to be a part of its reformation. I decided never again to let myself think of it as "their" church. It was *my* church too, and I was going to claim my right and responsibility in shaping its ministry. I would not let "them," whoever "they" happened to be, take the church from me, nor let them misdirect its purpose.

The second event that persuaded me to reconsider my temporary abandonment of the church was the United Presbyterian Church's grant of $10,000 to the legal defense fund of Angela Davis. Angela Davis, a university professor, had been charged with enabling a self-styled revolutionary to illegally obtain a gun with which he murdered a law officer. In those days of social unrest, the publicity surrounding the case and the public prejudice and pressure involved seemed to preclude a fair trial. In addition, from society's viewpoint, Angela Davis had three strikes against her: she was female, black, and Communist. (God help her if she had also been lesbian!) Reading of the Presbyterian grant in the newspaper, I admired our denomination's readiness to help insure a fair trial, though clearly the ideologies of the church and of Angela Davis were at odds.

I returned to church the following Sunday, though I later learned I was lucky not to be trampled by a stampede of disgruntled and departing Presbyterians. I found the church's action consistent with its policy of promoting social justice; others found it inconsistent with a narrowly-defined gospel easily colored by prejudice and national interest. Ironically, it was the church's stance in that controversy that helped bring me back into the fold; and it was I who helped surface yet a new controversy that would be referred to as another "Angela Davis": ordination of gays and lesbians.

Returning to church didn't mean the temptation to leave never again arose. Our congregation had forums every Sunday after worship that featured speakers invited to present social concerns. Reading in the *Los Angeles Times* of the formation of a new church which embraced homosexuals, I suggested that the forum committee, of which I was a member, invite speakers from this Metropolitan Community Church. The committee and subsequently the session (governing elders of a local congregation) approved the invitation. I contacted the new church and arranged for two speakers. But then a few elders objected, claiming that the session had not been fully aware of the subject of the proposed program. An emergency meeting was called that included the dissatisfied elders and members of the forum committee. Though initiating the program from personal interest and curiosity, I was far from ready to accept myself as both gay and Christian.

Yet now I would be called upon to defend our invitation to these gay Christians. In a sense, my defense of the program would be the one I would like to have been able to make years before on behalf of the Sunday school superintendent in my Baptist church.

Driving to the church for the meeting, I decided that if the invitation were withdrawn, it would be a sign for me to leave the church, using the occasion as a kind of fleece before the Lord. In retrospect, I believe I may have been looking for an excuse to leave, avoiding the burden, the cup if you will, that I sensed would come my way if I were to accept my sexuality within the context of faith. Though it seemed likely the program would be rejected, God didn't let me off the hook so easily. The Spirit intervened, and, to my surprise, even the doubting elders gave a hesitant nod to the presentation. Afterward I laughed to God in prayer: "You've made your point. You don't want me to leave. Now what?"

This was the beginning of what I consider my Jonah experience in the church. Jonah is the humorous Old Testament story of the world's most reluctant prophet who in the end enjoys the easiest success. Other Jewish prophets, more responsive to God's call than Jonah, were killed or ignored by their own people. Yet Jonah, by God's grace, preaches repentance to the Ninevites, enemies and oppressors of the Jews, and they immediately repent. Like Jonah, I have been a reluctant advocate for my people, gay Christians, yet, despite devastating defeats, God's grace has granted me miraculous responses and opportunities.

The forum went on as scheduled. How nervous I was meeting the speakers, how flustered I must have appeared as I feared they could tell I was one of them, how difficult it was to enunciate their names and their topic as I introduced them to the gathering! Those who would later bear a similar fate introducing *me* would evoke my profoundest sympathies!

A fear expressed regarding this particular forum was that the usual attendance of forty would drop severely. As it happened, an unprecedented attendance of eighty required setting up additional chairs! I don't remember the content of their presentations, but the speakers' gentle and joyful manner made a deep impression on me. The relative maturity of the subsequent discussion surprised and encouraged me. Even homosexuality could be discussed in church! I listened closely to the question from the pastor, Dr. Morse, about male and female complementarity available in heterosexual marriage. It would be years before I would discover firsthand how the male and female in each of us may complement the female and male in another, regardless of gender. Certainly both male and female aspects are integrated in God, and we are, each one of us, created in God's image.

Many left the church that day puzzled, challenged, wondering. Perhaps others left fearful or angry. And maybe a few felt as I did: emotionally exhausted, but spiritually uplifted. The sexuality and spirituality within me began to view each other less as competing strangers and more as potential lovers who together might bring peace to my troubled soul.

The reconciliation beginning within me would not surface immediately. I knew I was homosexual, but I wanted a different role in life. I developed an intimate relationship with a woman named Jill, an independent soul who enjoyed my lack of possessiveness, as so many women do who find themselves consciously or unconsciously attracted to gay men. I loved her, but was not "in love." We were drawn together by our mutual interest in process thought and our mutual ability to laugh at such serious, intellectual attempts to explain reality. Her mind intrigued me, but, though objectively attractive, her body did not. Yet our sexual encounters were highly pleasurable for us both because we were relaxed, warm, sensual, fun-loving, and enjoyed a sense of humor about it all. While making love, I was stimulated by picturing myself as a man making love to a woman rather than simply responding to her body. Nevertheless, I hinted at marriage, providentially discovering Jill didn't feel ready for marriage to anyone.

Deep within me I sensed a relationship with a man would be more fulfilling, not simply sexually, but emotionally as well, though I had no experience nor idea how to establish such a relationship. I couldn't tell Jill, but at my suggestion we agreed to be friends rather than lovers. I thought perhaps Jill sensed my dilemma when we once discussed bisexuality (in word but not in deed in vogue with the college crowd at the time), but when I explained to her one year after our breakup that I was gay, she laughed and said, "Oh Chris, you're not gay!" An hour of discussion was required to convince her otherwise! Homosexual people are often capable of imitating heterosexual interest and behavior, not necessarily insincerely or hypocritically, but because we have been taught that's what we're *supposed* to do, and that's what we *have* to do to be loved at all. Unless truly bisexual (as are many more people than society cares to admit), those who discover their homosexuality late in life, or who try to pass as heterosexual, or who claim through spiritual or other therapeutic means to have "become" heterosexual, find as I did that their hearts just aren't in heterosexual expression. Of course, many people keep their hearts tightly reigned in, perhaps the most common form of sexual bondage.

What was missing in my relationship with Jill I had experienced with my best friend, who recently had joined the Air Force rather than be drafted and face certain deployment to Vietnam. In high school, I had invited him to a Youth For Christ rally at which he accepted Jesus as Lord and Savior. I had since come to realize that what had originally presented itself as Christian compassion for his soul was additionally romantic interest. Fear of his rejection of me as friend kept me from sharing the nature or depth of my love, though the times and our youth allowed for expressions of affection. I realized being his very best friend had meant always being there for him, loving him even when he didn't love himself, always watching out for his best interests. In my mind, it also meant a refusal to exploit him, so I never fantasized about him sexually. Slowly, I grew to realize my love for him was good *and* a product of my homosexual orientation.

By then believing all ability to love ultimately comes from God, I felt led to the conclusion my sexual orientation was a gift from God. Like all of God's gifts, my choice was whether to reject it or accept and invest it as a good steward. I could hide it like the servant in the parable, who took the coin his master had given him and hid it in the dirt, or I could use it wisely as the faithful steward did for the master's glory and the benefit of all. Too many homosexual Christians feel compelled to hide their gift of same-gender love in unfulfilling sexual expressions or in self-serving piety.

This realization also called into question my stewardship as a minister. The recommendation of one of my professors had led the Congregational Church of Northridge to hire me as director of youth ministry, a ministry I enjoyed during my final years in college, as I found fulfillment working with young people and their parents. But I felt hypocritical: I encouraged the young people to be honest with themselves and open with one another, while I myself hid an important part of me for fear of losing my job. I counseled a young man who feared his homosexuality because he didn't want to be like the societal stereotypes offered as role models. How I wanted to share with him that I, someone he respected and loved, was homosexual. I would like to have served as a role model for him, because I so clearly remembered the lack of healthy role models offered me as an adolescent. Yet I believed sharing my own sexual identity would be unprofessional, if not dangerous. Again, I felt like the unfaithful steward hiding his treasure in the dirt.

I needed a friend with whom I could unburden a little by sharing all these feelings arising from within me. Jill was too directly affected, my friend from high school was in Texas for basic training, I didn't feel ready to trust my friends either in the Presbyterian or Congregational church, and I certainly wasn't ready to tell my family. One day, in one of the offices of the college's religious studies department, Jill and I found ourselves discussing bisexuality with a close friend named Kevin. The three of us had shared many conversations and experiences, so it was within an already established context of intimacy that the issue arose. I was keenly interested to hear both Jill and Kevin sound so open and relaxed about the subject, though admittedly in the theoretical realm. When Jill left the room, I seized what I considered an opportune moment to tell someone of my orientation for the first time. "I want to tell you something I've never told anyone before," I began, inwardly noting I felt so far removed from my voice it was as if I were speaking from another room, "but I have some homosexual tendencies." That was as far out of the closet as I cared to come. A long silence followed, a silence louder than words. Finally, Kevin replied, "I can see why you've never told anyone before." My heart came crashing down as I realized his horror at my confession, though a minute earlier we had been discussing bisexuality! He was not hostile, but his shocked response, not followed by any sign of support, was enough to make me crawl back in my closet for another six months. It was the beginning of the end of our friendship. In the weeks to come, in great pain I watched him pull away from me, expressing fear that I might expect more from him than he was willing to give.

Though the church could give sanctuary to so much of me and so many of my concerns, it was to the sanctuary of the seashore that I fled to reflect on the relationship of my sexuality and spirituality. I would drive to nearby Santa Monica, where I walked or ran down the wide aisle of sand between the palisades and the Pacific. Particularly at sunset and twilight, the colors of water and sky joined the rhythm of the waves to mete out God's grace in language both more primitive and profound than that of liturgies. No matter who I was, no matter what I may have done or failed to do, this experience of grace always welcomed me, offered hospitality, comforted me, and yet challenged and inspired me to be all I could become. I would be overwhelmed by God's love in this embrace of sea, sand, cliffs, and sky, and at the same time inspired to be more gracious, creative, and peaceful. In walks along the water or upon the cliffs, insights came and decisions were made. My yearning to share love with a man was but one of many prayers offered to God in this natural sanctuary.

I did not know how to meet anyone gay. The term itself had not come into common parlance. I'd always been taught the best place to meet a girlfriend was in church; but that hardly seemed a possibility in my search for a boyfriend. Yet another sanctuary would prove such a meeting place. On a long run along the beach one day, I stumbled onto a public meeting place for gay men under the abandoned (now demolished) Pacific Ocean Park pier in Venice, just south of Santa Monica. For a long time, I had enjoyed walking or running along the shore under the pier, watching waves crashing past pylons, some of which had fallen or were charred by fire. Sunlight streaming through holes and drains in the floor of the pier overhead created columns of light as they lit up the sea spray. The combined effect gave an intoxicating feeling of walking through ruins of an ancient Greek temple.

Passing now through this particular stretch of beach, I noticed a few men whom I sensed to be gay. Searching gazes combined with a secretive atmosphere should have served as obvious clues, but I was the new kid on the beach and as yet unsure. I circled back and slowed to a walk so I might explore the fearful and exciting possibility that I might have found a way to meet other gay men. Retracing my steps, I passed an attractive man walking in the opposite direction. He appeared to be my age, had long blonde hair, and was clad simply in a swimsuit as I was. We exchanged glances a little more than casual as we neared one another, and, at a little distance, we both turned for a second look, our eyes meeting. Adrenalin rushed through my body. Not knowing what to do next, I sat down on the sand to see if he might head back my way. To my dismay, he'd chosen to do the same, and we ended up eyeing one another discreetly from a distance. Mustering courage, I stood and walked toward him only to find him walking toward me; now neither of us could casually join the other on the sand. Desperate for some excuse to communicate, I lamely asked him what time it was. He told me, and after an awkward pause, we both felt compelled to continue walking in opposite directions. When I returned to my car, I mentally kicked myself for not initiating a conversation. Even my body felt frustrated: why the shot of adrenalin if nothing was going to happen? He must be gay, I told myself. So I walked back to the spot where we met. He was gone.

I returned on other days and did meet a few others there,

discovering, to my amazement, that sexual encounters occurred in the darkness far back under the pier. My only homosexual encounter had been with a friend I trusted and loved, though neither of us could admit to being homosexually inclined. To now witness strangers involved in similarly intimate activity was both a titillating and anxiety-producing revelation: this was a place for anonymous sex, not for finding a lover. When I expressed surprise at the taboo activities in such a public place to one of those I met, he was the first to explain the possibility of police entrapment. I avoided the place after that. This was not a safe sanctuary in which to meet other gay men, for, though one might assume the police arrested only those involved in public sexual activity, the reality was they arrested anybody who might be there.

The question how to meet other gays safely still burned within me. My political bias required an occasional reading of the *Los Angeles Free Press,*which was then an underground newspaper. A friend once advised reading the personal ads for a good laugh, and when I did, I found ads of homosexual people seeking friends. I thought a long time before answering one. Not interested in the blatantly sexual ads, I found myself intrigued by those "seeking sincere friendship" and "possible long lasting relationships." I answered three ads, but, fearful lest the police be on the receiving end in yet another form of entrapment, I typed my letters on a coin-operated typewriter in the college library. And I typed rather than signed my first name. If necessary, I could claim someone else had written the letters.

The first of the three responded by telephoning and inviting me to meet him at his apartment in Santa Monica. Flushed with a blend of nervousness and excitement, I drove to his place the following Sunday afternoon, and was met at the door by a smiling and friendly man dressed in jeans and a t-shirt. His face was average looking, his body hunky and muscled. As he offered me a beer and we chatted, I noticed ordinary furniture that might come with a furnished apartment, with the exception of a set of weights and barbells rather obviously exhibited in one corner. What struck me as particularly odd was that there was nothing on the walls with the exception of a prominently displayed, unframed *Playboy*-centerfold taped directly over the sofa. When I commented on this naked woman adorning his living room, he smiled and said that was to throw people off the scent as to his real interests. I considered it strange that he would be accepted as sexually normal by hanging a photograph I considered tasteless. While we spoke, a phone call came inviting him to a party for the gay son of a prominent celebrity. He told me this with pride, but insisted on being secretive as to the identity of the celebrity because he couldn't be sure if I was a trustworthy member of the "fraternity." After a half hour of not connecting conversationally, he excused himself to get ready for some other engagement, meaning it was time for me to leave. I guess I failed the interview, because I never got a call back.

Providentially, all three to whom I wrote were good people, even if ultimately we proved to have little to bring us together. The two others I met and saw several times. One gave a party that gave me the opportunity to meet other gay people. I found little in common with the people I met, mostly because they had long ago left my primary lover, the church. They found my working at a church curious, but admirable, my desire to be a minister amusing if not bizarre. I remember inviting those at the party to church the next day, but no one came. No lasting friendships nor romantic involvements developed.

God worked overtime, as a kind of divine *yenta*, connecting me to the gay community, sometimes through comical means. For example, two nongay college friends moved to San Francisco and unknowingly rented an apartment at the corner of 18th and Castro streets, the heart of the city's gay district. Gary and Michelle were both cosmopolitan in their attitudes, reared in Los Angeles by parents in the film and television industry. But while browsing through a newstand with them near their former home in Burbank one day, I had watched Gary pick up a gay newspaper, *The Advocate,* and express disgust at an article about the ordination of a gay man in the

United Church of Christ: "Now they're ordaining them!" As much as I wanted to read the article myself, I did not feel encouraged to share what was troubling me at the time.

Not until my second visit with them in San Francisco did I dare step into my first gay bar. Waiting alone for a bus one night on the side of Castro opposite their apartment, I said aloud (as if there were spies watching my every move!), "Might as well go in here for a beer." Pretending innocence, I stepped into the Midnight Sun, more reminiscent of midnight than of sun. Once my eyes adjusted to its dim interior, I disappointedly discovered only a few men in the place. I knew nothing of gay men coming out at late hours; nine o'clock in the evening seemed late enough for me. I perched on a barstool and ordered a beer. As I drank I watched an old, drunken street person going from man to man, presumably taking an offering for a drink. He looked diseased to me, with sores and a sickly complexion. When he came to me, he asked for a drink of my beer. Not wanting any trouble and certainly not wanting the intimate communion of drinking from the same bottle, I simply gave it to him. He asked to try on my gloves; hesitatingly I let him. Then he shuffled off toward the restroom, with me calling after him for my gloves. Plainly, he wanted me to follow. Thanks be to God, the bartender saved me: realizing my predicament, he retrieved my gloves, bought me a fresh beer, and ejected the unfortunate "villain." This not being a good introduction to a gay bar, I finished my beer quickly and departed from the sparsely populated tavern.

But, shortly before arriving at the home of another friend, I realized that in the excitement I'd left my gloves at the bar. By the time I had retraced my steps, it was so late that I hardly expected my gloves would still be there, in what by now must be an entirely deserted bar. To my amazement, opening the door revealed a bar packed with gay men. Animated conversation, laughter, cubes tinkling in drinks, cigarette smoke, and music filled the air. Just as eleven o'clock Sunday morning serves as the traditional hour of God for most Christians, so eleven o'clock Saturday night serves as the traditional hour of quite another form of communion for gay men. A beautiful, tall blond in his late twenties stood with a circle of friends: to me he was Prince Charming holding court and far above my class, so I didn't consider approaching. I found my gloves exactly where I'd left them, and began to leave, when I caught the eye of an attractive young man and found myself asking, "May I buy you a drink?" He didn't drink, so I bought us two glasses of orange juice. A student of philosophy from San Diego, he enjoyed literature and process thought as I did. Finally I'd found someone gay with whom I had something in common, and we talked for hours. Yet he was not ready to say he was gay, and, indeed, seemed to hold me a little in contempt for saying I was and that I found him attractive. Subsequently I wrote to him, but never received a reply.

(Ten years later I visited the Midnight Sun again during the annual summer Castro Street Fair and discovered its transformation paralleled my own: no longer dark and dingy, its interior was bright, colorful, and gay. A sign of the times, more recently, the bar has moved around the corner and is now high tech, video, and gray.)

During this visit I chose to tell Michelle I was gay and received an understanding, supportive response. Together we discussed Gary's less than accepting attitude toward this issue, though he was tolerant and progressive in other areas. Michelle wanted him to know, so we engaged him in conversation on the subject. During a not unfriendly but academic debate, he questioned and challenged my opinions. Finally, we broke it to him. Stunned, he regretted his negative position and sought to understand. Many years later, upon his graduation from an Episcopal seminary, he admirably refused ordination to the priesthood until women could be ordained in the Episcopal Church, writing me he would prefer to refuse ordination until gays also were ordained, but he couldn't wait that long! He addressed the envelope to the "Should-Be-Reverend Chris Glaser." He had come a long way from his previously disgusted comment, "Now they're ordaining them!"

Chapter 3

RECONCILING HOMOSEXUALITY AND CHRISTIANITY

LOS ANGELES
SUMMER AND FALL 1972

Kairos characterized the summer of 1972 for me. Facing my final semester of college, I needed to decide whether to apply to seminary and whether to become a candidate for ordination in my presbytery. *Kairos* is the biblical notion of God's time, a time of profound spiritual crisis and opportunity, and these months seemed such a time as I focused on whether God was calling me to professional ministry regardless of my sexual orientation. Coincidences so proliferated in so brief a time, I could scarcely fail to believe God's destiny for my life was being revealed. Grace prepared to hug me in passionate embrace, refusing to let go. Ultimately I could do nothing but surrender, and in so doing, experienced a peace that permeated my existence.

At the Congregational church the previous spring, the young man who feared his homosexuality reported a news story to me from the front page of the *Los Angeles Times:* The United Church of Christ, the denomination to which the church belonged, had ordained an "avowed" homosexual, the Reverend William Johnson, in the San Francisco Bay Area. The young man was both astounded and excited to find an alternative role model, but his excitement exponentially increased within me as a dream became possibility. I wondered if such were possible for *me.*

Yet I also wondered if I weren't overdramatizing my plight in my own mind. Perhaps I was unnecessarily exaggerating the conflict between my sexuality and the ministry. Perhaps it would not present quite the controversy I imagined and feared. I consulted a therapist for verification of my experience of reality, since I perceived immense obstacles to fulfilling my call. From a professor, I sought a referral to a former clergyperson who did counseling, because I wanted someone who could understand the church and yet be sympathetically critical. One visit confirmed many of my perceptions and relieved much anxiety and tension. For the first time, in a therapeutic setting, I was able to speak of my most hidden fears and dreams.

That visit opened a door for me. My family and friends were curious why I'd gone to a therapist; some of them still believed that only "crazy" people went to counseling. They wanted to know what was wrong. Obviously, if I'd been ready to tell them, I probably would not have gone to a therapist. For my family at least, and most of my friends, the question remained unanswered—for a time. Yet surely I was preparing to tell them I was gay, since I recall that I seemed to have made a point of telling them I'd gone to the therapist.

The curiosity and concern of my two closest friends led me to divulge my secret to them early in the summer. Both were nongay males, yet sensitive to the nuances of gender and sexuality. We enjoyed honest, open, and loyal friendships. My reservations in telling them grew from my earlier bad experience of sharing my inclinations with Kevin, with whom I had believed I enjoyed an honest, open, and loyal friendship. The truth was delivered to these friends when I perceived the safety of the environment in which it would be born. The birth image here is intentional; psychologically and emotionally, the pain of coming out as gay bore similarities to the physical pain of childbirth.

Henry Nichols, one of two college-age advisors to the junior high school group of the Congregational church, expressed much curiosity about my seeing a therapist. He sensed that he knew why I had gone, and, smiling, we together played a humorous kind of twenty-one questions as to why. The game began when I said that it concerned something in my personality which might interfere with entering the ministry; it ended when he asked, "Does it begin with 'h'?", meaning "h" for homosexuality. Once he knew for certain, he had all kinds of questions that, since he asked them in a friendly, inquisitive way (rather than a judgmental, inquisitorial manner), I was happy to answer. Although we had laughed and joked together, and although the whole process was casual and happy, I departed from the afternoon at his home exhausted. I was elated that a close friend now knew, but I feared what it might mean to the future of our friendship.

A few weeks later I came out to my other close friend, Don Eaton, son of the pastor with whom I worked at the Congregational church. As a folk singer, Don wrote songs about personal and societal integrity, and that, along with his interest in counseling and personal growth, made him likely to be receptive. I was housesitting for friends and invited him for dinner. After steaks on the barbecue, skinnydipping in the pool, and a giggling, nonviolent wrestling match in front of the fireplace, Don revealed some of his own growth process, which encouraged me to share what I was discovering about myself. He spoke of his own sexuality, finally venturing, "You're dealing with bisexuality, aren't you?" Smiling, but blushing, I said, "No, but you're warm!" "You're homosexual!" he shouted good-naturedly, as if he had just cracked a tough case by brilliant deduction, and we both howled with laughter. Suddenly my sexuality seemed friendlier to me, as if I had introduced a stranger whom I feared Don wouldn't like and Don had enthusiastically greeted him. Don held me in his arms in response to the disclosure, a silent, but most believable word of assurance. Here I was, literally and figuratively naked, and yet loved.

From both Don and Henry I yet feared a backlash, but the only afterthought both had was, "Why didn't you trust us enough as friends to tell us sooner?" I feared a drifting away, but, though geographical location separated us soon after, our intimacy grew from those moments of mutual risk-taking, encouraging the opening of a closet door. Many years later I would officiate at Henry's wedding, and a visit to Don and his wife Laura would be healing after the difficult dissolution of a love relationship. I feel we could still pick up our friendships where we left off, whenever we might be serendipitously brought together again.

Don's father, the Reverend Ken Eaton, happened to show me an article describing Bill Johnson's ordination, explaining to my surprise that a member of our congregation had been instrumental in Bill's ordination and had loaned him the story. Eagerly taking the article, I asked if I might borrow it. Not knowing its personal import for me, Ken hesitated, not having read it yet himself. But when I offered to get a photocopy, he kindly responded, "Go ahead and take it if it's that important to you." I didn't worry whether he'd guess why it was so important; gleefully I left the office and read the story carefully, discovering Bill had been ordained in the Bay Area to a "tentmaking" ministry right there in Los Angeles. (A tentmaking ministry is one in which the minister supports him/herself through other employment, just as the apostle Paul made tents to support his ministry.) My blood raced with excitement at the thought that he was nearby.

The summer had been one of prayer, reading scripture, and enjoying two communities of faith: the Congregational church where I served on staff and the Presbyterian church where I served as an elder. The chance to again housesit for friends gave me an opportunity for solitude in which to consider the call burning within me. When I had first felt that urge toward ministry in junior high school, it was a call to "save souls" from a literal hell. Now it was a call to heal others from symbolic hells of isolation, loneliness, and brokenness by reminding people of God's presence and love and hope for us. As I look back now, clearly that's what God was doing in *my* life: no wonder I wanted to imitate Christ in such ministry.

From within this context, then, I reached out of my own isolation, my own loneliness, my own brokenness to Rev. Bill Johnson, Christ's representative to my own as yet unknown community. Surprised that I could easily obtain his address and phone number from the United Church of Christ's regional office, I was disappointed to discover the phone disconnected. Later I learned this was because of threatening phone calls Bill had received. Instead of writing to him, because I was still fearful of putting anything in writing that would reveal my sexuality, I drove to his address, arriving at a small apartment in Hollywood. Nervously I knocked on his door, and, finding no one home, left a note with my name, the phone where I was housesitting, and a rather cryptic message about who I was. Back at the house, nervous tension sent me into a flurry of hyperactivity all afternoon as I waited, ear cocked to the phone, wondering if he'd call. When the phone finally rang in early evening, I virtually leapt at it. It might as well have been God calling. It *was* Bill Johnson! His voice sounded friendly as he explained he ordinarily wouldn't have responded so quickly because he received so many crank messages and visits, but he already knew who I was, having visited the Congregational church where I shared the leadership of worship. And yes, he'd enjoy meeting me and could I come to his place the next evening?

Hanging up the phone, I literally screamed and jumped with delight. At last! Thank God! At last, someone I could talk with! Someone Christian! Someone gay! Someone in ministry! I put on my *Jesus Christ Superstar* album and danced into the night, praising God, joyful tears streaming down my face. I could have been Miriam dancing after escaping the Egyptians through the divided sea, or David dancing before the Ark of the Covenant as it was brought into Jerusalem. Truly God was delivering me, truly God was restoring me to the covenant. "And you he made alive . . ." the apostle Paul wrote of the experience to the Ephesians. To someone who had felt a "stranger to the covenants of promise," I understood that "now in Christ Jesus you who once were far off have been brought near." Faith may have its abstractions that stimulate the mind, but it is faith's incarnations that move the soul. Bill Johnson was an incarnation of God's love for me. The Spirit was moving. Somehow, I once again *belonged!*

The next evening I arrived early at Bill's door. A bit anxious, I worried whether he would like me. I so needed a friend who was gay and Christian. I so needed someone similarly committed to the church. Over a bottle of Christian Brothers wine (both wine and name symbolic of a new communion), we told our separate stories. By the end of the evening, I had fallen in love; for Bill's part, we had become friends. Regardless of the hurt that would come for me later as I realized the dissonance of our feelings, God had given me a role model and hope for the future. And, from this experience of infatuation, I learned to empathize with whose who, in similar circumstances, would later become infatuated with me.

Bill explained to me that, because of some threats made on his life by those who strongly opposed his ordination, he preferred not to go out alone, and asked me to accompany him out dancing that weekend. Like a lovesick kid, I was thrilled, and jumped at the opportunity. I had never been to a gay bar in Los Angeles. Though I guessed they existed, I had no idea where. We went to a bar then called "Dude City," a rambling place with several rooms and a tree-shaded patio. One room was devoted to dancing; another across the patio served as a piano bar, usually featuring a black woman accompanying herself as she sang downbeat love songs. In those days, one could still see men dressed in coats and ties on the dance floor, and I remember being struck by how handsome they all seemed. If one imagined women dancing with these men, the scene would have been reminiscent of the all-American college dance that concluded many *Ozzie and Harriet* episodes. I half-expected to bump into Ricky or Dave Nelson!

The dancers looked happy. I envied their seemingly carefree self-acceptance. They did not look hurt, broken, disenfranchised, or alienated. They appeared prosperous, healthy, stylish. But in the years to come I would discover, through listening and interaction, that most had suffered, most were vulnerable, and most were survivors. In attracting a mate or friends—one of the central functions of gay bars—one does not use a grimace, a frown, or a scowl, but a smile. Those who reveal their pain, their sadness, their anger, are usually the ones sitting by themselves, perhaps drinking too much. I think, in our minds, we as a community believe there's enough of that negativity on the outside. Within the dimly-lit bars, within the frenzy of the fast-paced dance, within the amnesia of alcohol, and within the soothing comfort of a feminine voice (especially of one who has known suffering) singing love songs, there is an escape to a fantasy world in which our sexual orientation makes no difference, in which gays and lesbians are not bruised, in which commitment overcomes alienation. Yet, just as Disneyland is not safe from nuclear threat, the fantasy world of the bars is not safe from homophobia. It insinuates itself sinisterly when we least expect or want it to do so; our own homophobia catches our hands as we "reach out and touch somebody's hand," as Diana Ross sang so well. Subsequent generations of gays know less and less of what I've just described, thanks to societal maturation.

It so happened that the following week I was on vacation from my job at the Congregational church, and it so happened that the national annual conference of the Universal Fellowship of Metropolitan Community Churches (UFMCC) was to be held in Los Angeles the same week. The congregation that had sent speakers to our forum at Van Nuys Presbyterian had given birth to a nationwide denomination ministering to the needs of lesbians and gays in most major cities. Bill Johnson invited me to attend some of the public meetings with him, including the Sunday morning worship. To be Bill's "date" made me glow with enhanced self-esteem and pride. Bill was treated as a celebrity, and I shared his spotlight. More lastingly, Bill introduced me to a vast community of gay Christians.

The gay Christians I met at this conference provided a contrast to what I experienced at the bar the previous weekend. There were more women and more ethnic groups at the conference. There was a signer for the deaf who were also present. There seemed to be a greater diversity of educational and economic levels. Just as important, there appeared to be a diverse spectrum of feelings represented at the conference. Here was a community where genuine happiness found sanctuary alongside equally genuine, legitimate, though less attractive feelings of hurt, sadness, and anger.

The integrity of these lesbian and gay Christians welcomed me whoever I happened to be, whatever I happened to feel: no one would be turned away here.

Suddenly I saw the gay bar I'd visited and many churches in America in a different light: not every feeling, not every person was welcome. Some churches, even more than gay bars, require a superficial cheeriness, as if those who are Christian are not supposed to experience anything but joy. Most churches do not enjoy an ethnic mix; many are ghettoized on the basis of economic or educational status; few provide accessibility for the physically challenged, from those in wheelchairs to those who are deaf. But here at this conference, and indeed, at most Metropolitan Community churches I would later visit, this fledgling denomination proved sanctuary to the genuine feelings and conditions of a diverse assortment of God's children.

The Sunday of the conference Bill Johnson invited me and several others to his apartment for a blueberry pancake brunch before worship. As the guests assembled, Bill gaily exclaimed with an undisguised Texas twang, "It's the Lord's day!" Finishing this communion, we proceeded in Bill's battered old car to worship at the so-called mother church of the UFMCC, an aged structure located somewhere in a barrio of downtown Los Angeles that was the target of arson years later and burned to the ground. The church was filled to capacity with people and with light, the sunshine filtering through opaque and stained glass windows. Singing began at the behest of a white-robed, spirited, and dramatic songleader who led us in hymns reminiscent of my Baptist upbringing: "Jesus Saves," "Amazing Grace," "The Old Rugged Cross," and "Washed in the Blood of the Lamb." Eventually, the founder, the Reverend Troy Perry, preached, proclaiming the gospel with a charisma which transported us into God's presence and felt embrace. The people at worship revealed that though every feeling and every person seemed welcome here, the predominant feeling and common denominator blossoming from such integrity was the joy of belonging to God, to the Body of Christ, to one another. Moved to tears to witness gays, lesbians, and same-gender couples approach Christ's table during communion, access to which had long been denied us by a less-than-compassionate church, I received communion from Rev. Perry himself, listening closely to the individualized blessing given each communicant. This was a long way from the fearful, secretive darkness of the Greek temple of the Pacific Ocean Park pier!

Filled with food for digestive thought, I drove to San Francisco the following week for the wedding celebration of friends. While there, I visited Glide Memorial Church, a Methodist congregation blessed by an endowment that enabled it to carry out controversial ministries without worrying about reactionary financial cutbacks. Ex-offenders, prostitutes, senior citizens, gays and lesbians, people of all colors and ethnic origins, and street people blended into a congregation that worshipped creatively and witnessed prophetically. Though on later visits I would come to dislike its showier aspects, I enjoyed the worship because of its inclusiveness.

I returned to Los Angeles by way of Sequoia National Park, spending the night in a rustic cabin. Sitting on Sunset Rock as the sun glowed orange on the mountainous horizon, I wrote a poem entitled "Going Out." At the time I did not think of it as a "coming out" poem. Told in first person, the poem recounts the experience of an old man ending a business day by closing his shop's door, choosing not to switch on the store's outside neon sign because it would obscure people's view of the nighttime stars. The poem contrasts the effortlessness of the sun's departure and its extravagant display of colors with the old man's difficult and relatively mundane and unnoticed departure from work and, by implication, from life:

> Another end of another day,
> But an effort to close the door.
> Reluctant to go, I stand in the way
> As before.
> But leaving is hard for me!
> I close the door of all I own . . .

A year later I submitted the poem to a seminary publication, where it was placed, to my surprise, next to a photograph of a freestanding closet, created specifically for an art exhibit entitled "Closet Show." Now I believe the poem hints of the anticipated grief process that coming out of the closet partly entails: letting go "of all I own," including certain life plans and expectations. Movement toward any form of liberation may mean limitation in other spheres of life. To those who claim gay Christians are unwilling to sacrifice for their Lord, I say we have sacrificed more than the average Christian by acknowledging and accepting God's unique gift to us while risking the loss that doing so may bring. Gay activists particularly have sacrificed much in responding to our call: we have staked our lives, our loved ones, and our livelihoods on our willingness to be vulnerable in our passion to reform church and society. It is not surprising that my first sermon to a largely gay congregation (the Metropolitan Community Church of Hartford in 1974) would be entitled "Letting Go." Sacrifice and liberation, crucifixion and resurrection are the yin and the yang of faith.

After a two-week vacation filled with meeting Bill Johnson and other gay Christians, communing with the Metropolitan Community Church (MCC), witnessing Glide's inclusiveness, celebrating the love and commitment of friends, and being embraced by nature at Sequoia, I eagerly developed my sermon for the following Sunday worship service at the Congregational Church of Northridge, dividing it into two mini-sermons based on separate texts from the book of Acts. The first interpreted the familiar story of Pentecost, that undoing of the confusion of Babel, in which strangers visiting Jerusalem each heard the gospel spoken in their own language. The gift of the Spirit, I proclaimed, lay in the church's ability to communicate God's love and grace in everybody's language, and I boldly used MCC and Glide as examples of churches communicating the gospel in the languages of those often excluded from church and society.

The second mini-sermon interpreted the story of Paul and Silas singing hymns in prison, when suddenly God sends an earthquake to set them free. The prisonkeeper awakes, imagines the prisoners have escaped, and prepares to kill himself rather than face disgrace and punishment for his negligence. Paul shouts out to him, "Do not be afraid, for we are all here." The grateful man is moved to salvation by their care for his welfare. In delivering the sermon, I recounted how those of us who had felt somewhat imprisoned by the church may now experience liberation, but shout to those who might despair our departure: "Do not be afraid, for we are all here." On the other hand, those of us who consider suicide because we've not lived up to the church's expectations also need to hear the reassuring words, "Do not be afraid, for we are all here." The message was, we're all in this together, prisoner and prisonkeeper alike; nobody's going to leave nor should anyone do themselves harm, because we're going to learn each other's language and create a more inclusive church through the inclusiveness of the gospel. None of us can be free until all of us are free. My later interest in liberation theology was foreshadowed in this proclamation. In college I had read Andre Malraux's *Man's Fate,* in which the protagonist states he works for revolution to guarantee the dignity not only of those who are oppressed but also of those who oppress others. I believe any true reformation liberates the oppressor and the oppressed alike.

After the worship service, Don Eaton told me I all but came out of the closet during the sermon, causing him much tension on my behalf: "There are fingernail marks where I gripped the pew as you preached!" Bill Johnson, who attended, congratulated me on the powerful integrity of the sermon. And the rest of the congregation? Never had I received a warmer, more supportive response. The usual handshakes as people exited the sanctuary were transformed to hugs, one couple exclaiming I would never know what the sermon meant to them. I intuited one was gay, and they were dealing with it in their marriage. Later I was informed by an unflustered Ken Eaton that one couple had left in a huff, muttering about "planning to leave the church for a long time, and *now* . . . !" "One sermon by itself never makes anyone leave the church," Ken reassured me. Whenever I am afraid of preaching a prophetic gospel, I remember this

experience as evidence that taking stands on social and ecclesiastical justice issues in the pulpit at least provokes those
listening to consider and reexamine or reaffirm what they
believe. Frankly, I believe preachers are more likely to lose
members of congregations to boredom than by taking such
stands.

During my visit to Glide Memorial Church in San Francisco
I had discovered the church building housed the Council on
Religion and the Homosexual. There I spoke with Phyllis
Lyon about a November weekend conference the council was
planning entitled, "Lifestyles of the Homosexual." Totally unknown to me was Phyllis Lyon's legendary status in our community as cofounder with her lover Del Martin of the earliest
lesbian organization, Daughters of Bilitis. These two women
had been fighting for my rights since before I was in grade
school, and in 1972, the year I met Phyllis, their book *Lesbian/
Woman* was published. For me, the history of the lesbian/gay
movement was as yet an untapped resource of encouragement
and strength. Friendly and supportive, Phyllis encouraged me
to attend the conference, though designed primarily for nongay clergy and others in helping professions.

In November, then, I flew to San Francisco to attend the
conference. Happily it reunited me with Bill Johnson, one of
the conference presenters, whose move to San Francisco earlier in the fall had left me somewhat forlorn. As he greeted
me with a kiss on the lips in front of other registering participants, I delighted in the sign of affection while fearing the
others' reaction at the same time. I had not intended to offer
the fact that I was gay, yet I had also decided not to deny it
if asked. I disliked straddling the closet threshold, but I was
here as an observer, not yet a gay participant, nor a voyeur
unwilling to participate.

Many people find it difficult to understand that members
of disenfranchised groups often hold the same prejudices
that are held by mainstream society and that keep them
disenfranchised. This partly accounts for the failure of many
women to embrace feminist values. This dynamic also encourages those who live in economic ghettoes to commit crimes

against one another rather than to address the external source of their economic oppression. And certainly one reason gays and lesbians have trouble engaging in community organization is that they have been taught that homosexuals cannot be trusted. Further division is created by other prejudices: lesbian feminists may believe they cannot trust men regardless of orientation; gay men may believe they cannot trust women regardless of orientation; and lesbians and gays of various colors may find difficulty overcoming racial prejudices, not to mention divisions of age, class, physical handicap, economic status, political ideology, and religious beliefs.

For me, prejudices against Jews were overcome by attending high school with large numbers of Jewish students and teachers, and fears of blacks were overcome by attending conferences and exchange programs for both black and white students. In the same way, this conference on the lifestyles of homosexuals would help me overcome my own homophobia, evidenced in everything from my nauseous reaction to the Baptist youth worker's homosexuality to the dream described earlier in which I ran terrified from the gay man who tapped me on the shoulder. Ancient converts to Christianity were not told the significance of baptism or communion until after they had been baptised and received their first communion, because it was believed participation was required for true understanding of these sacraments. So, this weekend's immersion into the gay community and communion with lesbians and gays served as a prerequisite for true understanding. Years later, I would attempt to duplicate this weekend experience for others in similar conferences.

The weekend was evenly divided between the gay male experience and the lesbian experience, with a bisexual speaker placed in the middle for good measure. Speakers included a poet, a clergyperson, an attorney, and a therapist. Enablers for the small group discussions were, for the first half, lesbian women, and for the second half, gay men, all of whom reminded one of the girl- or boy-next-door. We dined in gay restaurants, drank in gay bars and lesbian bars, browsed in gay bookstores. In one lesbian bar I experienced for the first time women's protectiveness of their environments, as our mostly male group was almost asked to leave until the reason for our presence was explained by one of the conference organizers. Then we were warmly welcomed! Being a minority within a minority, women's bars are relatively rare and require a strong defense to prevent the invasion of nongay males and even well-intentioned gay males—that is, if the space is to remain a true sanctuary for lesbian women. We took a tour of men's bars one night. As we approached one of them I noticed men coming and going decked out in leather jackets and caps or uniforms. Naively, I guessed it to be a hangout for airline pilots. I'd never heard of a leather and uniform bar, nor of those who enjoy macho drag.

One morning, as we sat on overstuffed pillows on the floor of a room in the church basement, we were shown three films at a time, along with two slide shows. The films, from the series produced by the National Sex Forum, documented sexual behavior between a variety of real-life couples, ranging from geriatric heterosexual to gay or lesbian encounters. The slides projected romantic rather than sexually explicit images. There has been considerable debate over the ethics of such a desensitization process, which so inundates the senses and brain with input that societally implanted sensitivities are numbed. My view, and evidently that of the conference organizers, is that our sex-negative culture needs such radical therapy so we may *begin* to feel comfortable with our bodies, our sensuality, and our sexuality. The impression left by the films was that, generally, sexuality as an expression of true relationship between mutually-consenting adults was okay. Some Christians might then ask, what is sexual sin? Clearly, exploitation, rape, violence, and child molestation are not expressions of true relationships between mutually consenting adults. These categories might constitute sexual sin, were it not true that all of these really fall into another category of sin: abusive power and control. Often those most judgmental of so-called sexual sin are those most adept at or desirous of abusive power and control; Jesus' admonishment to those who would stone the woman taken in adultery (what about the man?) "Let one without sin cast the first stone" should stay the hands of all of us.

By far the most intimate experience the conference offered us was an evening visit to the homes of the gay and lesbian leaders of the event. Each small group went to a different home, and in the context of preparing and serving coffee and dessert and in the conversation surrounding this simple but profound ritual of hospitality, we caught a glimpse of the broader context in which these lesbians and gays—just like everyone else—must live their lives. We met roommates, lovers, children, and parents. We saw their books and their pets, sat in the furniture bought at garage sales or department stores, ate from their grandmothers' china, saw pictures of their families and friends, witnessed their prosperity or their poverty, listened to their favorite music. We thought less of their sexuality and more of our common humanity. They were not as different from us as we had thought!

The closing session of the conference revealed how the overall immersion into the gay and lesbian community affected the participants personally. As we took turns explaining what the weekend meant for each of us, one woman summed up the general feeling: "With trillions of stars and planets in the universe, and earth as one more speck in it all, how ridiculous to think of all these tiny little organisms on that speck we call human getting agitated because two other tiny organisms with the same genitals are making love!" In a spontaneous and imaginative way, this described the perspective we had gained. Sexual orientation had become in our eyes as morally neutral as color of skin, gender, age, and so on. We could now move on to the real and important moral issues. We were born again to a new communion possible through our baptism by immersion into the gay community. We were sensitized to society's trivial fixation on judging sexual variation, and we were sensitized to a vision of God's kingdom beyond such judgment. In Christ's communion and God's commonwealth, lesbians and gays were as welcome as everyone else. We ended the weekend by embracing one another not as gay and nongay, but as children of God.

As I flew home to Los Angeles, both exhausted and uplifted, I realized all that had transpired the previous summer and had been confirmed by this conference occasioned an integration of my faith and my sexuality. No longer separate paths, they converged on a third. No longer segregated by compartmentalization, they danced with each other, creating a newfound integrity from which I could approach life and ministry. I could affirm, with other human beings, that I am created in God's image. With other Christians, I could affirm reconciliation in Jesus Christ. The Spirit now led me into a future in which the only assurance would be God's presence in my joy and suffering. All this without renouncing the sexual orientation God gave me. All this without rejecting God's acceptance of me in Jesus Christ and the Body of Christ, the church. All this without refusing to follow the leading of the Holy Spirit in fulfilling the ministry to which she called me. I had previously accepted my ability to love another man intimately as a gift from God. Having integrated my Christian faith and my homosexuality, I now believed myself called to enable others to bring a similar integrity to their own lives and ministry. My ministry became one of reconciliation: to be instrumental in the Spirit's reconciling externally what she had reconciled internally within me, bringing the gay, lesbian, and Christian communities together.

Chapter 4

COMING OUT TO MY FAMILY

LOS ANGELES
NOVEMBER 1972

Upon my return to Los Angeles from the conference, I believed I heard a faint knocking on my closet door from my own family. A conference entitled "Lifestyles of the Homosexual" was bound to precipitate curious questions from them about my apparently more-than-passing interest in the plight of the homosexual. I sensed my family both did and didn't want to know the truth. A family's response is difficult for the gay person to gauge: often the most blatant hints dropped by a gay member of a family are somehow ignored; perhaps just as often, a gay member who carefully covers tracks may be known to the rest of the family before she or he has come to terms with it. Most gay people imagine the family's reaction will be more negative than it usually turns out to be. In my case, blatant hints about concern for the homosexual community were understood by my family as just one more liberal cause I pursued along with equality for blacks, Latinos, and Native Americans.

On my side were the memories of my parents facing the issue caringly in regard to the youth worker at our Baptist church. On the other side, my parents experienced my sister's divorce a few years earlier as a death in the family. What would they say to a son's homosexuality? In a dinner conversation after my return from the conference, my father, whom I believe felt almost as troubled about my becoming a Presbyterian as he would later feel about my homosexuality, surprised me by saying to my mother about homosexuals: "If they feel for each other what I feel for you, I can understand why they want their relationships." Though I found this re-assuring, I nonetheless feared my father might be less ac-cepting than my mother, who had proven fiercely and even irrationally loyal to her loved ones. Years before, the Christian school (where she taught and where I had attended school) had asked her for a story about an honor I had received. They also wanted a photograph of me for the alumni section of their newsletter, but then declined the picture because I had a beard. My mother refused permission for them to run the story, declaring, "He won the award with a beard, and if you don't want the picture, you don't get the story." Ironically, she herself had never been too happy about my beard. Now, in the same dinner conversation mentioned earlier, she inno-cently asked me, "Why are you so interested in homo-sexuals?" I avoided the central truth, citing peripheral truths of fairness, acceptance, and equality before God. But I be-lieved she unconsciously or consciously wanted an answer, and I knew it was forthcoming. On a previous occasion, I had intentionally requested their emotional support and prayers for what I thought might be a controversial and prophetic ministry. I had left the reason obscure, but they took it at face value and pledged their support, expressing belief that God had indeed called me to ministry. Now they needed to know the content of my calling.

I worried less about telling my sister and brother, who were, at the time, fairly liberal, though my brother would become increasingly conservative and, much later, my sister more moderate. At the time I felt closer to my sister: we shared similar political interests and biases. Years before, I had shown her the story I'd written about the homosexual youth worker, and we had talked about the situation comfortably. Though I grew to believe her divorce was a painful blessing for her, I initially believed it to be a sin, writing her a letter in which I pointed out that, though Jesus himself went beyond the law in many circumstances and was very forgiving, he personally condemned divorce. It was one of the subjects on which Jesus was unequivocally clear, I piously wrote. Of course I did not then know the context to which Jesus was responding, that is, that women of his day were being misused and faced financial insecurity because many men were wantonly divorcing wives to marry other women. And my desire to keep my sister biblically in line probably was fueled by my need to keep myself biblically in line. Thank God I never sent her the letter!

Throughout my upbringing, it seemed as if my brother always led the family politically. When he supported Johnson for the 1960 Democratic nomination, we did; when he supported Goldwater for President in 1964, we did; when he shifted back to the Democrats in support of Eugene McCarthy in 1968 in opposition to the war, we did. But, by the elections of 1972, we had gone our separate paths politically. Increasingly alienated from radical and liberal politics, he expressed discomfort with my open sympathy for certain liberal and radical causes. As my name appeared on more and more letters to the editor and commentaries in the college paper, and later in other places on behalf of the gay cause, he asked me to consider changing my name so my reputation would not reflect negatively on the family. Family loyalty has always served as cornerstone to our family unity, and my brother is perhaps the most loyal of all, always being there for family members when needed.

It had taken most of my twenty-two years for me to arrive at a point of self-acceptance and integration of seemingly paradoxical parts of my personality: my sexuality and my faith. I hardly expected my family—or anyone else—to affirm my integrity overnight. I knew whatever doubts, fears or pain yet lay before me, I needed to present my sense of call to my parents, both to be who God created me to be and to fulfill the ministry to which God called me, in the context of the faith we shared and with a minimal description of difficulties that lay ahead. In coming out of the closet, I spoke of current truth and truth yet to be. Yes, I accepted myself, but I continue to this day overcoming my own homophobia. Yes, I anticipated a single lifemate in a committed, faithful relationship, but I had yet to meet someone with whom I shared a common vision, a common commitment to the church, a common passion for social justice; and I knew the odds were not in my favor nor the societal support present for such a relationship. Yes, I anticipated the church would affirm God's call to me with ordination, but I knew it would be many years for the church to overcome the dividing wall of hostility between gay and nongay Christians. If, to my parents, I offered a description of things only as they were and not also as they *would* be, I believed I would not be presenting the full picture. The inbreaking nature of God's kingdom inspired Paul to speak in his letters of the Christian's call to live "as if" the kingdom were already here. This is what I attempted to do.

I intended to tell my parents before my brother and sister, but in a conversation with my sister I accidentally divulged my "terrible secret." She asked me why I'd visited a therapist. I replied evasively that it had something to do with a part of my personality I just couldn't talk about. Mischievously smiling, she abruptly guessed, "You're a homosexual." Stunned, I said, "How did you know?" Quickly she responded, "Oh, if you were a maniac going around killing people, you could talk about that, even write a book about it! But no one can talk about homosexuality." It was true. She thought a moment and then joked, "I always wanted a little sister!", a comment I received in the good humor in which she offered it, though uncomfortable with its implications. We then discussed how to tell our parents, who had already suffered two major shocks in recent years: her divorce and my father's cancer. (Within a few days of writing this description of our conversation, and reporting to my sister its contents, she confessed that, at the time, she had just made the "most wild guess" and, upon discovering she was correct, felt forced to justify it somehow!)

I decided to tell my parents my longheld secret by letter. Though some might judge it cowardly not to tell them face-to-face, I believed writing them a letter would enable more of a heart-to-heart encounter. I knew I expressed myself more clearly in writing than in speaking. I also knew that an exchange of letters, with all parties giving careful thought to what each actually wanted and meant to say, might avoid initial, ill-considered verbal reactions, exchanges, and mis-understandings we might later regret. Asking each of my parents to respond by letter would further insure obtaining their individual reactions rather than a single, perhaps com-promised response. I wanted to know how each felt, what each believed and concluded. To give them a full weekend to face it together, I left the following letter on their dining room table one Friday afternoon.

November 16, 1972

Dear Mother and Father,

This is the most difficult letter I have ever had to write; and it'll perhaps be the most difficult letter you will ever have to receive.

I love you very much. I firmly believe you love me very much. And that is why I feel the need to write this letter. I need to share a part of me that I have denied you most of my life.

You were curious why I took such interest in the cause of the homosexual. You've asked me that several times, and you've asked me countless other times in the past, "What's wrong?" I believe you genuinely want an answer from me; I've judged, rightly or wrongly, that you are capable of re-ceiving my answer. One of the reasons I'm interested in the cause of the homosexual is because I am a homosexual. And "what's wrong" is that I am a homosexual in an antihomo-sexual world.

For me there is nothing wrong in being a homosexual. In fact, there is everything right in it. I enjoy being gay. God has created me this way. I accept it. I affirm it. I thank God for it.

Being gay under oppression from a heterosexual world has sharpened my senses, my emotions, my intellect. As the op-pressed Israelites became stronger than their Egyptian op-pressors, so I have become stronger. My strength is the strength to live—and to live joyously. And my strength is the strength to love—and to love unconditionally.

I love you too much not to share this integral part of my personality with you, even if it involves taking certain risks.

To be fair to you and to myself, I decided to write this to you rather than tell you directly so we may both be spared your initial reactions. I am not so interested in your initial response as I am in your eventual, more carefully thought out response, a response governed by your love for me and God's leading.

I'd like both of you to respond *individually* to me by letter after you have given much thought to yourselves, to me, to my being gay, and to our relationship. I am certainly not afraid of God's leading in your decision. God has been with me in all of my struggles and has loved me through them all into self-affirmation. Somehow I believe that God has called me to an extraordinary ministry that requires my whole personality, and especially that area of my personality that has enabled me to *feel* and to be *sensitive* to so much: my homosexuality.

I ask you to respond separately so I may know what each of you really feel about this. Don't respond in a hurry—think about it. Search your innermost feelings. *I don't want to talk* to you or see you until I have received your letters. Don't think of the letters as your final decisions—your opinions will undoubtedly change. But continue loving me as you write!

I don't want you to feel that I am gay because of something you did or did not do. That reasoning doesn't work with me. I have always been gay, and will never change, and find no reason in our relationship that would have "caused" it. And once again, I am happy being gay.

I love you very much. Continue in the faith of our Lord.

Chris

Despite my request to avoid contact until their letters had been written, I received three phone calls from my parents that Friday evening. They were reacting typically for any major family crisis I could remember: my mother was hysterical, my father very, very calm. They wanted me to come over to their home, but I remained firm in my resolve. None of their phone calls were punitive in content, just distressed, flailing, wanting to reach out. Even with a good friend holding me, emotionally it was extremely difficult for me as well. I felt like I had abandoned them in the most difficult crisis of their lives; and yet, rightly or wrongly, I judged we needed to be separate to sort out our feelings. There would be time to communicate and respond to questions. I had intentionally chosen to tell them a full year before I would be leaving for seminary so that we would have many opportunities for dialogue. If I had waited till I left for seminary, it might have been too easy not to write.

Early the following week, I received their replies, both dated November 20. I waited to read their letters in the garden of the horticultural department of the college, wanting to be outside in a nurturing atmosphere. Though I winced at my parents' mistaken notion that psychiatry could change me, I read the following in fear and in faith transforming to joy. From my father:

Dear Chris,

To borrow a phrase from your letter of Thursday night, November 16, this too is probably the most difficult letter I have ever had to write. I honestly don't know if I am quite ready to write it yet. I only know that I must try.

The last two days have been such that there hasn't been much time for thinking of any thing except helping your mother get through the initial reaction. I won't dwell on the details of this, but I have never seen any thing quite like it. At times I thought we had lost her—that her mind was gone forever.

It is difficult to explain just how I felt during all this time. In a way, it might be likened to the time when your mother fell into the creek at Oak Creek Canyon. All the time the water was pushing us along that rocky creek all I could think of was, "I've got to keep her head above the water and hope and pray that the rocks pounding my back don't hit my head." And then it was over and I was sort of numb all over from the pounding. I don't think she would have made it then if I hadn't been there—but I honestly don't know this. You and Steve might have realized the danger in time, or if she took on water you might have been able to bring her around with artificial respiration.

But the thing is, she did make it then, and since she has written her letter to you before leaving for school this morning, she asked me to please write mine and to stamp and mail them today—I think, thank God, we can believe she has made it now—and again, I like to think that my being here helped. But in all honesty I must say that I don't really know.

However, now as then, for the most part I feel numb all over in a sense. Somewhere in this numbness there are feelings that will take time to come through: some may be good, some not so good. I hope and pray that *you* will forgive me of those that are not so good. I am sure there will be areas of disagreement between us as to what you should do or not do about the situation.

One thing that has come clearly through to me during the last two days is that I love you, Son, even more than I had ever realized. This surprising revelation came to me yesterday when I realized that through all this trying time since you gave us the bitter news that I didn't rant and rave at you like a maniac and try to shove all the blame on you. This doesn't say it very well, I'm afraid.

Another thing, I am truly proud of you for your courage in writing that letter and the courage to live that you have. If I may borrow some of that for a moment, I will use it to say this: My Son, I love you, whatever happens, or at least I think I could. I know definitely I don't want to lose you as a son. Just as definitely, as of now anyway, I want you to be as we are. Please give it some more thought. If you can bring yourself to try it, you will have all the support I can possibly give you.

As you mentioned in your letter, my writing of this letter also involves "taking certain risks." How you will evaluate what I have written, I don't know. If you take offense at my wanting to change you, please remember it is out of love that I want it. Love motivates changes throughout anyone's life. Every human being grows up, develops, becomes educated because someone loves him enough to bring about a gradual change from an unintelligible infant to a grown person capable of thought, feeling and living.

Chris, as they say "for openers" this is as much as I can honestly say now. Your mother has written her letter and I have written mine. Neither of us has seen what the other wrote, but I have an idea that the thought is about the same, only she probably said it better, or at least it was certainly in a more legible handwriting—ha! I have written this fast as it came from my heart without editing or copying it in more legible form.

The bakery strike is still on, so I will be working around home. Please come by and say hello or join me for lunch if you can find time. It was good to see you last Friday, even though the letter you left was something like a bomb.

It's a strange thing, but when I saw it there on the table I had the feeling that it was something that would make it a difficult weekend, and was tempted to open it before your mother came home. I didn't, but for awhile there I wished I had. Now, of course, I am glad I didn't. Together is the way we should read a letter like that. And together is the way we as a family should face the situation. Together with God, I should say.

As Jesus said, "The world will know ye are mine because ye love the brethren."

Love,
Father

From my mother:

Dear Chris,

This too is a most difficult letter for a mother to write. But maybe you can read between the lines and see the great love I have for you.

I've always felt there was no greater joy than to carry a baby; to know that inside me God was forming a new little life; and that I had that little soul very close to my heart so that every heartbeat would convey to my baby how much I loved him. I feel so sorry for women who resent the fact that they are women.

And I enjoyed my babies after they were born. I cuddled and loved you a little more because you were my last baby and I had more time. And everything I did for you was for the glory of God—your name, Sunday school, and even your day school.

But the Bible says the sins of the fathers fall upon the child, so I feel what has happened to you must be for my sins—I haven't been the best mother, I know.

My heart aches because while you were going through your problems you didn't trust me enough to confide in me. You went to everyone else first. So I know how much I have failed you. And I only wanted to love you. Can you forgive me?

Needless to say, you know how I feel about this problem. How can you be so sure? Have you sought professional help other than the one time? You can have every penny I make if you will go to a good psychiatrist. Would you try?

This needn't make any difference in our family relations because I shall always love you just as I did when you were next to my heart.

This is a poor example of my thoughts and feelings, but until I can think more clearly this will have to do.

Love,
Mom

P.S. I've just reread this. It all sounds so wrong. Just remember one thing. I love you and will help you in any way you'll let me. Can we talk about it sometime?

My parents' expressions of love and invitations to communication overjoyed me, though I felt troubled misunderstandings common in our society led them to believe psychiatry could change me and led my mother to blame herself, perceiving it as God's retribution. The years that followed—years of dialogue, reading, and growth—drew us closer together, enabling a fuller and more honest embrace, both in terms of mutual affirmation and our ability to speak together openly of both spirituality and sexuality, realms of intimacy considered taboo between many parents and children. My parents have also witnessed and even suffered for the cause.

Later, in 1976, when a consenting adults bill was before the California state legislature, their pastor preached against it, decrying homosexuality. My father took him aside and told him he didn't know the first thing about it, and bent his ear for an hour without revealing his son was gay, because he believed sharing such information was not his prerogative. Upon hearing of it from my mother, I told him, laughing, "The minister probably thought *you* were gay!" I felt deep pride in my father for taking the risks involved in correcting his pastor.

My public activity on behalf of the gay cause would test family relations in the years following this episode. Sensitive to my brother's concerns about unnecessary notoriety, I initially carefully guarded my media exposure. In a 1978 issue of the now defunct magazine *Inspiration,* I participated in a dialogue with Rev. John MacArthur, pastor of some of my brother's students, but requested my identity as a gay person be withheld and withdrew an argument from personal experience upon review of the typed transcript. Roger Ellwood, the publication's editor, broke faith with our verbal agreement and identified me as a member of the gay community in his opening column. At the same time, John Dart, religion editor for the *Los Angeles Times,* picked up a story written by Howard Erickson for the newsletter of Lutherans Concerned for Gay People. The story, which then ran in the *Times,* described my ministry within the gay community. John Dart had tried to reach me before running the story, but I was out of town. Upon my return my brother would not speak to me, evidently perceiving the publicity as both selfish and self-chosen. For almost a year he avoided me, a painful time for us both, not to mention the rest of the family. Finally I orchestrated a combined gift from my brother, sister, and me for my parents' anniversary, bringing us together at my parents' home for a surprise party. The reunion brought grateful tears to my parents' eyes, who were joyful that the enmity had been overcome.

But the publicity would take yet another toll on the family. My mother and brother both taught at a local Christian School, where I had attended elementary and junior high school. Though many of their fellow teachers proved supportive of them in the face of the news that I was gay, the school's principal did not invite my mother back to teach the following year. My brother, who taught in the junior high school, quit in solidarity. After thirty years of teaching first grade, it was especially disheartening and devaluing for my mother to have this happen so close to retirement. Sorely underpaid, she had sacrificially given of herself—her talent, time, and money—to help shape the school's early history and the lives of hundreds of her first-grade students, who frequently returned (often with their parents) for visits in which they thanked her for her efforts. To her credit and the credit of the other schools, three Christian schools immediately offered her teaching positions.

An aunt of mine who spent her life teaching high school in Coffeyville, Kansas, moved out to California upon retirement a few years before I came out to my immediate family. During my first year of seminary, she told my brother of a homosexual couple who lived in her apartment building. As often happened with this independent-thinking aunt, she surprised my brother by her open-mindedness. "Now, they don't like the term *homosexual*," she explained to him, "They prefer the word *gay*." My brother later asked me if her tolerance came from my coming out to her; I regret to say I never had the courage to tell her, and she died without knowing. She was very religious, and I feared disappointing her—she was so proud of my attending seminary. But I've wondered if she couldn't have handled it. As it turned out, when the gay couple in her apartment building broke up, she ended up ministering to the one who remained, as he spent many hours confiding in her all his feelings.

The rest of my extended family learned of my being gay through the media, certainly not the preferred way of coming out! I wondered if Pittsburg, Kansas, where many of my relatives lived, would continue as a second home for me. "He's still the same Chris we loved before," my aunts and uncles told my mother. And I wondered if I would enjoy the same gracious acceptance I previously received from my uncle in Texas. He is truly a self-made man, owner of his own construction company, very macho, and a conservative Republican. Upon learning of my sexuality, he typically kidded my mother, "You tell Chris I just want him to know that he's always welcome in my house—so long as he never votes Democratic again!" In more recent years, during a speaking engagement in nearby Houston, he affirmed me again by sending word through his son that he wanted me to do his funeral when the time came. I wished him a long life by returning the message: "May I be ordained by the time you need my services!" My uncle had worked with a gay professional whom he respected, thus enabling him to be open to me. Personalizing the issue for people is the best argument for acceptance that gay people can put forth.

Some final observations about my immediate family: my parents, starting from their conservative religious perspective, came a long way toward supporting me, my ministry, and my attempts at finding a lifelong relationship. In part, I believe, this is because they were not afraid to ask questions for which they needed answers. Sometimes I've wondered if my brother and sister have adequate answers to questions they refrained from asking. Some people, in a sincere attempt to be liberally accepting, stifle legitimate questions, concerns, and feelings, and later fail to understand the full dimensions of a gay person's experience. I've usually felt my parents were the more understanding of me, though indeed that may be so because they understand my commitment to faith and church, which may be more of a mystery to my sister and brother than my sexuality!

My whole family now embraces and enjoys my partner in life, treating him as another member of the family. The nicest Christmas gifts I've received in recent years have been: my parents' exchanging gifts with him our first Christmas together; my sister and brother exchanging gifts with him our second; my relatives from Kansas and Oklahoma asking to speak with him when they phoned the family our third Christmas; and the following Christmas these same relatives writing to invite us to visit them sometime and, in the meanwhile, to send them a photograph of us together for their family album!

We all still enjoy butting heads with each other over issues, but over more important ones, like who should be president of the United States! And my nephews have grown up in a different era then we did. Having a gay uncle accepted by the family, they are able, as my youngest nephew made a point of doing at a recent family gathering, to discuss the need for gay civil rights.

Chapter 5

LETTING GO: SACRIFICE AND LIBERATION

LOS ANGELES
DECEMBER, 1972–AUGUST 1973

Given the emotional trauma of coming out in the summer and fall, it's not surprising that I proved vulnerable to a severe case of mononucleosis early that December. Untypically for the disease, it affected my inner ear, throwing off my sense of balance and coordination. A combination of misguided medical advice and lack of rest permitted this pseudodrunken state to plague me for several months. Beyond the sudden burst of energy expended to begin coming out of the closet, enormous energy is required to keep the closet door, as well as communication with family and friends, open. The close friends to whom I entrusted so much of myself had moved: Don now lived on Prince Edward Island, composing songs; Henry had transferred to the University of California at Davis, and Bill Johnson lived in San Francisco. I did not yet have a reliable support group of gay friends. Between responsibilities with two congregations, I had little time or opportunity to reach out to MCC. I boarded with a wonderful older woman from my Presbyterian church, and though she proved supportive of me as gay, neither of us could understand or manage the whirlpool of feelings, searching, and events that surfaced as I came out of the closet. I abruptly moved from that living situation, figuratively running away from home, and rented a room from an older gay man, a friend of a friend. It became a lonely time for me in which I felt sorry for myself and resented my closest friends for being so far away.

Even now I find it difficult to write of this period; no words can adequately express the depression, ill health, and grief I experienced in this wilderness, as I grumbled ungratefully, "Is this the way to the promised land?" A friend formerly involved in hospice work describes the coming out process as a grief process: not only letting go of many life plans, but also letting go of certain perceptions and beliefs, and sometimes letting go of family, friends, community, or church. Nights often found me in gay bars, searching for a messianic lover to deliver me from my loneliness, insecurity, and fear. My desperation and intensity probably scared many away. I attempted to use creativity as a way out of the wilderness, but the dismal subject of one forty-stanza poem was a family of four whom our family had known—a family who had died one by one through plane crash, heart attack, and cancer over a short span of time.

The mononucleosis caused me to sleep all but two hours of Christmas day. Yet on that day the Christian message penetrated my self-pitying suffering, and words came to me in a semi-dreamlike state, from which I rose to write:

> Love is being crucified
> And rising again
> As if it never happened.
> That's love for you.
> That's love for *you*.

In other words, the Christian story is about love getting hurt and yet springing back, forgiving so completely as to forget. I felt hurt by the neglect of friends, the absence of a lover, the rejection (experienced and anticipated) of church and society, but my calling was to rise again as if it had never happened. This was how I experienced God's love in the death and resurrection of Christ. I believed myself called to love like that.

Jesus had called me forth from a tomblike closet, just as he called Lazarus. As religious authorities plotted the death of

Lazarus because he served as living proof of Jesus' spiritual power, so self-defeating forces within me plotted my death because I felt unworthy of a resurrected life. Those self-defeating forces, I believe, grew from the homophobia that permeates the fabric of our church and society. Though not as pronounced, the dynamic parallels the experience of those I've counseled who were abused as children: just as they question their worthiness of success and sometimes choose defeat instead, so I've been tempted to accept defeat by my own self-doubt. This leads me to conclude that homophobia and heterosexism (an exclusively heterosexual view of the world), alongside sexism, racism, ageism, and the like, are subtle and pervasive forms of child abuse.

Self-defeating forces seek to contain us like whitewashed tombs, keeping us under the power of gravity with the seduction of "resting in peace" rather than allowing us to break free and soar. In the words which came to me on Christmas day, I heard Jesus calling me forth from such self-defeating forces, asserting, "I am the resurrection and the life."

Throughout this difficult period, I somehow managed to continue ministering effectively at the Congregational church, serve the Presbyterian church as an elder, finish my college work, and plan for a trip to Europe, a dream for which I'd been saving for years. Although I had originally intended to travel and work in Europe for a year before entering seminary, Bill Johnson had so inspired me that I decided to travel only six months and enter Yale Divinity School the next fall. Even these plans were changed when I met Jeff.

I met Jeff at a gay disco; a little too quickly we became lovers and considered our relationship a marriage. In later years I decided we hadn't really been lovers, nor was our relationship a marriage: we were just two lonely people who desperately needed each other. More recently, I don't care to try to label whatever we had. Yes, we were each lonely and looking for someone, but we also loved one another as well as we could. Our dissimilarities would have eventually pulled us from one another's embrace, had Jeff not retreated first. I persuaded him to travel through Europe with me, cutting down my planned six months of traveling to two, so as to subsidize his trip. Soon into the journey Jeff made it clear he didn't want to visit any more cathedrals, nor was he interested in Christian symbolism in Europe's art and architecture. I hardly knew enough of such symbolism to have bored or burdened him with it, so I grew to believe his negativity arose from his recognition of an attachment and passion I had for the church that he did not share, something he rightly imagined would take me from him.

Traveling in Europe tempted me to remain there and avoid the ordeal I knew I would face in seeking ordination and serving the church. I dreamed I could live there, be myself, and live happily ever after in relative anonymity. Such a temptation was reminiscent of an earlier one to take a nine-to-five job, perhaps driving for the baking company for which my father worked, get married, buy a house, have children, camp on weekends. To live my life as everyone else seemed a happy alternative. But it denied so much of what was unique about me: my passion for the church, my extraordinary call to ministry, my sexuality, my hope to make a difference, my thirst for adventure. Ultimately, to be like everyone else would kill me, not literally but just as surely. But where would the road less traveled lead me?

Standing on the prow of a ferry from Brindisi to Corfu in the middle of the night, the inky-black Mediterranean merging in the distance with the misty blackness of the sky, I intuited the primitive fear that humanity must have felt as it rose from the sea's mud and saw the earth's horizon for the first time, and the exhilarating joy that space travelers must feel when they first break from the power of gravity holding down their bodies and imaginations. I wondered where I was being propelled, but relished the fearful joy of heading there.

The next day, seated on rocks beside a clear blue bay on the lushly green Greek isle of Corfu, I felt myself transported back to original innocence, to timeless and dutiless existence.

Though Corfu is too lush to be a typical Greek isle, the beach of Paleocatritsa embraced by towering cliffs resurrected Crete's Zorba within me, and I laughed as Zorba to watch a rooster chase a hen and mount her on the grounds of the local monastery perched high upon one of these cliffs. Despite such a commanding perspective, monastic life represented what I judged too quickly as a denial of God's gift of sexuality. Later I would understand celibacy itself as a gift, though one not so prolifically proferred as expected of Roman Catholic clergy and homosexual and single heterosexual Protestants and Catholics.

Even the idyllic and amnestic setting of Paleocatritsa could not erase the memory of the small green-and-white marble church on the outskirts of Florence, where I had found myself kneeling almost involuntarily in prayer as an organ lifted its voice in solemn praise. And I couldn't blot out of memory the unexpected tears I shed while visiting the tomb of Pope John the XXIII in the bier under St. Peter's Cathedral, the only grave in Europe that moved me so deeply. The neopagan within me wanting to revel in Bacchic delight of the senses was forever married to a Calvinist servant of God. Dionysian chaos bubbled from deep within me, like a sulphur hot spring warming the Calvinist cold and sobering water of the baptismal pool of my soul. Jesus and Zorba danced together a prayer of gratitude for God's grace on the shores of my experience. This did not seem inconceivable, remembering that both pagans and early Christians believed in the resurrection of the body, though the first sensualized the experience and the latter spiritualized it.

Jeff had no idea what I was experiencing, and I discovered no way to share it with him. He would not have been interested, nor would he have understood. It would have been like trying to describe the color red to someone who was color blind. My spiritual journey claimed my ultimate attention, though tempted to choose a lesser path. Upon our return from Europe that summer, Jeff suddenly turned cold, refused to consider coming to New Haven with me, and withdrew, I believe all as defense against possible hurt. My grief that summer was intense, as in the middle of ordinary tasks I would, without warning, stop and cry very hard. Now I am grateful Jeff recognized, as would many potential lifemates, that anyone in relationship with me would have to deal with another jealous lover, the church. Better to find someone who shared a similar, passionate commitment to the church; any marriage for me would have to be a *ménage à trois,* the third party being the church.

Jeff's withdrawal tempted me to stay with him, since I assumed my spiritual passion caused his protective alienation. But I knew fulfillment lay in another direction. Deep down, I believe, so did he. Packing my few possessions into my old Volkswagen, I drove from the home in which I'd grown up. A disc jockey on the radio quoted Thomas Wolfe: "You can't go home again." I cried passing the Los Angeles city limits, saying goodbye to family, friends, and lover. I sensed I was forever bidding farewell to the world as I had known it; if and when I returned, I would be a different person and see with different eyes. The pain of separation was buffered knowing my parents would follow in their car as far as Kansas, where we would visit relatives before I pushed on alone.

As a youth, hiking with a friend in the foothills surrounding my junior high school, I once slid on loose shale and somersaulted a substantial distance down a narrow gully to the bottom of the hill. When my friend reached me, he told me he thought for sure I'd been killed. My memory of the incident is clear: as I realized I'd lost control and could do nothing to prevent the fate awaiting me, I relaxed completely, probably accounting for my lack of broken bones or serious injury, though to this day I carry a scar on my left side from a deep cut acquired as I fell. I attribute my relaxed state to some deep, inner, intuitive trust that things would turn out, if not all right, at least the way they should.

Now, two days out of Los Angeles, I had a similar experience. Approaching Santa Rosa, New Mexico, during a driving rain storm in the middle of the night, I suddenly discovered my car was coming upon another car too rapidly. I stepped lightly on wet brakes that caught too quickly and sent me into a skid. I remembered to turn the wheels in the direction of the skid, but in the chaos of rain, darkness, and few reference points, I couldn't determine exactly which direction I was skidding. I lost control of the car, spinning like a top on the slick highway in the wet darkness, my parents a few car lengths behind watching in desperate horror. Unable to control the car, I let go of the wheel, and a remarkable sensation of calm and peace came over me. I relaxed as I had when rolling down the hill in junior high. I remember thinking, "Well, I wonder how this will turn out." Providentially no other car hit me, and I ended up in the wide median strip, unharmed. What touched me was the number of fellow travelers who stopped to see if I was all right and if they could help, including the driver of a big semitruck with two trailers. Only the starter motor was damaged, requiring these kind Samaritans, including my father, to help me push-start the car in the pouring rain. My joyful gratitude that other pilgrims stopped to give aid and that I'd been kept safe through the ordeal overwhelmed me.

In my years of ministry, I've seen the same peace and gratitude in many who faced death or other fearful circumstances beyond their control, and this I find comforting. Deep within us, I believe, runs a wellspring of intuitive trust and faith in the cosmos and Creator. For me, rolling down the hill or spinning on the highway served as parables for the nature of God's kingdom within my own life. As much as I wanted to be in control, it was when I let go, recognizing and trusting God's lead, that I felt the peace of the kingdom. "Thy kingdom come, thy will be done, on earth as it is in heaven," we pray in the prayer Jesus taught his disciples. My experience suggests to me that the kingdom or commonwealth of God comes to us when God's will is done on earth. Heaven is enjoyed where God's will and human action coincide. I do not believe God's will is detailed in content, but I do believe God's will has content: love of God, creation, others, and self are harmoniously brought together in the realm over which God is Sovereign.

That which is of most concern to us, such as vocational fulfillment or personal relationships, depends heavily on factors we cannot manipulate. As Kazantzakis discovered in his premature attempt to hatch a butterfly, I found I couldn't hatch my future on my own terms or along my own timeline. It had to be a gradual process of birth requiring both the readiness of the butterfly and the warmth of spring sun to dry its unfolding wings. To borrow another image, one from C. S. Lewis, the gates of heaven shut tighter when stormy feelings demand *entrée*. The future is not something which may be taken by force, nor is it something payable on demand. The future is a gracious gift, both quantitatively and qualitatively. Such an attitude alleviates angry resentment for what might have or should have been, and allows the experience of amazing grace in a lowly caterpillar resurrecting as a beautiful butterfly or being "surprised by joy" at the serendipitous opening of heaven's gates.

I had chosen to attend seminary for a year for the sake of my own spirituality, independent of my vocational goal. Ordination, too, would be among those things over which I would have little control. Those in certain human potential movements who claim they are in control of everything that happens to them are correct in a limited sense. People do need to take more responsibility for their actions. But to be ordained would have required me to be duplicitous, deceptive, and hypocritical at best, and at worst to tell outright lies. But the divine dimension of experience sometimes calls us forth where we would choose not to go: God's spontaneous and serendipitous future sometimes puts us out of control, like a messianic banana peel thrown in our path on the way to our goals. My banana peel on the way to ordination was the church's homophobia, not my homosexuality. My homosexuality was an occasion for God's glory and grace to be manifest in yet another human experience. The church wanted to cast off that manifestation, like an unwanted banana peel. As I slid on the peel and continue to slide on it, I am out of control and wonder how things will end up, but I experience peace and some inner, intuitive trust that things will turn out all right. This gives me stamina, a priceless gift in any movement.

Slipping on the banana peel is a comical image reminiscent of clowns at the circus. Witnessing our faith as gay and lesbian Christians has given us what the apostle Paul considered a high calling: the opportunity to be "fools for Christ," fools to the church because of our sexuality and fools to the gay community because of our continuing commitment to the church. The humor is at our expense; people forget the careless culprit who littered our path with the slippery banana peel of homophobia. The litterer in this case is the church. But we, at our best, don't play victim. Our redeeming sense of humor and God's redeeming sense of grace put in proper perspective the human folly of attempts to control the Spirit. The Spirit of God often leads us where we would rather not go, whether into a lonely wilderness of open oppression, which makes enslavement to the closet look good, or into an impassioned ministry for the excluded and dispossessed, which requires sacrificial confrontations with religious and political authorities. Providentially, there may be a friend nearby or other travellers willing to help us in our journey, as my friend in junior high who found me at the bottom of the canyon or the Samaritans along Interstate 40 who braved the storm to help me get started again on the road I was traveling. Ultimately and intimately, at the center of the somersault, in the eye of the spinning storm, there is available to us a peace that passes all understanding, deep within and far beyond all human experience. I believe this is the beginning of faith in God.

After visiting relatives in Pittsburg, Kansas, I left for the unknown of the East. My parents returned to California a few days later. With the exception of my cross-country flight and brief stopover at John F. Kennedy Airport on the way to Europe, I'd never traveled east of the Mississippi. The adventure of the journey almost balanced the deep loneliness which met me behind each motel room door. I felt as if something had been torn out of me. Coming out of the closet of the West, I emerged fearful of what lay outside the familiar, friendly, and homely.

Arriving in New Haven late one humid night, finding what I initially considered my dismal room, meeting a cynical second-year student—all led me to make a desperate phone call home expressing regret for my decision to be there. Having experienced joy leaving the loneliness of the sexual closet, finding new community with family and friends, and tasting love with a lover, I felt all the more keenly my aloneness now as I seemed to have returned to square one. Here would be new friends, but without a long past history together they might be less accepting of my being gay, or might refuse friendship and intimacy. They might expect what society expects, that all belong to the majority *hetero*sexual culture. Yet, at the same time, they would not have personal expectations of me based on past behavior that might have reinforced their mistaken assumption. While I did not intend to make an issue of being gay, I had decided not to hide it. I wanted to share my gay experience as any nongay person would share his or her unique experiences and perspectives of the world. As a member of a feared, hated, and disenfranchised minority, I also believed my insights, perspectives, and experience might add to the milieu of preparation for ministry.

Chapter 6

SPIRITUALITY AND MINISTRY

NEW HAVEN
FALL, 1973

Providentially my seminary roommate had be-friended a gay classmate in college, so that he brought his own sensitivity and this previous experience to our quickly developing friendship. But his friend had become emotionally dependent on him, and, experiencing deep inner turmoil, ultimately attempted suicide. David described finding and carrying him in his arms to a nearby hospital. "He wouldn't believe I loved him," David agonized over the friend's lack of self-esteem. "I wish he had your positive self-image," David would say as he shared depressing letters from the friend, who now attended seminary at Princeton, which apparently reinforced his negative self-image. Understandably, this intense experience kept David at a distance from me, lest he be caught in a similar dilemma of emotional dependency. To me the distance seemed unnecessary and felt painful; I did not want to be judged by his experience of another of my kind. Despite the barrier, our friendship became important to each of us—perhaps even *because* of the barrier, since I did grow to be a little in love with him, as so many who knew him did.

Despite this friendship, at first extremely close, and the friendships of a number of others, women and men, in my dorm, I felt a deep loneliness. I missed my lover. I missed gay people. The only gay gathering place in New Haven at the time was a restaurant and bar called The Pub, and that only became gay after 10:00 P.M. on weekends. And the weekly meeting of the newly-formed Gay Alliance at Yale drew sparse and erratic attendance.

In loneliness, when one is tempted to reach outward over-much, it is time to reach inward. It is deep in the soul, I believe, that we find relationship. The content of the soul gives form to our relationships. A soul full to overflowing gives rise to full, abundant relationships. Those cut off from the fullness of their own souls are cut off from the fullness possible in their relationships. I believe that we as gay people, along with women, people of color, the disabled, and other disenfranchised groups, are frequently cut off from the full-ness of our souls. For so long we have been carefully taught there is nothing or little there, that we believe it, and fail to look inward, scorning our own spirituality. Or we have been taught that to delve into spirituality requires rejection of our bodies, whether because of their color, gender, erotic attrac-tion, experience, emotions, or condition. But a soul is not a disembodied spirit: it combines the so-called duality of spirit and body, a Hellenistic notion later baptized into Christian faith. Spirituality is far more dependent on embodiment than is generally believed. Bodily experience, whether sensual, emotional, political, or prayerful, is spiritual experience. Soulfulness sees, suffers, and celebrates this relationship. The black concept of soul captures this truth, and brings us closer to the experience of ancient Jews and early Christians.

Needy as I was, my hunger began to be satisfied upon listening to a tape of professor Henri Nouwen speaking of loneliness in a course entitled "Discipline and Discipleship." "We keep looking for someone or something to take our loneliness away," he said, "then we realize no one and no thing can ever take our loneliness away." Later he would speak of transforming loneliness into creative solitude as one move-ment of the spiritual life. Significantly, I dropped a course on church history to take Nouwen's class. Almost with Huck Finn's disdain for what he could learn from Moses upon discovering that the latter was dead, I was more interested at the time in where the Spirit was leading rather than where it had been. Later, however, I would recover my balance be-tween history and the present as my fascination grew for the faith stories of the "clouds of witnesses" from the past.

Father Henri Nouwen's lecture notes for the course became the basis for his book, *Reaching Out: Three Movements of the Spiritual Life*. As he spoke of moving from loneliness to creative solitude, from hostility to hospitality, and from prayer to community, I knew these were answers to unarticulated but heartfelt questions of my own. Two papers he distributed also spoke profoundly to me. One paper appeared as a chapter in a book edited by Dwight Oberholtzer, entitled *Is Gay Good?* (*Philadelphia:* Westminster Press, 1971). In this paper, "The Self-Availability of the Homosexual," Nouwen spoke of the need of gay people to be able to be fully themselves in any given situation, just as anyone else. The other paper was Ashley Montagu's story of the "Elephant Man," since popularized in play and movie form. I identified with this grossly disfigured man, who was feared, hated, and exploited simply because of the way he was created. I cried for some minutes at the conclusion of his story, as he died trying to sleep horizontally like everyone else. How many of us have died or killed a part of ourselves trying to be like everyone else!

Several years later, another social and ecclesiastical misfit would be the subject of a Nouwen course during my final semester at Yale: "The Life and Ministry of Vincent van Gogh." Van Gogh had been a Calvinist minister for three years to the coal miners of the Borinage. Church officials ousted him from his post because he identified too much with the plight and poverty of the miners, descending into the mines with them, giving up possessions to them, and going so far as to give his bed to a sick woman. After an idle period of trying to determine what to do next, van Gogh decided to make paintings his sermons, hoping they would have "the same consoling effect the Christian religion used to have." My joy was completed in this course as I wrote my final paper at Yale, a story of a woman in transition ministered to by a painting of van Gogh's. It called forth from me creative writing in prose and poetry, analytical thought, theology, spirituality, ministry, and art. Writing it was an integration of all I valued, an experience infrequently enjoyed in seminary or in church. I felt a sense of integrity in the process.

Seminary would further increase my access to and sensitize my awareness of the messages of scripture, add the perspectives of liberation theology to my theological horizon, and give me a vital, ecumenical community in which to be challenged, nurtured, and nourished. But the single most valuable gift I received was a deepening understanding of spirituality. Students, faculty, and administrative personnel took active interest in daily chapel, as well as special opportunities for worship and prayer. The spiritual life was much sought after as a foundation for study, personal and communal growth, and ministry. With Henri Nouwen and others as inspiration and spiritual guides, I grew within this milieu of spirituality called Yale Divinity School.

Spirituality is the truth of the connectedness of all things. Some would limit this to living things; I choose not to, because to me it does disservice to God's creation of matter and spirit, the inanimate (at least as we perceive it) and the animate. The spiritual life is the cultivation of the consciousness of this truth of interconnectedness, interdependency. Our prayer life becomes authentic spiritual life when it moves from magical thinking or manipulation to the transcendent realization of our relationship with God, with others, with creation. Prayer is a lifting of these relationships as living offerings to God. As we do so, we seek God's will in these relationships, whether it be in relationship with Middle East terrorists or in relationship with family members. We do not pray because we *know* God's will, we pray because we *seek* God's will in and on earth as in heaven. We pray questions more than answers, problems more than solutions. Jesus the Christ lived his whole life as a prayer, the climax of which was offering his life on the cross, a problem to which God alone could offer a solution.

I do not believe the spiritual development I experienced in seminary was accidental. I believe God's providence was seeing to it I had the spiritual resources to face the ordeals of coming years. Growing up, I had spent hours talking with

God about all I experienced. Now, I continued to talk with God, whether during long walks at all times of day and night in all kinds of weather, or sitting alone in the prayer chapel underneath the main chapel at Yale Divinity School. But more and more, I was learning how to listen. I'd been taught as a child to listen for God's voice in the dramatic happenings of life, yet now, like Elijah, it would be beyond the earthquake, wind, and fire that I came to believe I might hear God's still, small voice. I needed times of silent solitude to listen. Spirit, scripture, spiritual direction were always available for guidance, but it was *I* who had to create the time, the silence, and the solitude. Quieting my heart and mind, I could listen more to the hearts of others and seek more the mind of Christ. This has been the toughest responsibility of my life. It's so easy to let work, the expectations of others, my own personal desires or distractions, recreation, or sleep prevent me from protecting, defending, and asserting this spiritual time. Yet when I have maintained a disciplined prayer life, I have best been able to *respond* rather than merely *react* to life, and to do so with greater amounts of love, hope, and peace. After all, if God's will can transform the problem of Christ's crucifixion into an opportunity for love, hope, and peace, so God's will can transform *any* problem or question into similar spiritual opportunity.

This is why, in working with churches, I would later insist that worship and prayer must come first in parishioners' lives; if they had to choose between committing time to a church committee or attending Sunday morning worship, the latter should be their first priority. As with the practice in some traditions of priests receiving communion before distributing it to others, so I believe one cannot give in ministry what one has not first received in prayer. Called to preach forgiveness, reconciliation, and acceptance to the gay community, I could hardly do so authentically at times I myself did not feel to some degree forgiven, reconciled, and accepted in prayer. Called to preach humility, repentance, and inclusiveness to the church, I could hardly do so sincerely when I did not feel humbled, repentant, and inclusive in my own prayer life.

Clergy, perhaps unfortunately, are professionals, so, as is expected of professionals, they are often able to preach what they have not personally experienced or felt. But most clergy seek integrity in practicing what they preach; even in my own failure to reach such integrity, I have recognized that prayer makes it more nearly possible.

Rooted in spirituality, authentic ministry takes place. My first purpose in seminary was to grow spiritually, especially since I had no assurance that the church would affirm my call to ministry. My second purpose was to prepare for ministry within the particular community to which I felt called: the lesbian and gay community. I hoped such a ministry would occur within a worshiping congregation, as I could not imagine ministry cut off from a local church, particularly if its central purpose were to bring the gospel that churches are called to proclaim.

Knowing I would need skills in community organization in such a ministry, I registered for a field work course called "Community Organization and Theology in the Midst of Social Change." Despite the impressive title, I found to my disappointment that the field work opportunities would be of little help in developing such skills. So I approached the professor with an alternative proposal of organizing a Christian ministry within the gay community. Not surprisingly, it required a minority person to understand why I believed myself called to ministry within my own minority. The professor, a black pastor named Robert Jones, proved receptive and recommended that Yale fund my proposal with a grant of $1,000, to be applied to my tuition. During this project, Rev. Jones and I discovered similarities between the black and gay communities, among them the central role that such disparate locales as bars and churches serve as social and political centers for our respective minorities.

The ministry began on the main campus of Yale University. The Gay Alliance at Yale (GAY), drew members mostly from Yale's graduate and professional schools. Undergraduate Yale had a macho image to maintain, especially in view of the recent admission of women to its ranks. Mixed with the sexual ambiguities of youth, the pressures of present peers as well as future careers, homophobia maintained an effective barrier to the involvement of undergraduate students in GAY. Recognizing that there were a lot of lonely gay undergraduates on the other side of the ivy-covered wall, GAY resolved to remove such isolation through a speaker's bureau, a peer counseling program, and gay dances. Those who would not attend regular meetings could see and hear gay and lesbian role models who contradicted stereotypes in class presentations; they could speak anonymously and confidentially with a gay counselor by phone or by dropping into the office, or enjoy the gay-sponsored dances that nongays frequented too. These nonthreatening activities enabled undergraduates who were gay or questioning their sexual identity to know they were not alone, without making the political statement implicit in membership within the organization. Of course the speaker's bureau and the social events fought homophobia within nongay people as well. I participated indirectly in the development of the counseling program, and headed up the speaker's bureau, organizing and appearing on panels for courses in the medical, divinity, and undergraduate schools. Often we spoke to classes or course sections with such titles as "Abnormal Psychology," feeling much like guinea pigs or pathological models literally looked down on from tiers of students seated in lecture halls shaped like Roman amphitheaters.

But where were the religious gays? Inside the closet or outside the church: these seemed to be the alternatives. Most religious gays whom I met felt so alienated from organized religion that their faith had become a private affair, with all the attendant dangers of such idiosyncratic individualism. Unsupported and uncorrected by a faith community, these people often held esoteric if not bizarre mythological or philosophical views, views which frequently prevented self-transcendence. One might think, nonetheless, that these separate religious viewpoints might be more liberating than religions from which they were derived. But unfortunately they often contained similar if not harsher elements than those found in mainstream religion, partly because those holding such views had left the mainstream in childhood or adolescence, when emphasis on the punitive aspects of religion is the greatest, and partly because of the homophobia that the gays themselves had internalized.

Churched but closeted religious gays often needed to compartmentalize their sexuality and their faith, thus failing to achieve the integrity sought in the spiritual life. This accounts for the phenomenon of practicing gays who at the same time are practicing biblical literalists or fundamentalists, an apparent contradiction. It also helps explain why practicing gays may participate in local churches whose congregations and/or pastoral leadership condemn homosexuality. Those gays who most desperately need to maintain this compartmentalization, or to suppress their sexuality altogether, frequently join conservative or charismatic congregations, as do their heterosexual counterparts, who similarly need to compartmentalize or suppress their sexuality. More open, progressive, and liberal churches endanger this compartmentalization or suppression process, as they allow for freer expression, enabling sexual feelings and experience to find integration in the broader context of spiritual life. An irony I've discovered since first recognizing these phenomena is that compartmentalization frequently leads to obsession with sexuality and compulsive sexual behavior, the very thing that those who compartmentalize or suppress wish to avoid. Those encouraged to accept and integrate their sexuality within their life of faith tend to experience and express sexuality in ways appropriate to their well-being.

Initially I found no gays or lesbians who were both churched and uncloseted. Because I found fewer points of identification with unchurched-but-religious gays whose spirituality was often noncommunicable, I chose to focus on closeted, churched ones with whom I at least shared a common vocabulary, milieu, and commitment to spiritual community. Eventually this led me to ministry almost exclusively on my own campus, Yale Divinity School.

Auditing a course on "Homosexuality in Contemporary

America" offered at Yale's undergraduate school, I learned that Rev. Troy Perry had been invited to speak to one of the class sessions. I asked Rev. Joan Forsberg (at the time the seminary's registrar and unofficial "friend of students") and a Methodist student to join me in petitioning the Community Life Committee to invite him to address the Divinity School as well. That committee agreed to extend the invitation, but when the student body president heard of it, he fought unsuccessfully to have the welcome withdrawn. He told me, "I'm tired of these minority concerns! It's time we remembered that most of the student body here are white, male, and straight!" An argument that those straight, white males might be ministering to various minorities, including lesbians and gays, did not sway him.

Arranging the invitation was the most public act I had engaged in as a gay activist at the Divinity School. I experienced deep emotional pain, as if I were being born again, coming out of the womblike closet of secrecy and anonymity. The night before Perry was to speak, I lay in a fetal position in my bed, feeling actual physical pain. The fright I felt was akin to what I imagine I'd feel being pushed from an airplane ten miles high. I hyperventilated. I cried. Finally, I fell asleep. When I awoke, I felt renewed, strengthened, encouraged. God had ministered to me in sleep.

It was Thursday, October 18, 1973. Troy spoke to a responsive group in the small undergraduate seminar. That evening he ate dinner with selected Divinity School student leaders and faculty, who expressed fear that attendance for his evening lecture would be small and offered their condolences. Several good explanations were given for the anticipated small audience: evening lectures seldom drew as many people as daytime lectures; many people did not sense the importance of the issue; others would be discouraged by its controversial nature. As it turned out, over one hundred people crowded in to hear Perry, a number far beyond expectations. Though remarkably few of the divinity faculty attended, divinity students were present in large numbers, as well as faculty and students from the greater university. A few community members attended, too.

"Homosexuals are the last minority in America that people can persecute openly and still get away with it," Troy told the gathering. With characteristic humor and Pentecostal punch, Troy broke the ice by describing his own pilgrimage and the founding of the Metropolitan Community Church. "Nobody loves me!" he recalled hearing someone cry in gay bar. "Jesus loves you!" he had sincerely responded. Reflecting on the episode led Troy to start a church for homosexuals. Applause and laughter punctuated many of his statements as he carried the audience to a greater acceptance by personalizing the abstract issue with more humor than pathos. "At least now we can talk about it," a student from Australia said afterwards.

The following weekend I had arranged a personal retreat at Mercy Center on the shores of the Long Island Sound in Madison, Connecticut. Emotional exhaustion drove me to seek sanctuary after the personally draining ordeal of Troy's visit. The Sisters of Mercy who run the center truly ministered to me in my need to be in a supportive environment where I could nonetheless be alone for God's healing Spirit to surround me. Even the news of the "Saturday night massacre"— President Nixon's firing of special Watergate prosecutor Archibald Cox—did not seem so disturbing in this placid place. I had missed the sanctuary of the Pacific shore; my little room afforded a view of the sound, and the brisk fall weather yet permitted long walks along its beach. It had been one of New England's most spectacular falls, and the colored beauty of the leaves still lingered on tree branches or danced with the rhythm of the wind along grassy or sandy ground.

Henri Nouwen, who regularly retreated at Mercy Center, was there the same weekend and honored me by asking me to look over a sermon he was preparing. Since Nouwen had attended Troy Perry's lecture, I eagerly took the opportunity to ask him what he thought of it. Hesitant at first to comment, Nouwen finally told me that, though the purpose of the presentation may have been achieved—that is, everyone may have become more comfortable with the gay issue—he himself had been searching for something deeper as he listened. He wanted to hear more of Perry's feelings in the description of interactions with people and with the church. He wanted to know more of Perry's spirituality: how being an outcast had affected his faith, what his spiritual resources were for contending with seemingly insurmountable odds in church and society. I believe Nouwen's gentle critique arose from being on a different level than most members of the audience, who apparently appreciated the lighter approach to an as yet uncomfortable subject. But I realized that though Perry's sexuality and commitment to preach God's word of love were certainly evident, the spirituality necessary to keep him going remained to some degree hidden.

Nouwen's comments shaped my own presentations on the subject in the years to come. My faith had to come out of the closet along with my sexuality. I would try to draw out the deeper, universal implications of my experience as a gay Christian to benefit everyone's spirituality. This itself would become an argument for the inclusion of lesbians and gays in the church: our spiritual gifts, not the least of which is our stamina, are vital to the church. I learned in the process that to share honestly one's faith and one's doubts is a far more intimate activity than sharing one's sexual orientation. In today's American society, many of us find it far easier to talk about sexuality than spirituality.

Though I had not introduced Reverend Perry and served only as unofficial host, word got around that it was I who initiated his invitation to speak. Upon my return from my weekend retreat, more gays and lesbians came forward with their own stories: a man who painfully served as best man at his college lover's wedding; a lesbian who had successfully served as student body president of her prestigious alma mater but remained closeted; a married man who'd been through half a dozen years of Freudian psychoanalysis with a therapist who had convinced him that his homosexuality was really fear of castration. Nongay people came forward too: a woman who had felt threatened by another woman who had made a pass at her; a woman in love with a gay man; a self-confessed homophobic man concerned with how to counsel future parishioners who might be gay or lesbian. The burden of homophobia on gay and nongay alike grew heavier and heavier as I listened to dozens and dozens of unique individuals. To keep myself sane, I relied more heavily on friends; but then there was a brief disappointment.

Someone told me that David, my roommate and closest friend, was considering a move out of the suite we shared. At a time when I needed a friend, I felt hurt that he had discussed this openly with others before telling me. When I confronted him, I learned the truth of the matter. The student body president had offered him another dorm room, since he'd "gotten stuck with" a gay roommate, and a gay activist at that. And some of our mutual friends had consoled him for having to live with a gay man. Out of loyalty to me, he had declined the offer to move and had set our friends straight about his preference to live with me. I was grateful to learn of his steadfastness, but hurt that the student leadership and our friends would consider this a difficulty. None of them had ever consoled *me* having to live with a *straight* roommate! I felt foolish having trusted these friends with my identity, and I felt forsaken having had that trust betrayed. I took a long walk through the brisk autumn darkness cloaking New Haven that night, feeling more alone than I had felt in a long time.

Returning very late to the campus, I wanted to enter the intimacy of the prayer chapel, only to find the building locked up. I didn't let that stop me. I slipped through an unlocked window. Finding the chapel, I opened the door to the darkness within. Stepping inside and closing the door behind me, I chose neither to switch on the light nor light a candle. The comfort of the velvet darkness was like a safe womb, not barren, but fertile in function. More than any other place on campus, this small, octagonal, grey chapel served as empty space, a kind of walled wilderness that served no purpose other than to facilitate prayer. Unlike the larger New England-style chapel above it, it hosted no preaching classes nor liturgical practicums. No antiphonal organ interrupted its silence. It boasted no large windows through which the beauty of the trees' seasonal changes could distract. Its two, porthole-like windows were placed so high, one might glimpse only a patch of sky. Like two giant eyes looking outward, their only function seemed to be to let in light. Now, as my eyes adjusted to the darkness, the light that these windows invited from moon and stars far above illuminated this house of prayer with a soft, gentle, homey glow. To be alone here did not feel lonely; to be alone here made me feel fully present to myself and fully present to God.

I filled this empty place with spoken words, emptying myself of hurt, of pain, of anger. I was answered with silence: not a stony silence as if I had said nothing, not an indifferent silence as if what I had said were unimportant; and not an empty silence, as if no one were listening. The silence I experienced was as if a friend wanted to speak, and didn't know what to say, or better: knew there was nothing that should or could be said, but felt it important that I put my feelings into words, thereby dissolving their potentially self-destructive power.

It dawned on me that part of fulfilling my ministry would be to make others feel more comfortable about my sexual orientation. I thought of Susan, a friend who challenged the limitations that cerebral palsy had placed on her ability to walk and speak. She understood what it meant to make other people comfortable with a perceived "handicap"—in her case, her braces, crutches, and slowness of speech. And I understood what she meant when she described herself as "damn tired" of helping other people overcome "her" disability. In different ways, we shared an experience of hurting and yet having to help the very people who, through their ignorance, apathy, and fear contributed to our suffering. Was this the message from the cross of "Father, forgive them, for they know not what they do"? Was this another aspect of redemptive suffering?

I had once suggested to Susan that perhaps those who felt nervous about her awkward movement or who interpreted her slow speech as a sign of intellectual disability were truly the handicapped ones. When the church discussed racism in the sixties, we soon discovered the "black problem" was really a white problem. As the church began discussing sexism in the seventies, we began recognizing it more and more as a male and patriarchal problem. As the church has just begun dealing with issues related to the physically or mentally challenged, we realize our own disabilities. Now, as the church faces the "problem" of homosexuality, we are learning that the real dilemma is homophobia and the broader phobia about sexuality. Of course, racism occurs within the black community, sexism within women, physical or mental perfectionism among the disabled, and homophobia in gays and lesbians. But each of these communities is trying to root out that which holds it down, and each community struggles to establish and affirm its integrity. To maintain its own integrity, I believe, the majority culture in each instance must do the same, though direct benefits may not be readily discernible. Jesus' truism may be paraphrased to say that one may have to lose life as it is known to find the integrity of the life to come, the life of God's kingdom or commonwealth—whether the one is an individual, a community, or a dominant culture.

In the stillness of the prayer chapel, I felt led to the conclusion that my ministry entailed making others feel comfortable with both me and my ministry. I recalled how enthusiastically divinity students spoke of their ministries and inquired after the ministries of others, while avoiding mine, as if my ministry were as taboo a topic as homosexuality itself. The ministry itself required interpretation. The *ministry* had to come out of the closet.

Chapter 7

COMING OUT AT SEMINARY

NEW HAVEN
WINTER-SPRING, 1974

Winter transmuted a vividly blue autumn sky to shades of greys and whites; the descent of orange, yellow, and red leaves gave way to falling snow, with occasional ice storms transfiguring the abandoned branches to crystal chandeliers illumined with sunlight by day, moonlight by night. Awed by these changes in New England, I was equally dazzled by the California contrast upon my return to Los Angeles for Christmas holidays: everything seemed so green, the sun so warm! But geophysical climate was not the only contrast I experienced. Having felt somewhat embarrassed revealing my feelings and sexuality at Yale, it bolstered my self-confidence to enter again an environment that climatically and culturally invited and welcomed openness. Going home may serve as a reality check, a chance to place recent experience in perspective. Touching base with my personal history (recalled by my return) enabled me to affirm the direction I had chosen in my new home; looking back confirmed that I was still on the same path, though further along. I returned to Yale after the holidays with renewed vigor and determined boldness. The ministry *was* going to come out of the closet! I posted signs on Divinity School bulletin boards and listed notices in the student paper reading: "Gay? Have some gay feelings? Meet and share with other gay Christians. Call or write Chris Glaser" and bravely included my mail box and telephone number.

Up to this time I had considered Yale Divinity School, while not exactly "fermenting for freedom," to borrow a phrase from liberation theology, still liberal enough to be tolerant. I was surprised, then, when my signs were ripped down and tossed, mutilated, into trash cans. Either naive or incredulous, I at first thought someone may have believed the signs to be poor practical jokes at my expense, and were tearing them down in my defense. But when replacing the signs became a daily task, I realized the true origin and intensity of the hostility behind the destruction. More representative of the Divinity School community were those who came to my defense, from Barbara Brown, who personally lettered new signs for me, to Kim White, who wrote a letter decrying the actions to the Divinity School paper. I was interviewed on a Divinity School video magazine. People stopped me in the halls to offer support.

Ironically, the hostility provided opportunity to reach more people than would have been possible otherwise. Hostility expressed toward me, when unreturned, became an invaluable instrument of conversion of those previously apathetic or unaware. If I returned hostility for hostility, I could be dismissed. I began to experience firsthand the political and spiritual power of redemptive suffering, as lived by Gandhi and King. The basic principle of redemptive suffering is simple: nonviolently allow or provoke an opponent to express his or her violent reaction to you without returning violence for violence. Unreturned violence calls forth the conscience in opponent and observer alike, as both must reevaluate you and their reactions to you. Gandhi and King and their followers endured bloody, physical confrontations with their oppressors. We lesbians and gays have sometimes endured bloody, physical confrontations with our oppressors; but more often, we endure psychological, emotional, legal, spiritual, and biblical beatings at the hands of those who oppose us. There have been exceptions, but I've found I have most often failed in communicating my message when I've forgotten the old Proverb, "A soft answer turns away wrath, but a harsh word stirs up anger." Verbal violence, too, requires nonviolent response to be transformed.

Remembering that my own "difference" engendered my empathy for the black cause, I was therefore disappointed to learn it didn't necessarily work the other way around. I learned that some of the black students angrily opposed toleration of homosexuality; in my presence, one raged in front of one of my signs about "these damn eunuchs." Other black students were fearful that yet another movement on campus might compete with their cause for student activity funds, a complaint already raised against the campus Women's Center. It is unfortunate that those with money and power, such as student councils, private foundations, and governments, are thereby enabled to divide minorities from one another in the continuing competition for funding and other support.

When I met with fundamentalist opposition I was not surprised; what surprised me was to find fundamentalists on the Yale Divinity School campus! One wrote me anonymously, quoting Leviticus and Romans, uncritical of the perfectionism of the holiness code in the first, and unaware of the central theme of God's unearned grace in Jesus Christ which dominates the second. I responded to the letter in the Divinity School paper, encouraging future correspondents to fear nothing in identifying themselves.

A professor stopped me one day to explain he had finally connected the "Chris Glaser" of the signs to the "Chris Glaser" in his classroom. Then, referring to gays, he asked, "What right do we have to tell these people they shouldn't be ashamed?" Incredulous, I responded, "What right do we have to tell them they *should* be ashamed? And we've been doing that for years!" Another professor chose a sermon at the main university chapel as a forum to critique the feminist movement and attack "gay liberation." I felt compelled to storm out a side door in protest, startling the professor. Not even worship felt safe!

What most disconcerted me was the anger I met with at the hands of the few men at the Divinity School who had already identified themselves to me as gay and interested in a support group. "How dare you call attention to us!" they reprimanded, fearful others would be more suspicious as to who might be gay, now that my ministry was out of the closet. Perhaps Lazarus in the tomb, also embarrassed by his condition, might have preferred darkness, anonymity, and resting in peace to being called forth publicly. I had betrayed no one's confidentiality; I had merely brought the issue of homosexuality out of the whitewashed tomb of the seminary and personalized it in me, incarnated it, if you will, so neighbors and Lazarus alike could see there was nothing to fear.

But the same individuals who feared the limelight with all its attendant dangers did not affirm my courage for being willing to stand in the light. Perversely, they claimed I did it for my own ego, a claim that made me doubt my own motives. That they considered the attention dangerous to them and yet somehow beneficial to me did not strike them as contradiction. Their lack of trust of my intentions hurt me deeply at the time, though now I realize pervasive homophobia clouded their judgments, the judgments of those who, one might have assumed, would have known better. But, just as I had once concluded I could not let my youthful certainty serve as an excuse to do nothing about the Vietnam war, I similarly decided that, even if certain ego needs were being met in the process, I couldn't let that keep me from doing something about the oppression of gays and lesbians. Psychological and spiritual reflection on one's motives is crucial, but when a child is being murdered it is better to stop the perpetrator and later examine motives and process. Some people are so fastidious in determining their priorities, motives, and process, that the child may be long since dead and buried before they act.

Despite all of these negative reactions, the signs had their intended effect: others came to me, telling their own stories. Yet, for everyone who came forward, probably ten kept their distance. The memory of one still haunts me. I vainly try to recall his face and his identity, but remember our conversation and his departure as if it occurred yesterday. Our conversation circuitous, he never quite told me he was gay. He concluded by putting on his jacket and leaving with the cryptic words, "I admire what you're doing, but some of us live in too many closets." I watched through the window as he disappeared through the snow blanketing the campus, the red of his jacket eventually fading into the pure whiteness as if it were fresh blood in frigid snow. "Go, sell your closets, and follow me," Jesus might have said. And the young man rich in closets went away sorrowful.

A woman at the seminary once explained her difficulty joining in some prayers of confession during worship. "They often have to do with the misuse and abuse of power," she said, "Whereas I, as a woman, need to confess failure to assert my own power." This spiritual insight prompted me to consider what gays and lesbians need to confess before God. Those who accuse us of being "unrepentant" simply misunderstand the needed direction of our confession and repentance. Gifts of God require no repentance, though repentance is required when we refuse them, hide them, bury them, misuse them, or in other ways prove unworthy stewards of these gifts. Sexuality, whether heterosexuality, homosexuality, or bisexuality, is a gift of God. Perhaps, I thought, what we need most to repent of is our closet. And since a closet is not only constructed from the inside, those who have helped construct it from the outside must also repent.

Lazarus needed his neighbors to roll the stone from the tomb and unbind his death cloths; Jesus then called him to new life. A developing spirituality helped me hear that call to new life, not only for me, but for others. Dismantling closet-tombs is a job for those both inside and outside them, requiring neighbors. While trying to prove neighbor to other gay seminary students seeking liberation from closet-tombs, I found them reluctant to prove neighbor to me. They avoided me in public for fear of guilt by association, and in private often demanded my attention rather than offering theirs. Most alternately perceived me as having overcome all my own problems or as making the biggest mistake of my life, neither state requiring their support.

If the gay men, with whom I had the most experience, did offer sympathetic understanding, it often served as prelude to attempting seduction. Many were such needy people that offering my affirmation made them misperceive me as their best friend or potential lover. I went so far as to try to be each one's best friend, an emotionally tiring and impossible task. When that was not enough, and I did not "come through" in the way their mistaken expectations led them to anticipate, a few tried to make me feel guilty: "You're not a friend!" or "You led me on!" Outside of becoming a lover, I found it difficult to decline any demand, for fear of failing them. It was as if I were faced with a hungry child, and gave the child everything on my plate, going hungry myself. I soon felt emotionally exploited and abandoned.

After spending time with me, a married student wrote:

> You affirmed me in a way I haven't experienced in a long, long time. I have also been left feeling frightened and seriously trying to see what future there is. Let's face it, I am paranoid, a closet case. I cannot afford to become labeled. You aren't, you're honest and open, and I admire your courage. We will not be able to spend much time together.

Another gay student to whom I devoted much time claimed I was unnecessarily stirring things up with my openness and asked, "Can't you see yourself as ever getting heterosexually married?" Indicating that was his intent, he added, concerned for my career, "This openness is dangerous for you." I appreciated their admiration and concern, but I wanted their availability and support. I would receive enough question- ing and criticism from our opposition. I didn't want to fight this war on two fronts. How little I then realized that a war of independence and integrity requires battling on many fronts.

In the midst of all this, I received a call from a New York gay activist concerning the broadcast of a *Marcus Welby* epi- sode planned for airing the following night in New Haven. The plot involved a male high school teacher's sexual liaison with a male student. At this relatively early point in the present gay movement's history, this was just the kind of unsavory association we wished to avoid. The caller, whom I didn't know, encouraged me to do what I could to dissuade the television station from broadcasting the segment. I felt like David to the television station Goliath, though I had none of David's optimism and faith as I phoned the station the next morning. To my surprise—another Jonah experience!—the station officials encouraged me to gather together a representative sampling of members from the gay community to view the episode in advance of broadcast and offer our comments to the programming executives. Almost as amazingly, I easily rounded up a good group of people, who, on this very short notice, made room in their schedule to attend the screening and the meeting afterwards.

The episode we previewed had been done with a certain amount of sensitivity, though the line between pederasty and homosexuality seemed vague, and the fatherly Marcus Welby appeared disapproving of both, which may have been a realistic portrayal of his character. The television executives, always cordial, asked first for comments, then for recommendations. Unanimously we recommended the station not air the program. They had already informed us they would not reach a final decision until after we left, and we would learn their decision at airtime. I believe we all departed feeling we had done what we could, but that the program would probably air as scheduled.

That evening I'd been invited to speak at a forum of nearby Quinnipiac College, where I experienced frustration persuading the young and intolerant audience that homosexuality and marijuana-smoking were vastly different! They argued both were "choices" for which one had to pay the consequences, and, since people suffered "equally" for both, the homosexual should receive no special attention. I explained sexuality is far more integral to personhood, and stressed how gays suffer overwhelming discrimination from childhood through old age not because of choice, other than the one to be who they are. The dissimilarities proved elusive to their comprehension. Angered by the simplistic and judgmental approach of these youth, I eagerly escaped back to my own campus to discover the results of our lobbying effort that afternoon.

Running into my dorm, I dashed upstairs to one of the few televisions on campus. I asked the student who owned it if we could change channels to see if *Marcus Welby* were on, and she said, "This is the channel it's supposed to be on. But there's some documentary on instead." I couldn't believe it! My heart thanked God as I danced downstairs to a friend's room to share my joy. Our friendship had grown from shared convictions about social justice. He had also come to my defense when signs about the gay support group were ripped down. As I told him of this victory, however, his face grew dark and he verbally lashed out at me in anger, "You interfered with the freedom of the press!" I was devastated, a credit to how highly I valued his opinion. I offered flustered explanations, then retreated to my room. Years later I would realize, as did he, how wrong he had been. I had merely expressed my views with no power to coerce; I had simply helped inform the television executives' decision.

But, at the time, my celebration became a wake. After all the criticism I'd endured, after all the misunderstandings I'd tried to correct as recently as that evening at Quinnipiac College, my friend's words stunned me. It was too much. An apparent victory was transformed to self-questioning and self-doubt. I phoned Roy Birchard, a good friend and the pastor of the Manhattan Metropolitan Community Church, and described my dilemma. Speaking of the gay movement in general and my participation in particular, I plaintively and sincerely asked Roy, "What if we *are* wrong?" His response has stayed with me throughout the years: "It's God who brings the kingdom in, not us. Even if we find ourselves involved in 'egolatry,' we must keep faith that God will nonetheless bring in God's kingdom." His words comforted me; reared to concern myself with personal salvation, I knew I now valued more highly the kingdom, which would be the world's salvation. I must do what I believed was right, but Roy lifted a burden by placing my work within the larger perspective.

I awoke the next morning feeling empty and lifeless. As I stepped through the dormitory hall to the showers, I heard beautiful music. I followed the sound to its origin, another friend's room, and entered his open door quietly as if entering a sanctuary. I sat in a pew (actually, a wooden chair) and listened in awe and for the first time to Pachelbel's *Canon in D Major*. The theme and its repetition seemed to summarize my life—I can't explain why. I cried, I smiled, I hoped, I loved: all in the presence of this minister, this music. As the Psalmist described, it "restoreth my soul." When it was finished, I departed as reverently as I had entered. I could not find the friend whose room it was, but it didn't matter. The music had fulfilled its ministry. Pachelbel's *Canon* sung integrity to me as it harmoniously blended polyphonous sounds over and over again, bringing its theme home to my heart. The peace I experienced listening to it, I decided, is the same peace available in the presence of integrity. This music, this integrity, was perfection.

All my life I had wanted to be perfect: the "best little boy in the world." But there was at least one area of my life that would never conform to the world's concept of perfection: my homosexuality. Would this be my "tragic flaw," or would I exchange the whole notion of perfection for a different goal, integrity?

In the Holiness Code found in Leviticus, separateness and integrity are the characteristics of holiness, so I had a scriptural basis on which to stand. But wouldn't integrity become another expression of perfectionism? The way I view it, perfection is following the rules in a linear fashion, never stepping out of line, never stepping on any lines. By contrast, integrity may take one outside the rules, stepping on or outside lines, as an interpretative dancer might move to the music rather than a particular form of dance steps. What governs such a dancer's movements is an internal response to external inspiration, in other words, the music. What governs the perfectionist is largely external, punitive, and prisonlike, intimidating and coercing the inner soul of a person into submission, with the inevitable byproducts of guilt, anxiety, and frustration. The gospel inspires; the law coerces.

In the New Testament, when Jesus speaks of being "perfect, even as your Father in heaven is perfect," the word translated "perfect" really suggests "maturity," in this case, spiritual maturity. Maturity, I believe, is the continuing integration of all one is, does, says, knows, thinks, feels, and believes. It is a never-completed process, if only because new data or new situations require fresh integration. The way we consider God as "the most . . . ," God would have the greatest integrity. God wills us to be as mature as God is, which means imitating God's own integration process.

When a person who is gay leaves the closet, she or he moves toward the integration of sexuality with other components of her or his personality and existence. There is severe temptation to seek safe haven in another closet. For example, the forces of Jerry Falwell become strange bedfellows with those gay ideologues most hostile to the church when both proclaim, "You can't be both gay and Christian." In other words, one cannot have integrity in these two important areas of life. So a person might be tempted to abandon faith to express sexual urges and emotional needs, entering the closet of a secular gay lifestyle. Similarly, while acknowledging homosexual orientation, a person might refuse to express it on "biblical grounds" and become celibate or behave unnaturally as heterosexual, entering the closet of an antigay church. Yet another might choose the dual closets of compartmentalization, described earlier, in which behavior and belief are strictly divided. Such compartmentalization may lead to distorted forms of sexual and spiritual experience and expression. A person might aggressively participate in antigay religious activity, while having homosexual encounters. More likely, a person might simply participate in a religious community condemning homosexual behavior while continuing to have homosexual encounters. If asked in church about homosexuality or asked in a homosexual liaison about church, the response is likely to be evasive, as the person tries to keep religion and sexuality separate. Anxiety results if the person is asked to choose between them, or encouraged to integrate them.

Many gay Christians consider themselves biblical literalists, affirming the inerrancy of scripture. They need to believe scripture says nothing about homosexuality, when, in truth, it does, and speaks negatively, even if rarely. Many put a lot of weight in an argument from Jesus' silence on the subject. In order to discount the negative biblical remarks about homosexual behavior, though they be a handful, one must recognize that not every word in the Bible proceeds from the mouth of God. I've never met a self-proclaimed biblical literalist, gay or nongay, who truly believes every word of scripture: most delight in lobster, wear polyester and cotton blend fabrics, earn interest on savings accounts, and allow women to speak in church, though these all are more clearly and more frequently condemned in scripture. So a Christian who affirms the inerrancy of scripture not only in belief but also in practice is truly remarkable. A gay Christian who affirms the inerrancy of scripture is similarly remarkable. Such a person compartmentalizes homosexuality and the belief in the inerrancy of scripture. Such a person lacks full integrity. Yet such a person may achieve greater integrity by accepting homosexuality and affirming the inerrancy of the essential spiritual truths of scripture rather than the inerrancy of particular stories or specific applications. The Holiness Code and Paul's letter to the Romans contain inerrant spiritual truths for the Christian, but their specific applications may be culturally limited. A homosexual person may be faithful to herself or himself, and yet be faithful to scripture by this understanding. Indeed, being faithful to the spiritual intent of scripture is a greater faithfulness than simply believing that every word proceeded from God's mouth, since the former requires a wrestling with scripture's meaning, much as Jesus wrestled with the true meaning of the law.

Though often associated in people's minds with the more conservative side of the religious spectrum, compartmentalization is just as much a temptation for liberals. Many gay and lesbian Christians who advocate social justice and who are progressives with respect to other causes often refuse public identification as friendly to, let alone champions of, gay rights. They fear losing their livelihoods, choosing rather to sacrifice their integrity. I've met more *nongay* clergy willing to risk their jobs on behalf of the gay movement than I've met gay clergy willing to do so. Even in private, I have found gay clergy reluctant to come to the aid of gay Christians. We would probably think less of a black person from the ghetto who completed medical school or seminary and then chose to work exclusively in a rich, white community than we would think of one who maintained ties with and offered help to other black people. Yet I am shocked at how little gay clergy in mainline denominations do for their own kind, often defending themselves by saying, "I've got to minister to all of the people—I can't be limited." Reminiscent of the priest and the Levite in Jesus' parable of the Good Samaritan, they pass by on the other side of the road to get to their congregations, rather than aid the one most significantly in need, the lesbian woman or gay man. They refuse to accept their own "scandal of particularity" as Jesus accepted his—that is, taking the gospel first to his own people, the Jews. They lack his integrity. They compartmentalize their courageous stands on social issues and their identification (or lack thereof) with their own gay community. Of course there are parallels to this phenomenon among lay Christians who are gay and among nonreligious gays and lesbians.

Because I believed gay people have been pushed around quite enough by the church and society, I have hesitated in the past to write or to say much that might be interpreted as a "should" to closeted gay Christians, clergy or lay. But now, for their own sake, I share an insight that has proven therapeutic for me. Less integrity *actively* lessens self-esteem. The lesser the integrity, the more it wears at the soul and the God-given valuing of self. The opposite of integrity is disintegration. The enemy of integrity is hypocrisy.

We all live with a little bit of disintegration and hypocrisy. Because working toward integrity is a lifetime process, we sometimes fill in the gaps in our paths with the pitch of hypocrisy, to make the going easier. During the earthquakes or storms of our lives, the filler material separates from our main substance, and the gaps widen. If there are too many or they are too deep, our path may disintegrate, causing us to lose our way. The greater the integrity of our path, the better chance we have not only to survive, but to get to our destinations.

Beyond ourselves, we make paths for others alongside and behind us. Regardless of the threats to livelihoods and life itself, the less integrity with which one constructs one's road, the more dangerous it will be for those who follow. Centuries of (at least seemingly) necessary hypocrisy and disintegration have resulted in gay and lesbian contributions to religion, history, and culture being unknown, ignored, and forgotten. To remedy this requires even greater sacrifice for those who follow.

Closeted lesbians and gays are facing a crossroads. They will build a road with greater integrity or follow the cheap and easy street of hypocrisy or the slum road of disintegration. Each will receive his or her due reward. What is fearful for those who face this crossroads is the signpost: the cross, symbol of the fullest integrity. Yet our faith may help us see the direction to which the cross points: past itself, past the cross of integrity to new life possible. Eternal life is not just a matter of quantity; an eternal perspective transforms the *quality* of life. The path one makes must have its quality informed by an eternal perspective. The quality of the path one makes will also be *judged* from an eternal perspective. Martyrdoms along the way become a witness to the value of seeking integrity: it's worth living for, it's worth dying for. Eternal life is a life of integrity.

A life of integrity is not free from suffering and pain; in truth, viewing the cross as a symbol of integrity suggests the life of integrity is a way through suffering and pain. But notice it is a "way *through*." Suffering and pain are inevitable; integrity facilitates our fullest experience of them, at the same time integrating them into our path, placing them in context, allowing us to see them in perspective, and using them as alloys to reinforce the roadway toward our futures. Integrity similarly enables us to fully experience and integrate joy and pleasure without feelings of guilt, unworthiness, or self-indulgence.

Exchanging perfection for integrity as a goal was not a conscious choice for me in coming out more and more as a gay Christian minister. Indeed, it has taken over ten years for me to understand retrospectively the path I chose. Perfection is an idealistic goal and, as such, impossible; but integrity is authentic and possible, although never completed. Choosing integrity over perfection is not simply a pragmatic choice; it is a choice for spiritual health. Striving for perfection creates debilitating anxiety ("If I can't be a perfect saint like Mother Teresa, I won't pray regularly!") or undue pride ("I'm on the road to perfection while these other slobs are wasting their lives.").

Accused of being a glutton and drunkard, Jesus did not live up to the ideal of ascetic prophet. The external things of life were not ultimately important to him; internal things were: "Not what goes into a person, but what comes out of the person's heart." True perfection lies not in following the demands of an external law, but rather in the way in which a person receives, integrates, and gestates what is given and in response gives birth to loving actions from the heart. True asceticism acknowledges this point: at heart, external things ultimately cannot take control nor be determinative in the spiritual life. "Why should I live by another's scruples?" Paul rhetorically queried the Corinthians. "If I partake with thankfulness, why am I condemned for that for which I give thanks?"

Rev. Bill Johnson had once told me he believed every minister experiences some loss of integrity approaching ordination. By denying some part of one's self to please those with the power to ordain, or by telling them what they want to hear rather than what one actually believes, almost every ordinand feels compromised in the final laying on of hands. What could be a service (or, in some traditions, a sacrament) of integrity, may, in the most extreme case, become a sham of conformity. In any case, it never *confers* integrity, though one might wish it could both call forth and be a celebration of the integrity of both minister and church.

Of course, the common perception of ordination is quite different, as if, of itself, ordination proferred an aura of spiritual authority and integrity. Even Protestants have set aside their own tradition to adopt a view of clergy at which their Reformed ancestors rebelled: that ordination sets one apart morally, implying moral superiority. Hence we are least forgiving of a clergyperson involved in some impropriety, especially one that is sexual in nature. Calvin's belief that the worthiness of the vessel does not affect the validity of a sacrament does not deter us from our moral perfectionism when it comes to clergy. In my own ordination process, for example, the church became preoccupied with my sexuality, and asked little of my theology or spirituality.

A seminarian struggling for ordination as a woman within her own denomination helped me clarify what I already knew deep within me: ordination is not necessary to minister; my ministry had already begun. In truth, my struggle for ordination would itself be ministry. Though I did not intend to make my sexuality an issue as I approached ordination, I knew the church might make it *the* issue. Remembering my own lonely, adolescent search for acceptance as gay, I decided that, if discussion and debate over my sexuality enabled *one* parent to respond with love and understanding to a gay son or lesbian daughter, all the struggle would be worth it. The success of my quest for ministry could not be predicated on ordination, else, if ordination were denied, I would experience abject failure. My success had to be determined by whether "the blind receive their sight, the lame walk, lepers are cleansed, and the deaf hear, the dead are raised up, the poor have good news preached to them."

A fellow student I didn't know very well wrote to me after hearing a sermon I preached at the Divinity School the last week of the school year. For a long time, he wrote, he had had a liberal attitude toward homosexuality, but he was further sensitized to the issue when the woman he loved and had hoped to marry revealed to him that she was gay and severed communications with him. Though he understood her need to do this, it nevertheless caused him much pain.

"Although you have had no way of realizing it," he wrote, "In no small way you have helped me to understand the difficult situation in which a homosexual person finds himself or herself. . . . I look to a day when every person will be valued not for their race, religion, political beliefs, or sexual orientation, but for their qualities as a person. . . . I look forward to the day when we will be colleagues in the ordained ministry."

Chapter 8

COMING OUT TO THE CHURCH

LOS ANGELES
SUMMER 1974

The new pastor of my home church, Rev. Bob Rigstad, was on the phone. We discussed the special meeting called later that week by the presbytery committee "charged with the care and oversight of candidates for the professional ministry." Atypically, the committee had but one agenda item: *me*, particularly my ministry with gays during the past year. Equally unusual, the committee had requested my pastor to be present. The pastor, who knew I was gay, guessed the purpose of the meeting and said, "Looks like this is it!"

During the year I'd written to the woman who served as my liaison with the committee. I had told her about my seminary experience, including my ministry within the gay community. Her response was curious and amusing. She replied:

You sound like you are happy and well integrated into the situation. We will want to hear more about your work with the homosexuals as well as exactly who is going to be your Presbyterian sponsor. I do hope that you get involved in *Presbyterian* work somewhere, since again the homosexual work seems to be interdenominational.

It seemed odd that she responded to the ecumenical aspect of the ministry, rather than asking the nature of the ministry, a question she surely pondered. It was not till years later, when I acquired the files kept on me as a candidate for ordination, that I discovered my letter had prompted her to carry on a personal investigation of my sexuality within my home church, an investigation which was both indiscreet and unnecessary.

When, in college, I had sought the endorsement of the elders (governing council) of Van Nuys Presbyterian Church as a candidate for ordination, I had not informed them of my sexuality, though I had told the pastor. We both believed their education on the subject should precede any disclosure on my part. When they proudly endorsed my candidacy as one of their own (since I had been ordained as an elder in 1972), my joy at their support was compromised by the question that had plagued me since childhood: would they still support me if they *knew*?

The process had then required my taking standard psychological exams, followed by a consultation on the results with a psychologist. The psychologist carefully watched my reaction as he reported that I had rated high on the "feminine side" in one of the tests. Apparently his intent was to shock me either into a confession or a revealing confusion; but I calmly replied I had expected it, since the so-called "feminine" qualities are those commonly associated with the requirements of ministry: sensitivity, listening ability, emotive capability, as well as a desire to be cooperative and nurturing. What a shame there's been such opposition to the ordination of those who have traditionally been assigned such traits: women and gay men!

When I had then met with the presbytery committee for an initial interview, several of its members took exception at my choice of a non-Presbyterian seminary, Yale. "Why not Princeton?" someone asked. I responded that, since I believed education to be a cooperative effort, I didn't believe I'd fit into a school then deeply affected by the fundamentalist "Jesus movement," a cultural phenomenon of the late sixties and early seventies. Privately, I doubted such students would accept me as gay as well. "Are you born again?" another asked. Surprised, I replied, "I haven't heard that question since I was a Baptist. Yes, I'm born again every day. Each day is an opportunity to experience life and my faith anew. Conversion for me has always been a gradual process. I can point to significant moments along the way, but conversion is a lifetime process." After being excused from the room for the committee's deliberation, I was invited back and told the committee had voted to recommend the Presbytery of San Fernando take me under care as a candidate for ordination to the ministry. However, they added that I needed to work on my "intolerance," illustrated by my remarks about Princeton and Baptists! I was offended that the committee had sized up my character in a ten-minute interview; my seeming "intolerance" was really intolerance of the intolerance I anticipated at Princeton or from someone who might ask me if I were "born again"! I smiled to myself as I wondered, "Wait till they find out I'm gay. *Then* we'll see who's intolerant!"

Now, during the summer following my first year in seminary, the "wait and see" meeting had arrived. I felt uneasy as I entered the lion's den of the committee room, though grateful to have a supportive pastor beside me. Like my early childhood dream, I would have to take off my shoes and show my naked feet. I would be vulnerable to these committee members who were yet strangers. But, like rolling down the hill in junior high and spinning on the highway en route to seminary, I experienced remarkable peace as the meeting began—a meeting that might be stormy and mean my downfall. My calm derived from an intuitive feeling this meeting *had* to take place, like learning to walk as a child: difficult, even traumatizing as one risks falling, yet necessary for all but the physically handicapped in order to proceed. Again, it was *kairos:* standing on my feet as a gay Christian, and taking a step forward toward the ministry to which I believed myself called by God. I was grateful my first steps had already been taken in more welcoming environments.

The meeting lasted several hours, the first half devoted to my ministry with homosexual persons, my views of homosexuality, my concern for justice for gay persons, and my belief they should be included in the church and its ministry. A few questions were asked about my preparation for the ministry and my theological and biblical perspectives, but like a curious adolescent drawn to explicit diagrams of genitalia in a medical encyclopedia rather than to the whole book, the committee's questions gravitated repeatedly toward sexuality.

The chairperson tried to ask his questions neutrally, but I sensed God had not yet softened this Pharaoh's heart regarding lesbians and gays. That wouldn't happen to this otherwise sensitive man until the plague of the first-born, when his own son would come out to him as gay years later. Over an hour into the discussion, he finally posed the question all had been wanting to ask: "Chris, I'm not sure if you're telling us you are gay, or not. Are you homosexual?" It struck me that the members of the committee suspected anyone interested in ministry with gays must be gay too, a touch of homophobia that prevents many from bringing up the issue and doing similar ministry. I responded "Yes," and we talked for another hour and a half.

"Why didn't you tell us this before?" someone asked. I answered, "I didn't view it as an issue. Though I would want a congregation hiring me to know, for my own sake as well as theirs, I didn't believe it was your business. I felt that if the issue were to be raised, it would have to be *your* issue." A pastor on the committee concluded the discussion by telling me I didn't have the "chance of a snowball in hell" of being ordained in that presbytery.

To their credit, the committee members chose to avoid rash actions. Ultimately, they decided to keep me under their care, understanding that the denomination as a whole would deal with the question of the ordination of gay members. Because of turnover in committee membership, however, a new committee member would be assigned as my contact person almost every year, requiring fresh initiative and energy on my part to inform the individual about myself and about homosexuality. It seemed I fell under closer scrutiny than other would-be clergy, ironically receiving more "care" than most, yet at the same time feeling personally lost in the shuffle of committee members and in the controversy of homosexuality. I experienced the committee less as grand inquisitors than grand inhibitors, and considered their contacts with me as casual and transient as they characterized gay sex. Though I urged them to educate the presbytery on the issue, what was done would be too little too late.

Providentially, I've never identified the church primarily with its bureaucracy. That summer the church manifested itself in three congregations. Once again I worked for the Congregational Church of Northridge. I resumed attendance as a member of the First Presbyterian Church of Van Nuys on Sunday mornings, when my work didn't require my presence at the first. But, on Sunday evenings, I eagerly anticipated worshiping most intimately with the Metropolitan Community Church in North Hollywood.

This was my first experience worshiping with gay and lesbian Christians on a regular basis. As such, it served as my first ongoing opportunity to witness the ingathering of lesbian and gay Christians from the world's longest and most intense diaspora. Gays and lesbians of all ages, of disparate religious backgrounds, unknowingly separated from one another by the homophobia and heterosexism of both church and society, were at last able to "sing the Lord's song in a foreign land" together. When the Babylonian empire exiled the children of Israel from their homeland and dispersed them throughout the world, the Babylonians believed this divide and conquer tactic plus separation from their homeland would prevent any rebellion. But the faith of the Hebrews grew stronger not only in spite of but also because of this strategy, as the faith was more conscientiously and intentionally remembered and preserved in the heart of the family. When African slaves were sold and bought in the United States in another experience of diaspora, families themselves were wrenched apart, yet black children, adolescents, and adults could at least visibly identify members of their community.

The lesbian and gay diaspora allowed neither of these options. We did not grow up in gay families, nor could we identify by visible sign those with whom we shared our condition. We endangered our relations with what family and community we had if we voiced our difference, and yet, unable to be ourselves fully in those contexts, we experienced isolation even from those to whom we felt most attached. Gay and lesbian children, adolescents, and adults therefore suffered a more intensely personal form of diaspora, leaving scars which will take generations to disappear.

At Metropolitan Community Church, I witnessed healing as we told our individual stories of how we kept our faith in isolation from one another and under persecution from the majority culture. Just as the faith of Jews and blacks deepened in the face of exile and oppression, so had ours. And, just as life came to be celebrated and life's rights came to be valued in the religious lives of Jews and black Christians, so gay and lesbian Christians and Jews have come to celebrate life and value human rights in their respective congregations more keenly than their nongay counterparts.

Never had I felt so deeply the emotion described in the hymn "Amazing Grace" as I did when we sang it together at this church. For God's grace *had* "brought me safe thus far" to this community of faith. I regret the experience of many lesbian women and gay men whose only exposure to others like themselves are environments that often fail to promote adequate community: bars, business, and politics, all of which are more likely to engender competition than community, whether competition in appearance, finances, or power. Though community-building occurs within these environments, it often happens in spite of the law of survival of the fittest. The church at its best is a place where one does not need to be perfect, where one may fail and find forgiveness, where one may receive the prayers of others and be reminded of one's own God-given high hopes for self and world. Cruise bars require performance, competitive business and politics expect no mistakes, and the latter demands ideological correctness. The church loses its unique identity when it requires a particular performance, forgives no errors, and demands absolute conformity of belief. As the church is more in touch with God's amazing grace, it becomes more amazingly gracious.

Representing the Presbyterian Council on Theological Seminaries, Rev. Jack Meister once visited Presbyterian students at Yale. I knew nothing of his prestigious history of service to the Presbyterian church, nor of his disheartening defeat at the hands of William P. Thompson when both ran for election as Stated Clerk of the General Assembly, our denomination's highest parliamentarian and then most powerful position. (Thompson would later prove himself an opponent to the ordination of gay people.) In my meeting with Jack Meister, I tested the waters by asking him what he thought of homosexuals in the church. Without a pause, he smiled and replied, "I think we need everyone we can get!" I thanked God for his inclusive vision. What a different church we might have been had *he* been elected Stated Clerk. I grieved upon learning he died of cancer a few weeks after our encounter. His amazingly gracious attitude has stayed with me all the years since, ministering to me when I faced doubt, reminding me of God's grace.

The church misses an opportunity for increasing its faith when it fails out of fear to incorporate the deepened faith, joy of life, and valuing of human rights which often characterize a dispossessed minority's spirituality. That August I was invited to preach my second sermon at the Van Nuys church. My first, entitled "Conflict and Unity in the Church," had paraphrased Jesus' words: "One who saves one's [church] will lose it, and one who loses one's [church] for my sake and the sake of the gospel shall find it." I proclaimed that to be faithful to Jesus Christ meant taking certain risks with the church as institution, risking stability and comfortability in reaching out to those in need. Now, the second sermon, "Not Just Another Interruption," described how, through faith, we may discover meaning in the interruptions of our lives. If we are listening, we might hear God's call in the midst of such interruptions. Of course I had my own experience of interruption in mind: my acceptance of my sexuality certainly interrupted my life, and yet I discovered within that "interruption" a unique call. But I was not ready to make that explicit to a congregation also unready to hear it.

The following summer I preached about yet another interruption in a sermon entitled "A Still, Small Voice," in which I related a personal experience avoiding a subway bum who tried to help me find my way in the subways under Brooklyn: ultimately, I realized his directions (which I had ignored) were correct, and the directions of a subway official (which I had followed) were wrong. It had been a religious experience for me, as I felt I had met Christ himself under the streets of Brooklyn and had ignored him because he looked diseased and wore tattered clothes. I compared the experience to Elijah's hearing God's still, small voice where he had not expected it, and the church's need to listen for God's voice where we might not expect to hear it: the voice of the stranger. I knew I was leading up to something. Though my preaching was popular, that was the last sermon I was invited to give at my home church. By the next time I was available, I had come out to them as a stranger.

For in 1976, I wrote the elders to tell them of my homosexuality and the unique call to ministry I heard. The pastor reported to me that this had prompted a hot debate at their next meeting, but those most opposed had been surprised to find their number less than anticipated. A decision was postponed to a later meeting, at which, after a calm discussion, the elders voted unanimously to sustain their previous endorsement of my candidacy for ordination. This was remarkable, for, given the diversity among the elders and the broader congregation, it was unusual to gain unanimity on any issue. Nonetheless, there were those in the congregation who disagreed, one member saying if I even walked into the church he would walk out. It was considered too controversial to invite me to preach the following summer. I remember the pain I felt being allowed to serve only as liturgist one Sunday, and the Sunday following hearing a colleague of mine, also home from seminary, deliver the sermon. I had recommended him for a position at the church when we were both in college. During his time on staff, he'd been rather casual about letting the youth group know that he spent nights with his girlfriend. Yet his heterosexuality gave him access to a pulpit denied me.

However, after a communion service one Sunday later that summer, the pastor informed me that the member who had threatened to walk out of worship if I attended had been there and had stayed. "Not only did he not walk out," he said encouragingly, "He took communion with you!" Once again, Christ's broken body had proved reconciling.

Chapter 9

EXPERIENCING HOMOPHOBIA

NEW HAVEN
FALL 1974–SPRING 1975

Though I continued my gay activism during my second year of seminary, I was nonetheless relieved and renewed by taking a youth ministry position at the Congregational church in nearby Thomaston. The need of ministry in this small town parish was not necessarily less than what I experienced in ministry within the gay community, but, unlike the latter, it afforded me a certain distance and detachment. First, it was geographically an hour's drive away and culturally less diverse and hectic. Second, though I cared for the young people with whom I worked in Thomaston and for their parents, I was emotionally more detached than was possible with gays and lesbians, for whom I felt the most keenly and from whom I experienced the greatest demands. Third and most important, I did not feel the constant need to prove myself as a gay minister or show myself worthy as a gay person. My personal life I kept in New Haven. Yes, I was back in the closet and enjoying it!

Of course it wasn't quite the same; I had been "out," in reality *was* "out," but, just as I might choose not to tell a person seated next to me on an airplane about being gay, I chose not to inform either the pastor or members of the congregation. I realized it was an unreal and temporary estate, for I believe ministry cannot be done as authentically from outside a community as from within. If I were to become the pastor of a congregation, I would need to live nearby, with all the lack of privacy that that would entail. This is not to say that a degree of privacy is not possible and necessary in ministry, but the choice of a lifemate, with whom one lives, is difficult to conceal—although not impossible, as many semi-closeted clergy demonstrate, clergy whose discretely uninquisitive congregations choose to believe in the myth of ten- to thirty-year "roommates."

I had been an invisibly gay person before, but this time was very different. Coming out had greatly enhanced my self-esteem and self-valuing as a gay man. Now I could observe homophobia and heterosexism with less personal damage, easier recognition of its destructive power, stronger assertiveness in my response, and greater ability to laugh at its absurdity and to cry at its tragedy. The vignettes that follow from my second year of seminary serve as evidence of how homophobia attacks.

Invited to join a family gathering for Thanksgiving weekend, I felt privileged to observe (more objectively than I could my own) three generations gather and interact with one another. There was love, and there was joy, as well as an undercurrent of expected behavior that was not overly restrictive. At one point grandfather, two sons, grandson, and I were in the living room of the grandparents' home. Music played on the stereo, and the little grandson began dancing to the music like a ballet dancer. We were all amused at his playful antics, which continued until one of the sons, the boy's father, suddenly commanded, not unkindly, "Better stop dancing like that or your grandpa won't love you anymore." The boy stopped, and things continued normally.

But I felt as if ice water had been poured down my back, chilled by the meaning of the father's statement. There was every indication that the grandfather enjoyed the boy's dancing, had even encouraged it. Why, then, this comment from the boy's father? Had he himself been kept from dancing at the boy's age, metaphorically or literally, by a father who now enjoyed the boy's play as grandfather? The clear message of the father was that the behavior was inappropriate for a boy, because of the perceived "effeminacy" of the style of dance.

Some observers would consider this an example of gender control rather than a matter related to sexual orientation. But the two are inextricably linked, especially in a child's experience. If a little boy's fulfillment of a desire to dance ballet risks losing grandfather's love, perhaps fulfillment of other desires perceived as effeminate may risk the same loss of love.

I wonder which one of us there actually felt the boy's mimic ballet was inappropriate? Did the father hide his own feelings behind grandfather's supposed feelings? Did the father anticipate grandfather's or society's feelings and feel compelled to control his son? Could the father have been expressing hidden anger at grandfather's other expectations, while at the same time subscribing to gender conformity? Who was hurting and who got hurt in this exchange?

Whatever the answers to these questions, what passed for others as an innocent comment I perceived as homophobia and heterosexism subtly and serpentinely insinuating themselves into this loving atmosphere. I wondered what devastating effect the comment had on the other son, the little boy's uncle, who wanted so much to be able to tell his father and brother of his homosexuality. He and I exchanged understanding glances as we listened to the one tragic flaw in this otherwise noble day.

Having worked with youth groups before, I felt prepared to deal with "fag jokes" and the indiscriminate use of the words *fag* or *faggot* as general pejorative terms of abuse. The teen-age members of the church soon learned I did not approve of hate words applied to gay people, nor applied to anyone perceived as different. (I find words like *redneck* and *hardhat* similarly offensive.) The young people were also made aware that comments, stories, and jokes in which lesbians or gays were stereotyped or put down might be hurting gay people present who had not yet accepted or revealed themselves.

What I was not prepared for was a conversation with the

pastor of the church and his wife about the subject. While somewhat cosmopolitan in their attitudes, the pastor's personalized stereotype startled me. Telling the story of how kind an older gay couple had been to him in seminary, he attributed their generosity to sexual interest. A little too cockily, he observed, "I don't know what it is about me, but I seem to be overwhelmingly attractive to homosexuals. They just can't leave me alone." I was shocked, as I had often wondered what his attractive wife saw in him physically. I was tempted to reply, "*I* don't find you attractive at all." I did ask him if possibly he unconsciously flirted with gays to see if he could attract them.

Homophobia caused him to make assumptions and possibly mistake the motives of a couple he otherwise described as very helpful. Kindness that he probably would have accepted from anyone else without sexual implications he understood as sexually suggestive from gays. I believe this man's macho arrogance also would have led him to see sexual overtones in the kind acts of two "spinsters," and would have blinded him to the possibility they might be lesbian lovers. That would have been heterosexism rather than homophobia, however, as heterosexism is an exclusively heterosexual view and interpretation of the world.

Back in New Haven, I enjoyed a friendship with a first-year student who was also a writer. We spent time sharing our poetry and short stories. Mike had been a truck driver, and his writings nostalgically recalled his experiences and praised truck drivers' simple virtues: straightforwardness, loyalty, hard work, and support for one another. This struck a receptive chord in me, because this is the way I experienced my father, who had begun as a truck driver, become a sales driver, and later a sales supervisor for a bread company. One night Mike "escaped" the seminary environment to breathe the grease-filled but relaxed air of a local truckers' cafe, explaining to me how he missed that part of himself in the midst of what he considered the intellectual masturbation of Yale. Mike's uniqueness fascinated me; his soft southern voice caressing his well-chosen words had a hypnotic effect on me. I respected his integrity, his talent, and his call to ministry.

Mike was not gay, but he seemed tolerant. Occasionally he asked questions about my experience as a gay man and what I believed as a Christian. Of course much of the writing I shared with him had to do either with my experiences as a gay man or as a Christian, especially the poetry, which I frequently wrote as therapy to express the heights of fulfilling love or the depths of unrequited love. I never thought not to trust Mike with the limited intimacy available in the early stages of friendship, that is, sharing some of who I am, what I believe, my loves, my dislikes.

One evening, after I had read him one of my love poems, Mike asked abruptly and harshly, "Why do you always have to remind me that you're gay?" Thrown off guard, I immediately felt vulnerable, even naked, as if I had stripped before someone who was embarrassed or disgusted rather than interested in my body. A slight sense of panic rose in me, as if I now had to say the right incantation to preserve the friendship, for I sensed in his tone strong disapproval. Flustered, I made several attempts at explanation, basically telling him, "For the same reason you always remind me that you were a truck driver." He refused to see the comparison, as if my life experience as a gay man could not be as worthy or appropriate a subject for writings as his life experience as a truck driver. Much to my dismay and total surprise, this became the last time we shared our writings, as well as our final conversation. It was as if a squall had arisen on a peaceful sea, completely unforeseen, but able to capsize our boat and send us swimming for safety in different directions. How I wished Jesus could have been there saying, "Do not fear" and "Peace, be still" before disaster struck and I lost a significant friend.

The squall was homophobia. Mike evidently didn't want to be reminded of what he considered the one flaw in the character of someone he gave every evidence of loving. Perhaps he was "loving the sinner but hating the sin," which felt to me like homophobia in sheep's clothing. Whatever the case, I was devastated. After having lost one close male friend in college and another my first year in seminary, I was beginning to doubt the possibility of close friendships with straight males.

A friend once gave a party to which he invited his supportive straight friends from one church and his gay friends from another. The gay friends came, the straight friends did not. My friend was disappointed and saddened, as he had been trying to avoid ghettoization by giving a party that might reflect his intended integrity. The same dynamic between Mike and me was at work. Straight people wonder why we gays and lesbians keep to our own, why we ghettoize. It's not entirely our choice. A wall of homophobia separates us from would-be friends, as well as from old friends; I believe it is far less of our construction than that of the mainstream culture.

During the fall semester I fell in love with a man with whom I believed I would spend my life. I'll call him Joe. Joe combined northern efficiency and southern charm, having been reared in the South but educated in the North at a prestigious college. He was dedicated to the church (a necessary component to keep my interest, I would learn in later years) and determined to find success in a professional church career. He was good-looking, but more importantly, he incorporated the solid, honest, middle-class values I appreciated, having myself been reared by parents with similar values. He dressed well, kept his room extraordinarily neat, and placed a high value on an ordered life.

His passion for order complemented his passion for his work. But one passion threatened his tidy existence: his passion for the local seminary gay activist: me. It was a passion that he could control only in limited ways. I experienced a similar passion for him. But I also experienced love, a love which I believed he shared. Passion and infatuation choose you; you choose to love. Falling in love may be primarily infatuation and its resulting passion; it may grow into love, but my experience confirms the concept that authentic love is choice more than feeling. In Joe's case, he had the feelings and the passion for me, but ultimately chose not to love me because of homophobia.

I'd spent a long weekend at his family's home, designated simply as "a friend from seminary." The pleasure in meeting family members and friends was mutual. Afterward, when Joe's parents wrote him, they told him they had enjoyed meeting me and were pleased he was finding such nice friends at school. At Christmas, I returned to California and Joe to his parents' home. By this time we were so attached we could not hold back tears at the prospect of being parted at this special time of year. I wrote him what I hoped would be a comforting letter from California, feeling forced to delay its mailing lest I arouse his parents' suspicion. We avoided the telephone, though I did feel I could justify calling him on Christmas day to wish him a merry one.

Despite our precautions, Joe's mother became suspicious, and, ironically, as Joe and his father worshipped one Sunday at the church in which he had been nurtured to adulthood, she rummaged through his things to find and read the letter I'd written. When Joe and his father returned from church, his mother confronted him with the question: "How long have you been gay?" Then she raged for days, threatening to prevent Joe's return to Yale and my "influence." Thousands of miles away, I got fragmented reports of the crisis from Joe himself or from a closeted gay family friend who lived in the small town. What I felt was akin to what a wife feels hearing her husband's battalion is locked in mortal combat in a far-off war: I felt frustration at lack of information and my inability to reach out and help, panic that my loved one might be hurt, and sorrow that I might not see him again. I knew I could not underestimate the power of a parent's influence.

One call that came from the family friend delayed my arrival for an appointment with the liaison of my ordination committee. I was grateful that he proved forgiving and understanding of my dilemma, but at the same time I was keenly aware of the contrast between the supposed hurt the church would suffer were it to accept gay people and the actual, everyday devastation lesbians and gays face in a homophobic society.

"Who is my neighbor?" Jesus was asked. Jesus replied with the parable of the Good Samaritan: a neighbor is both the one who needs help and the one who offers help. In the story, the priest and the Levite (a lay priest) pass by without helping the one who needs help, possibly to avoid being rendered ritually unclean on their way to worship in the temple at Jerusalem. Fearing defilement, the church similarly passes by wounded lesbian women and gay men, failing to prove itself neighbor and failing to recognize us as neighbor. Joe's pastor turned out to be both exception and Good Samaritan to him in his need.

During a time that should have been filled with joy, visiting family in Los Angeles and friends in San Francisco, other emotions predominated: grief for Joe's emotional anguish at his parents' reaction, guilt for the exposure of his sexuality as a result of my letter, fear that he might be prevented from pursuing his education and career, and sorrow that I might lose him. Finally I'd found someone with whom to share my life and my commitment to the church, and now I might be denied him and his love by external, homophobic forces. My only relief was that I could pray for him, and even if I lost him, could always embrace him in prayer.

When we returned to Yale after the Christmas holidays and to each other's arms after the terror-filled separation, we spent the whole day holding one another, skipping classes, reaffirming our love despite outrageous pressures, relieved we had not been torn asunder. But it was the beginning of the end. Joe's mother refused to communicate with him; his father wrote letters urgently pleading that Joe bring peace to the family by breaking off our relationship. One letter said, "By now you've gotten rid of 'C' "! We both laughed at how my name had been reduced to an initial, as if as loathsome to spell out as "cancer," reminiscent of stories of beating "the big C." Yet it was a nervous laughter for me, wondering what effect such comments would have on Joe and on our relationship. Joe told me he had placated his parents in his letters and phone calls, leading them to believe what they wanted to believe: that no, he was not gay, and no, he was no longer in relationship with me. His feisty, independent spirit at his parents' home now weakened at a distance.

Then Joe began finding reasons why we shouldn't continue our relationship: "For example, I like nice things," he would say, "Like nice furniture, and that isn't very important to you. Our priorities are different." His concern about keeping his sexuality closeted surfaced again. I remembered nightmares he described earlier about other students finding us together in intimate embrace. In the fishbowl of seminary, I'd been surprised that he had believed our relationship was not apparent. Indeed, in those early days he had asked that we not see each other for a week, and I agreed, though he recanted within three days. I wrote a poem for him then, the concern of which resurfaced in the latter days of our relationship:

> My lover is walled up in the church.
> Yes, within that brick is a beating heart,
> Yearning to love, yearning to be loved,
> Yet unable to reach out, transcend that stone,
> Held back and held down by nails and cross
> > And years of tradition.
>
> He bears the weight of that church
> Like a millstone 'round his neck
> It keeps him from rising to heaven.
>
> I pity him. I love him.
> But can *I* free him?
> If I march 'round the church walls,
> Will they fall down?"
> And if they do, will my lover die in the destruction?
>
> I ask *you* to roll the stone from the tomb,
> I say a prayer, and I shout "Come forth!"
> And I wait with a fearful, faithful Martha
> And a crowd who marvels at my tears:
> > "See how much he loved him!"

And doubting Thomas cries from within,
"Unless I see the prints of the nails,
I will not believe you escaped
Or loved, which is the same thing."

Joe wanted a professional church career. He wanted to keep peace in his family, satisfying their need to see him in a particular way. His passion for me got in the way, and the only way Joe could get over the one thing that apparently disturbed the neatness of his life was to replace the object of his passion. Before ending our relationship, he began dating a male student from another graduate school at Yale, a student who also wanted to remain closeted and who shared Joe's ambition to do as well as he could in his field. For me to see him do this (their first date was dinner at the Divinity School dining hall) was like undergoing major surgery without benefit of anesthetic. As he wrote me later, Joe chose "mind over heart" in replacing me with another.

Joe and his lover live together to this day; Joe's parents and the church that employs him both choose to believe they are simply roommates. When I was in their city a few years ago, I paid them a visit; they entertained me hospitably in their tastefully decorated apartment. I was amused to see that Joe still seemed to be finding reasons why our relationship "would never have worked out anyway." As he returned an album to its jacket, he said, "See, you never put your records away. We would never have gotten along." I didn't bother to tell him I had subsequently adopted this simple practice myself. He needed every *reason* to believe it would not have worked out.

Although there may have been other factors that would have interfered, I was convinced then and am even more so now that the relationship was a casualty of homophobia. That's why I cringe whenever a self-righteous person decries gays because we "can't maintain longterm relationships." Lesbian and gay love promotes relationships; homophobia tears them apart.

In the family Thanksgiving gathering, in a working relationship with a fellow minister, in a friendship with a fellow writer, and now, in a love relationship, homophobia sought to destroy that which was holy: covenant relationships of family, coworkers, friends, and lovers. These and thousands of similar stories, in my life and in the lives of friends, parishioners, and counselees, have led me to conclude that homophobia is a pernicious sin.

Chapter 10

BEGINNING A MINISTRY WITH GAYS

PHILADELPHIA
FALL 1975–SPRING 1976

Like others with broken hearts, I couldn't bear staying on the same campus with Joe, especially if it meant watching his new relationship grow and blossom. When the recruiters for the Christian Association, an umbrella Protestant ministry of the University of Pennsylvania, appeared at Yale two weeks after our break-up, I signed for an interview. The Christian Association (usually referred to as the CA) had initiated a campus ministry internship focused on ministry with gays the previous year, but I had declined the CA's invitation to apply, feeling unready with only a year of seminary behind me. This time I went through the initial interviews, then found myself invited to Philadelphia for follow-up interviews with the rest of the staff. Upon meeting everyone involved in the CA and experiencing the beauty of Philadelphia in spring, I knew God had provided a paradise. The collegial style and enthusiastic support of the staff members, plus a mystical recognition that I somehow belonged in Philadelphia the coming year made me feel that God was calling me to this new home. I'm glad the staff felt the same way and invited me to serve there during the 1975–76 academic year.

I spent a hot and humid summer in New Haven, where I endured an intensive course in Hebrew. After a brief visit to Los Angeles, I returned to New Haven to drive myself and my belongings to Philadelphia. I had arranged to rent a room in the home of a young gay couple just across the Schulkyll River from the university. The narrow, red-brick rowhouse was on South Street, blocks and blocks of which seemed like a ghost town rather the border between an Irish Catholic ghetto and a black one. Plans to put an expressway along that route had been defeated after years of court battles, but by then houses and businesses had been abandoned by the dozens. Ours was among the first of the houses to be reclaimed and renovated. When I arrived that evening, another gay man, who also rented a room in the house, helped me move my things up three flights of stairs to my little room, which had a view toward the rear, a twin bed, no light, and a small closet. Fortunately, I had left most of my files and books in storage at Yale. The room and its closet were quickly filled in two trips from the car.

He took me to dinner, then out for a walking tour of parts of the city, a walk that increased my love for Philadelphia. The nation's fifth largest city seemed much like a small town; the gay district further downtown intensified this effect as I got to know many people in that community. In the midst of that evening's introductions, I providentially met a Roman Catholic priest who, much to our mutual surprise, became a significant friend in the months to come.

The following week I eagerly embraced my new work. Up to that point in my life I had been a worker/student, feeling the tug of two roles, feeling guilty when one claimed my attention over the other. Now I could focus on one: the work, the ministry. Immediately I fell into a happy camaraderie with the other staff members, to their credit. Our collegial approach to ministry meant each of us took turns chairing staff meetings, taking minutes, working in the front office (directing phone calls and providing information), and participating in program decisions, though only two of the staff were ordained clergy. I have never since experienced a staff situation as ideal as this turned out to be. Even in moments of tension, basic support and care were never withdrawn. Staff members trusted one another's commitment; no time clock was punched. We were not perfect in our attempt at collegiality, but for me it served as a taste of the kingdom, God's commonwealth. I blossom when I experience trust and support in a work environment, working sacrificially, creatively, joyfully. I wither in an atmosphere of suspicion and distrust, in which I feel forced to account for my time and justify my existence. At the Christian Association, I blossomed.

Ministering from within this nonbinding embrace, I had the equal delight of working with my own: gay people whom I could more readily understand, with whom I could identify, and for whom I had a passion to be of help, because of my own experience. Just as Jesus brought the gospel first to his own people, I, as a gay man, felt similarly called to bring the gospel first to my own kind: lesbian women and gay men. My ordination committee back in Los Angeles seemed scandalized by such a focus in my internship, though it would last only an academic year. I daresay the same committee would have had no problem with a ministry exclusively with a white, surburban, middle-and-upper-middle-class congregation (which typifies much of Presbyterianism), or a ministry exclusively with fundamentalist students (such as Campus Crusade or Intervarsity). The committee approved my taking the position only when convinced of the full range of ministry available within the Christian Association and when convinced of the association's local Presbyterian financial support.

The city, the home in which I lived, the staff members with whom I worked, the lesbians and gays for whom I worked, and the opportunity to fulfill a vision of ministry I had been given—all felt like heaven to me. I have long believed heaven is a time and place where God's will and personal will coincide. Jesus taught his disciples to pray, "Thy kingdom come, thy will be done, on earth as it is in heaven." Heaven, to me, is where God's will is done; true human happiness is predicated on bringing one's will in line with God's. Not surprisingly, everyone's understanding of God's will varies, but even with such varied understanding, when one's will coincides with one's perception of God's will, happiness results. Naturally and ultimately, history and the God of history determine whether one's perception of God's will is true. But we may be limiting our understanding of God's creativity to believe in only one truth that excludes other truths. Perhaps seemingly contradictory truths may exist side by side. Surely that lesson may be drawn from the very different yet profoundly meaningful world religions.

In my state of perceived paradise in Philadelphia, it was not so surprising that I found an ideal companion. The Roman Catholic priest whom I had met my first evening invited me out to dinner; our evening concluded with an intense and in-depth conversation lasting several hours. Again, God had provided someone equally committed to the church, and our shared interest in spirituality and faith heightened and intensified our mutual emotional and physical attraction. Unfortunately, the fact of his priesthood meant, in my mind, that he was married to the church and celibate. He viewed his celibacy more lightly than I did, seeing it as part of Roman Catholic red tape on his way to doing ministry. He rightly understood celibacy as a gift bestowed by the Spirit rather than an automatic or necessary ingredient for ministry. And yet his tradition expected it. As I wondered what future there could be to our relationship, he explained he had been considering leaving the priesthood. This possibility gave us permission to fall in love.

Within three months, however, the direction of our relationship shifted abruptly. Partly from an increased awareness of his call to ministry that grew from our relationship, and partly because of an affirming experience in a charismatic Catholic movement, he decided to end forever any dream of our making a life together. I was crushed. I was happy that he chose to reaffirm his priesthood, because that was an essential part of who he was. But I grieved that that meant denial of another essential need: physical and emotional intimacy with another person. And I felt devastated that it meant automatic rejection of me as anything more than friend. Nonetheless, we became and remain loyal friends, enjoying a friendship that is spiritually and emotionally significant for us both to this day.

Revealing conflicting and jealous feelings, though, he angrily departed from my life for nearly two months when, some time later, I began seeing someone else. He wanted intimacy, yet his seminary training had carefully taught him to avoid "particular friends," thus preparing him for ministry with all kinds of parishioners with whom he might or might not feel close. Celibacy is supposed to be an exchange of intimacy with one person for intimacy with a spiritual community (and thus with God), but my priest friend never seemed to have such a spiritual community. The system failed him, and fails millions like him. Ironically, a disproportionate number of gay people become priests and nuns partly to avoid questions of sexuality, preferring to be celibate or to appear celibate rather than deal with the expectations of a heterosexual society.

Though my friend found little spiritual community within the church, I found spiritual community within the lesbian and gay community of Philadelphia. This was the first time I had worked side by side with gifted and mutually-supportive gay and lesbian leaders. Though there were ideological and political differences among us, there was yet a sense of family: acceptance, appreciation, encouragement, and belonging. The significance of a Christian organization hiring a gay person to provide ministry with lesbians and gays was not lost on the broader lesbian/gay community, nor on those on the campus with whom I worked most closely. I served as a kind of living anachronism, an incarnation of reconciliation between gay and Christian that was yet to be accomplished in church and society. The Christian Association had been supportive of Gays at Penn, the campus student group, providing office and meeting space not available in the university. Yet even more important was the CA's investment in hiring gay seminary interns over a period of several years, demonstrating a valuing of gays and lesbians which went far beyond mere hospitality.

In addition to this witness, my internship's purpose was to educate me and, through me, the broader church. Apprenticing myself to the gay community, I would learn better how to minister within it. What follows is what I learned.

First, I learned to withhold judgment. At a preliminary meeting of Gays at Penn before the beginning of the school year, members discussed preparation of a listing of services, bookstores, bars, and restaurants available for gays in Philadelphia, thus helping newly-arriving gay students find their way. Someone suggested listing "tearooms" too, which are men's restrooms in which cruising and (sometimes) sexual activity occur. Privately I objected on aesthetic more than moral grounds, finding the idea of meeting someone in a restroom—let alone having sex there—distasteful. But publicly I protested on political grounds, arguing that tearooms were signs of our oppression, because married men frequented such places for sex, exploiting gay men with whom they refused to identify. This and other arguments opposed to the listing of tearooms prevailed.

Weeks afterward, I learned a couple of active members of Gays at Penn had found their way out of the closet via tearooms, and now felt uncomfortable with me and could not approach me for counseling because they feared being judged for their past experience. I regretted my statements, valuing my approachability more than my bourgeois attitudes. Certainly there are more fulfilling sexual expressions than those available in restrooms, but isn't *some* sexual expression better than suppression, and *some* reaching out better than isolation? I realized the need in my ministry to postpone broad judgments, exploring issues on a case-by-case basis and not rejecting out of hand any attempts to reach out beyond the closet.

When Virginia Ramey Mollenkott once asked Father John McNeill for a two-minute crash course on counseling gays, he said simply, "Never, but never, put down anyone's attempts to love. Show them there are better ways, perhaps, but not at the expense of their developing self-esteem."

Years later, gay parishioners would criticize me for not stating more strictly what God permitted and what God abhored with regard to sexuality, but the utter presumptuousness of doing so and the desire to remain available to everyone kept me from doing more than suggesting general guidelines. I have not been hesitant, however, to proclaim the greater desirability of certain expressions of love, because I have found among those I've counseled an almost universal desire to learn better how to love. Interestingly, 95 percent of those believed higher forms of love were most possible within committed, faithful relationships.

Another observation I made related to the sensitivity of gays and lesbians. I knew my own hurt at being different had sensitized me to others' hurt. But I didn't fully realize how delicate were the sensitivities of lesbians and gays until I saw it again and again during the year in Philadelphia. Repeatedly I witnessed gays and lesbians minister to their friends and families, who were often unaware of why they were able to empathize so well. I had once heard an older, closeted gay man quote Thornton Wilder at the conclusion of a sermon: "In love's service, only the wounded can serve." He certainly knew wounding: he and his supportive wife had been paying blackmail for years until they decided to call the extortionist's bluff. They were greatly relieved when their tormentor chose not to reveal the minister's homosexuality to the congregation he had served thirty years.

But sensitivity is two-edged. One day in the office, believing I had some free time, I decided to go to the university pool for my regular swim. As I pulled the office door shut behind me, a counselee walked up expecting to see me, having made the appointment the week before. I confessed to the unprofessional sin of not checking my calendar before leaving. The look of shock and hurt apparent on this man's face as he realized I had forgotten our appointment sobered me. I opened the door, and together, sitting in my office, we spent the next hour discussing his feelings about this incident. Although he was a competent graduate student, who knew I liked him very much, he was devastated that I had forgotten him. Once revealed, however, the wound proved the more available for healing.

A friend who has been involved in gay chapters of Alcoholics Anonymous for years describes a phenomenon he associates with alcoholism, though I think it applies to gays and lesbians as well: "I can go to a meeting where there are a hundred people," he says, "Ninety-nine of them will give me a hug, but I become preoccupied wondering why the one did not!"

Another friend, a former Jesuit now turned therapist, sums up our sensitivity in this way: "It's as if a group of injured hospital patients try to love each other. They want to embrace one another, hold one another, even make love. But casts and crutches and past wounds get in the way, making such loving difficult, awkward, and painful."

Such sensitivity may lead to antisocial behavior. Some pout in silent martyrdom. Others exhibit passive-aggressive behavior, saying one thing to satisfy another but doing something else to please themselves. The "bitchy queen" syndrome is employed by yet others who believe the best defense is a good offense, and so with attitude, gestures, or tongue they whip imagined opponents before an opponent may strike. Others express generalized anger, particularly evident in a few strident and extremist activists. Their anger derives from a keen and valuable sensitivity to sexism and homophobia, but it is a sensitivity unrelieved by humor, perspective, and self-discipline. Finally, perhaps the most common response is self-destructive behavior, which arises when gays consent to society's judgment that "we are bad people, should be hurt, and if we can't get someone to hurt us, we'll hurt ourselves." Overeating, alcoholism, drug abuse, careless sexual activity (especially recently in the face of AIDS), staying in the closet, sabotage of relationships, heterosexual marriage, celibacy, and sado-masochism may all become ways of reinforcing our sense of unworthiness.

Though people in general may be aware of such *destructive* behavior within the gay community, they tend to be unaware of the much more common *constructive* ways in which we respond to our hurt. I've already mentioned our ability to empathize, listen, counsel, and help others. Another grace is our ability to transform personal hurts into art, literature, music, theater, ministry, architecture, agriculture, fair business, medicine, therapy, and social reform, to name but a few examples. Leonardo da Vinci, Gertrude Stein, St. Aelred of Riveaulx, Helen Keller, Tchaikowsky, and Eleanor Roosevelt are but a few of the more famous examples of those involved in same-sex relationships who made this transformation. If the church only knew what I've seen of unsung contributors to the well-being of family, friends, church, and society who are lesbian or gay, it would throw open the doors to welcome the gay community, laughing and grieving at its own foolishness in rejecting such people's offering of compassion, insight, and creativity. Ironically, even the figuratively blind and deaf, from Jerry Falwell to the General Assembly of the Presbyterian Church, have benefited enormously and unknowingly from the gifts, resources and talents of lesbians and gays in key positions.

I witnessed sexism within the gay community. I was dancing in a popular Philadelphia bar with a friend when suddenly the lights came up, the music stopped, and some drunk started shouting, "There's too many women in the bar." I commented to my friend, "Where did that character come from?" As we wondered what happened to the music, the lights went down again and the music started. We assumed there had been some problem with the music system and the lights had been needed in order to repair it. We continued to believe this when it happened twice more. But each time this drunk took advantage of the silence to shout, "There's too many women in here. Some have got to leave." My anger at this obnoxious man turned to humor a short time later as I laughed about the incident with another friend. The friend corrected my impression. "That 'drunk' is the owner of the bar," he said, "He was trying to get some of the women to leave." I was astounded. I did not need to ask why. I had been told that the previous year, when Gays at Penn had invited a famous lesbian activist and author to speak at the university, she had been denied entrance to this same bar. She could not produce enough pieces of identification to satisfy the doorman that she was old enough to enter, though well into her fifties! Now I witnessed this discrimination firsthand, and I was disgusted. I avoided the place after that until one evening, showing a straight woman friend around Philadelphia's gay scene, I decided to try getting into this popular disco. My friend was denied entrance, and I was so infuriated I demanded to speak to the manager, but this didn't help. He was nasty and threatening, refusing to acknowledge the injustice that he was perpetrating. (Later, in Los Angeles, I joined in a boycott for several years of a popular disco whose owner boasted of his "quota" system which allowed only a small percentage of women and people of color to enter.)

I've heard unconvincing arguments from bar owners who discriminate against women; their arguments include "protecting the rights of male patrons" and "women don't drink as much as men, so we don't make enough profit." But I believe the truth is that the bar owner's attitude reflects the desire of many gay men to avoid women socially. I suspect this avoidance originates from unchecked male sexism combined with understandable resistance on the part of gay men toward society's thrusting of women upon them as desirable. A gay man's repugnance at such an idea may be similar to that of a nongay person who experiences a gay advance, or that of a woman who endures the unwelcome advance of a man. In addition there are women who believe they can make a gay man straight, a messianic pretension to a "salvation" that most gay men do not welcome or at least realize cannot be achieved.

Lesbian women often similarly wish to avoid men socially, even refusing to associate with gay men. At the university, Gays at Penn was a primarily male organization, and lesbians on campus preferred associating with other women at the campus Women's Center. The shared experience of oppression as women was often considered more significant than their oppression as lesbians, and the fact that they could be required to leave a gay disco supports this conclusion.

Despite this separation, my experience in Philadelphia (and in the years of ministry to come in other locales) taught me that our sensitivity as lesbians and as gay men made us more aware of our separation and our sexism than the nongay majority culture. My disappointment that an oppressed minority could still oppress others has been alleviated by my pleasure that we are challenging our sexism more intentionally than mainstream society.

The value of peer counseling was another important part of what I learned in this year. Experience taught me that overcoming homophobia required the presence of gay and lesbian friends, family or community members who personalized the issue of homosexuality. This is no less true for lesbians and gays, who have their own homophobia to unlearn. Gay ministers, therapists, or peer counselors, then, may automatically become a healing presence simply by virtue of who they are. And, as for almost everyone, nothing matches shared experience in feeling understood.

Drawing on my experience with the Gay Alliance at Yale in its establishing a peer counseling program, I gained the support of Gays at Penn, the Women's Center, and the Christian Association for such a service on the University of Pennsylvania campus. The Gays at Penn office could become a center for both phone and drop-in counseling. I screened volunteers who expressed interest, frankly discouraging those who I sensed were not good listeners or who offered ready-made solutions. Because I had served as a resource to the classes of the Marriage Council of Philadelphia, that organization readily agreed to offer our volunteers a four-session training course in listening skills and developing comfort in discussing sex-related issues. An outside phone line was installed, regular hours established and covered by a weekly schedule of trained volunteers, and the easily remembered phone number advertised widely in publications and through fliers. A log of phone calls and visits was kept, and I met regularly with the volunteers to discuss them.

Use of the service began slowly, but by year's end had justified the energy and time committed to the project. There were occasional calls critical of our service from a moral or religious viewpoint, a few crank calls, and one caller who claimed to have planted a bomb in the office, requiring an evacuation and search by police. But generally the calls and visits were sincere requests for information and help. For a timid first-year student afraid to attend a meeting of Gays at Penn, or a graduate student so protective of her career goals that she couldn't attend any public gay event, or a professor troubled by a heterosexual marriage, the anonymity of a phone call eased their access to someone who might understand. The establishment of this Gay Peer Counseling Service prompted the university counseling center to call a meeting of all who did counseling on campus in order to coordinate better all of our efforts and to become aware of referral possibilities.

Almost ten years later I would return to the Christian Association for a brief visit after a speaking commitment nearby. I already knew Gays at Penn had since found housing in university student facilities, the initial denial of which had caused their presence in the CA's building. I found the CA had been through several spectacular changes: the lobby and front office had been remodeled, the basement "eatery" transformed into a modern cafeteria, the women's bookstore converted into an elegant restaurant and bar. Most of the staff with whom I worked had moved on to new career opportunities. But, tucked away in the same corner office, I was gratified to discover the Gay Peer Counseling Service still there. The two volunteers staffing the office didn't quite know what to make of me as I explained why I was so pleased to find them there!

I discovered some "walls of hostility" between the church and gays. The Christian Association was affiliated with four nearby congregations: Episcopal, Lutheran, Methodist and a federated Prebyterian/United Church of Christ. One of my goals during the year had been to be invited to preach in each of them to explain needed ministry within the gay community. All but one of the pastors clearly supported my ministry. I wondered where the Lutheran pastor stood, so I phoned for an appointment with him.

His voice turned cold as I explained my purpose over the phone: to tell him a little about my experience in ministry with gays and lesbians. As he kept me waiting in his office at the time of our appointment, I noted a sign on his desk which read: "Yes, you may smoke . . . OUTSIDE!" Though not a smoker, I felt put off by this method of discouraging smoking in his office. When he finally arrived, the distance I experienced between us made me feel as if we were in two different rooms. I was reminded of the time when I came out to my college friend Kevin and felt far removed from my voice as I admitted to homosexual tendencies. Now it was not my voice that felt far removed; it was this man's ear!

When I told him I was available as a resource and a speaker or preacher if he thought his congregation would be interested in the subject, he replied, "No, nobody's interested. Nobody's ever brought it up." I explained the onus placed on anyone who might express interest: "If someone did raise the issue, your church council might think he or she were homosexual." "Well," he answered, "It doesn't really matter. In this church there's 'neither Jew nor Greek, male nor female, slave nor free.' We're all equal here." I reminded him that that might be true of God's future kingdom, but that we weren't there yet. By that time I knew our discussion was pointless: he was the proverbial brick wall.

That night, after a Gays at Penn meeting, I found myself in an increasingly intense debate with a graduate student about the church. I couldn't fathom the depth of his hostility as he recounted the familiar historical litany of church evils. I knew the same history, I reflected to myself, yet I didn't share his anger. Finally I asked about his own religious background, and the anger found explanation. He described some crushing, personal experiences as a gay youth being reared in the Lutheran church.

The next day, a young man came to my office seeking referral to a counselor or psychiatrist who would respect his integrity as a homosexual person. I gave him several names, and then, noticing how tense and nervous he was—he was evidently experiencing a crisis—I cautioned him that he might have to wait a few weeks to get in to see any of the therapists. I explained I would be available in the meantime. "Oh no, thank you," he replied almost deferentially, "Listen, I had enough of a problem just bringing myself even to come into something called the *Christian* Association, let alone talking to *you*—I mean, why, you're almost a *minister*!" And he said that somewhat accusingly! As we explored his churchphobia, I discovered he had suffered many bitter experiences growing up in the *Lutheran* church.

The providential irony of meeting these two disenchanted Lutherans just hours after my unsuccessful conversation with the local Lutheran pastor was not lost on me. That afternoon, I wrote the pastor a letter describing my recent experiences, adding that perhaps the reason no one in his congregation had raised the issue of homosexuality was because lesbian and gay Lutherans left the church before they could participate in a university campus congregation. The pastor never responded to my letter.

The story has a final twist. A member of his congregation who became an enthusiastic and supportive friend encouraged me to speak with her pastor about my ministry. I explained I had already done so and described my experience. She was surprised: "He can be so sensitive, and he's been so heavily involved in all kinds of liberal causes—I just can't believe it." When she was similarly rebuffed, she told me she'd keep working on him. Though her efforts apparently had no effect on him, when he moved to a job with another parish that same year, she managed an invitation from the church council for me to preach. During the sermon, I shared the whole story of a "local, liberal minister" in a disguised form from the very pulpit he had once occupied. The gospel text for that Sunday was John's description of Jesus as the Good Shepherd. I entitled my sermon, "Other Sheep Not of This Fold," and spoke of how lesbians and gays were among the other sheep of which Jesus said, "I must bring them also, and they will heed my voice. So there shall be one flock, one shepherd."

Finally, during this year I became more aware of the oppression that gay men and lesbian women suffer. I've always hesitated applying the word *oppressed* to my experience, partly because of a tendency to celebrate what's good and partly because of a reluctance to put my troubles in the same category as hunger, torture, imprisonment, total disenfranchisement, or dispossession. But, just as encounters with blacks and Jews made me aware of the oppression they suffer, however subtly, so my encounters with lesbians and gays during my year in Philadelphia made me aware that we too suffer oppression. Lesbians and gays *do* suffer widespread political, legal, and economic discrimination, but we do not for the most part have physical wounds whose bleeding make good media copy. Yet invisible wounds to the psyche, the spirit, and the emotions we suffer in abundance.

By the end of the year, I found myself comparing our experience to Job's in a sermon for Tabernacle Church, the federated Presbyterian/United Church of Christ congregation with which the Christian Association was affiliated and with which I regularly worshiped. In the sermon, I pretended Job had sought me out for counseling the previous week, and I discovered that his pain at being made to suffer despite his innocence and goodness was similar to the experience of others I counseled. Job felt "like a slave who longs for the shadow," either a shadow of restful shade or a shadow caused by the sunset, meaning the end of a long day of suffering. Many of the people with whom I ministered similarly longed for the shade, or sanctuary, of the church, and yearned for the end of their day of unjust suffering. I will elaborate here on one example from this sermon.

A twenty-two-year-old man began attending meetings and functions of Gays at Penn. He was a local resident, not a student, but was welcomed as part of the group. I witnessed him gradually emerge from his protective cocoon, trusting others, beginning to be himself and enjoy himself. He relaxed around the issue of his sexual orientation, while still maintaining the values that his working-class, Catholic family instilled in him. Physically he was not attractive, but as he smiled more, he revealed a heretofore hidden beauty within. His mental capacity seemed limited; he explained later he was mentally handicapped, having the mental age (so doctors told him) of a ten-year-old. From time to time we chatted briefly, but we never had a long conversation until the crisis.

The crisis arose out of his evolving interest in the gay community. He had brought some sexually innocent though politically explicit gay newspapers and brochures home, where he lived with his family. He carefully hid the material under his mattress, reading it only when he could do so alone and uninterrupted. As he later told me, trembling in my office, he wasn't sure what had happened: either he had accidentally left the material out, or his sister had uncovered it. She took it directly to their parents, who raged at him. I could imagine him cowering like a puppy under their hateful barrage. They threatened him with both a psychiatrist and a priest, saying, "We'll see what Father So-and-so has to say about this." It's a sad day for the professions of psychiatry and priesthood when they may be used in parental threats! Finally, the mother seemed to calm down a bit. She said to him, "Remember that time when you were twelve, when you had the bike accident, and we rushed you to the hospital just in time to save your life?" His hopes, he told me, were renewed, thinking she might yet relent and express her love for him despite the discovery. Timidly, he had offered the expected "Yes?" The mother responded, "We should have let you die *then!*"

I fought back the tears as he told me this story, stone-faced. Stunned, my eyes watered, my voice smothered by a choking feeling deep in my throat. My memory fails me here, as the memory of a tragic accident might be blocked. I don't recall what I said, how I counseled him, what further conversation occurred. Not often in counseling situations have I had to fight so desperately to control my feelings. This poor young man, trying so hard to overcome his mental disability and the social isolation and rejection it entailed, trying to appreciate his sexuality while remaining faithful to his religious principles, was now humiliated and degraded and made to feel unworthy of life itself.

No, gays and lesbians do not generally carry scars of physical torture, but inside we carry scars from deeper, psychological wounds. Our bodies may not be painfully thin from lack of food, yet, as children and adults, we starve unseen for affection from those who could nourish us. Though we may not suffer economic deprivation because we are able to hide our difference, lesbians and gays for the most part live with the painful fear of discovery: a telltale matchbook cover, a potentially revealing gesture, look, or vocal inflection, a suspicious silence about personal lives—that could cause us to lose in an instant a job, a promotion, a client, a customer. Unlike other minorities, we usually suffer these things alone, without support of family, church, or community. When we reach for support from the church, as I did when invited that same year to address a United Church of Christ Association meeting, we are told, as I was by one of the "ministers" present, that we are "injustice-gathering individuals"! A church and a society intolerant of valid criticism choose to blame their victim.

Just as the young man in this example was beginning to blossom, a late frost chilled his resolve. I never saw him again, never was able to learn the outcome of his story. The one warming ray of grace was that the priest with whom he had been threatened turned out to be more supportive of him than of his parents.

Gazing out my office window after that conversation, I could see the resurrection of crocuses on the ground below, a delight after Philadelphia's snowy winter. I recalled a seminary chapel service the previous spring. A student praying agonized over the late frost that had killed the first crocuses just beginning to appear. At the time I thought, "Only here in this safe sanctuary of seminary could one have the luxury of mourning flowers." It was not a cynical thought, but an approving one. The church, after all, should be concerned with "the least of these," as Jesus enjoined his disciples.

Now I mourned for this young man, and my grief was deepened, knowing that many of the same people who had a tender place in their hearts for the safe coming out of crocuses had no place at all in their hearts for the safe coming out of people like him. Their attitudes, their fears, their rejection, all chill us. I had seen the late frost of disapproval or hate destroy gays and lesbians—those who simply sought family acceptance and those who sought broader societal acceptance. Yet I believed in my heart that, despite the late frosts, spring had already arrived for lesbians and gays.

Chapter 11

BECOMING A GAY RIGHTS ADVOCATE WITHIN THE CHURCH

BALTIMORE, PHILADELPHIA,
AND WEST HOLLYWOOD
SUMMER 1976

Though politically unwise, there may be something spiritually appropriate about approaching religious councils with a certain naïveté, an idealism unchecked by probabilities while drawn forward by possibilities. Despite gospel-writing hindsighters, I wonder if Jesus knew for sure what would happen when he approached Jerusalem for the last time. Doubtless aware of risks, he nonetheless must have held some hope that the Sanhedrin might recognize the truth he spoke and lived. A few commentators on his life have gone so far as to suggest that Jesus planned it all, much as a savvy political figure might calculate the effects of his or her own martyrdom on the future of his or her cause. Traditional theology would have you believe *God* planned it all, as if God would not have been satisfied with something less than Jesus' death to bring about our salvation.

But I don't believe in that kind of God. I believe God would have been delighted if the people, including the religious leaders, had been delivered from their legalistic, idolatrous, selfish, and self-righteous ways simply by Jesus' words and deeds. Jesus' death was God's last resort, the last line of defense, so to speak. It was the *people,* not God, who demanded (and continue to demand) Jesus' death. Confirmation of this comes from our faith's claim that God did not leave Jesus in the grave. God always chooses life for us and for the prophets; it is we who, in our brokenness, often choose death for ourselves and God's prophets. Jesus lived, died, and lives again to redeem us from this brokenness, this condition called sin. In being broken himself, broken by compassionate identification with our condition, Jesus demonstrates how God's grace alone restores us to life, to community, to God. This restoration is both spiritual healing and resurrection.

Believing spring had arrived for lesbians and gays after a long, homophobic winter may have been a politically unwise attitude with which to approach the Baltimore General Assembly, but, retrospectively, I believe that it may have been spiritually appropriate. The apostle Paul encouraged early Christians to live "as if" the kingdom were already present. This proleptic lifestyle echoed Jesus' own understanding that the kingdom was already inbreaking: "the kingdom of God has come upon you." William James described religion as a set of "over-beliefs" in which the very action of belief helps create the believed reality. If I meet someone expecting her to be friendly, I probably will behave in a way that will elicit the very response I anticipate. If I believe she will be hostile, I may choose behavior that encourages that response. In a parallel but profound experience, neither the Gospels nor Acts nor the Epistles claim that the resurrected Jesus appeared to any save those who believed. (Paul's conversion on the road to Damascus falls into the category of mystical vision rather than resurrection story.)

Christians who live out liberation theologies (whether in the Third World, or in American black or feminist communities) speak of a "memory of the future" that informs their present action. The "remembered future" is God's ultimate victory, giving faith and encouragement even if today's battles are lost. The remembered future has its roots in a community's historical experiences in which God kept faith. In Gethsemane Jesus affirmed, "God's will be done," even though it meant risking life as he knew it. The roots of his nonetheless hopeful memory of the future lay in the history of his people as well as in his unique calling to preach: "Repent, for the kingdom is at hand." Whatever happened, God's kingdom was already being established.

It was with this unchecked hope, a desire to life "as if," and a memory of the future casting light upon the present that the Presbyterian Gay Caucus came to the Baltimore General Assembly in 1976. As individuals we already had had a taste of God's kingdom in which spirituality and sexuality harmonize, God's will and creaturely will coincide, and integrity of spirit and body is achieved. We had been called out of closets into the kingdom or commonwealth of God. And now we were to live out our calling as a ministry to the church. We believed the church ultimately would live up to its own high calling "to keep abreast of truth," as an old hymn declares.

And we had begun to experience some history together as a community which contributed to a collective memory of the future. The founding of the Metropolitan Community Church in 1968 and the ordination of Bill Johnson in 1972 within a mainstream denomination had generated publicity throughout the country, alerting the diaspora of religious gays and lesbians that they were not alone. Letters and phone calls began coming in from everywhere, both to MCC and to Johnson, revealing the stories of lesbian women and gay men from every religious tradition, denomination, and sect. In 1974, Johnson asked the Reverend David Sindt of Chicago to coordinate the Presbyterians who had contacted him.

In turn, Sindt sent out a letter to gay and lesbian Presbyterians inviting us to coalesce into a group initially named Gay United Presbyterians (since we were all from the largest stream of Presbyterianism, the United Presbyterian Church). When we had our first ministry of presence at the 1974 General Assembly in Louisville, Sindt was among the handful representing our infant organization. By 1975, he submitted the first annual report of the new group to the Cincinnati General Assembly, which rejected it, even though acceptance would confer no official status. During the floor debate, one commissioner ridiculed it, saying, "If we were to accept the report of this group, Cincinnati, the Queen City, would become known as the 'City of Queens'!"

Gay United Presbyterians would change its name three times in five years, confusing even its membership. But each time the change was intended to reflect our inclusiveness.

Since "Gay United Presbyterians" sounded exclusively gay, leaving out nongay friends and supporters, we changed our name to the Presbyterian Gay Caucus, under which name we became a nonprofit corporation. Again, this came to sound exclusive of nongays, so we became Presbyterians for Gay Concerns, keeping the same initials (PGC). Later, with increasing awareness that many, though not all, gay women preferred the term "lesbian," and wanting to be more inclusive of women, we eventually became Presbyterians for Lesbian/Gay Concerns (PLGC).

Though our organization was concerned about gays in pews as much as pulpits, we failed to be viewed as a priority until there were openly gay seminarians seeking ordination. New York City Presbytery had queried the Baltimore General Assembly for "definitive guidance" on the ordination of "avowed, practicing homosexuals" because it had such a person seeking ordination—Bill Silver, a student at New York's Union Theological Seminary. A Manhattan church had offered him a specialized ministry in the arts.

When I met Bill Silver at a meeting of the northeast chapter of the Presbyterian Gay Caucus a month before the assembly, he reminded me that we had been introduced before. I'd been visiting Union Seminary's local gay activist when Bill stopped by. I had found Bill's appearance and bearing forbidding and hostile. I was therefore shocked when my friend commented about Bill after the brief encounter, "He's going to be so much happier when he accepts he's gay!" I hadn't gotten the slightest hint that Bill was gay; indeed, I thought he had regarded us judgmentally.

By the time of our second meeting, at the PGC meeting he was hosting, Bill had come out as gay in a big way: he had sent "birth" announcements to his friends, he had cut his longish hair short, trimmed his beard and dropped forty pounds of unneeded defense. A relaxed, slimmer, and friendlier Bill greeted me at the door of his and his lover's New York apartment. He certainly was happier; later he told me he had repainted much of his artwork in brighter colors as a result of his self-acceptance. Small wonder I didn't associate him with the brooding, uptight seminarian I had met years before! Now, as the local PGC group strategized for the Baltimore Assembly in his home, I smiled at the transformation. If the Assembly delegates could have witnessed this resurrection, this meeting would have been unnecessary.

I was one of the first to arrive in Baltimore. The unfamiliar surroundings accentuated my feelings of loneliness. I was alone on the second floor of Kirk House, a former manse owned by the First and Franklin Street Presbyterian Church, where I had acquired free housing. My loneliness grew from having completed the fulfilling ministry internship at the Christian Association the week before. I had not only said goodbye to a number of friends at term's end, but I had also broken off a relationship with a man whom I will call John, a name that means "The Lord is gracious." I had met him shortly after my wounding over the decision of my priest friend to pursue no more than a friendship. John, a graduate student, had sought me out for a relationship. His presence in the months that followed comforted me, though the heights of love experienced with the priest were not yet available for me with him. While he respected and admired my commitment to the church, he was not similarly inclined, and this limited the depth of the relationship for me. On the other hand, though severely closeted, John at least was not inhibited by the church. At the close of the spring semester he completed his studies and returned to his home in California, where he intended to become a millionaire in his chosen career, a priority I did not share. Unblinded by passion, we made a mutual and rational decision to bring our relationship to a close, since I would only briefly be in California before returning to New Haven for my final year of seminary. But something happened as I drove him to the airport: he cried. I had never witnessed his poker face display emotion. I was moved, and fell in love with him for the first time. He *was* vulnerable, capable of an intimacy never before revealed. Then he was gone. Lost love frequently prompts me to write, so I wrote him a poem. I did not know it would rekindle our love, but I hoped that it would.

Now as I sat alone in Kirk House, I wrote a prayer to God in which I cried, "Gay activism is such a lonely business. Send someone with whom I may share this." Bill Silver arrived the next day, and we found ourselves thrown together, strategizing the new wave of activism of the Presbyterian Gay Caucus. David Sindt, the founder, had practiced a kind of passive activism at previous assemblies, reflective of both his gentle, nonaggressive personality, as well as his political acumen, which told him that a ministry of presence was initially appropriate. Bill and I were quite different. Not content to wait till commissioners (Presbyterian for "delegates") sought *us* out, we actively approached them, offering our views, experience, and suggestions. Neither of us had attended, let alone lobbied, a General Assembly before, but we learned quickly and worked well together, harmoniously effective and efficient. Mutual respect and admiration spiraled. God had sent me a significant friend, if not a significant other.

Late one evening, walking back to our lodging, we discussed our amazement at how well things seemed to be going with our lobbying efforts. Arriving at our destination, to our consternation we saw no light in Kirk House, which meant no one was home to let us in. One of us tried the door. It was locked. The other rang the doorbell, but in vain. "Everyone must still be at that party," Bill observed. We too had been invited to a gathering in someone's hotel room, but we had been too tired from the long day's activities to attend. "We should have gotten a key," Bill said, stating the obvious. "Look, there's an open window," I pointed out. "What? Are you crazy? On the second floor?" Bill continued, "How do you propose we get up there?" I defended my idea, saying "Maybe there's a ladder somewhere."

We stepped to the rear of Kirk House, and lo and behold, there was a ladder. "See? God provides," I laughed. But a large, vicious dog disagreed. Stirred from sleep by my comment, he growled, barked, and lunged for us, providentially restrained (somewhat) by a now-teetering wire fence that looked as if it might come down any minute. Momentarily my "dog-phobia" paralyzed me. Growing up, I had occasionally been bitten by the family dog, the memory of which yet gives me pause at the sight of any potentially threatening dog. "Let's get the ladder and get out of here!" Which we did.

Planting it firmly between ground and windowsill, I remembered yet another fear: acrophobia. Though willing to fight it to climb to the open window, I gratefully accepted Bill's offer to do so. As he climbed, I anxiously kept an eye out, fearful lest the Baltimore police come along and ask us what we were doing. I could already see the headlines: "Gay Activists Break into Presbyterian Church!" That would not help our cause. It might have been difficult explaining that we had a right to be there. Providentially, the operation was successful: Bill unlocked the front door, we returned the ladder apologetically to the infuriated dog, and then we laughed over the whole episode.

Years later, invited to preach at the church that had owned Kirk House, I reflected on the incident as a parable of our experience as gay and lesbian Christians seeking entrance to the church. Neither the absence of light nor the presence of locked doors and growling dogs in the broader "kirk" can keep us from providentially finding an open window, turning on the lights, and unlocking the church's door. After all, we *belong* there.

The "locked-door, open window" incident proved prophetic of the final outcome of the Baltimore Assembly. The members of the Assembly committee brainstormed a spectrum of postures toward the ordination of "avowed, practicing homosexuals," settling on words in the middle of the list: "injudicious" and "improper." Given the historical stance of the church on homosexuality, they concluded, it would be "injudicious, if not improper" to proceed with such ordination. (Later, I would draw a cartoon for the PGC newsletter depicting Jesus on the cross with the words "Injudicious, If Not Improper" tacked above his head.) Yet also, given the ignorance and strong feelings on the subject of homosexuality, the committee would recommend to the full Assembly the establishment of a task force to lead the church in studying the issue, because "God hath yet more light to break forth from his word." Here they quoted both a hymn and John Robinson's counsel to the Pilgrims seeking religious liberty. To many the quote became the most illuminating statement of the document.

There was a last ditch effort to scuttle the work of the committee through a substitute motion, believed to have been authored by one of our most vociferous opponents, the Reverend Jerry Kirk of Cincinnati. Though not himself an elected delegate, he was permitted to present an alternative on the floor of the full Assembly in which whatever study done would be biased toward changing homosexuals. His professed love for his "dear" homosexual brothers and sisters came across as empty and insincere to many. Anyone who smiles all the time cannot convince me either of sincerity or compassion. He glowed in the spotlight of assembly attention, but the superficial light in which he basked, from my perspective, vulgarly contrasted with the inner light emitted from those I experience as truly spiritually mature. The latter light is warm and welcoming; his I experienced as cold and distancing. Kirk House in its dark and locked emptiness had seemed more accessible and inviting than Jerry Kirk.

Presbyterians traditionally have faith in their committee process; this faith plus the shadow of doubt that Kirk's endorsement cast on the substitute motion led the Baltimore General Assembly to approve the committee's recommendations: ordination of homosexuals was deemed inappropriate, but a task force would shed more light on the issue. The door to ordination was locked for the time being, but the window of education was opened for more light.

In July 1976, before moving from Philadelphia, I took my car for servicing and, as usual, waited for it in a nearby cafe. During a prolonged breakfast, I wrote of my experience to that point as a gay minister. At this relatively early time in my ministry, I already found myself describing a feeling that a primal scream lay buried within me—a scream that expressed the cumulative pain and birth as described to me by hundreds of gay sisters and brothers. I felt like their vessel, a vessel of their feelings, their stories, their hopes and fears entrusted to my care; and I felt as if I would burst if I did not write out their feelings.

The cafe waitress was unusually gregarious and solicitous, equally generous with coffee and conversation. She picked up an ongoing conversation with a regular customer, evidently begun when he was last in, about methods to avoid crib death. She had a new grandson to worry about. Now they turned to discussing an article in the paper about women as priests: she said "Why not?" but he was opposed. She spoke her mind plainly, without fear, as one might in a friendship of trust, in which the parties agree to disagree. She had already learned my intended profession, so she shouted over to me, "Hey Rev, what do you think of women priests?" I said I agreed with her, that women should be priests.

She brought me more coffee as a reward and whispered about her other customer, "He don't like women, that's his problem. Two divorces and can't find anyone to marry him. Not surprising!" She said this matter-of-factly, not meanly. Even more compassionately she added, "Y'know, the other girls warned me he didn't tip when I started to work here, but I decided to be just real friendly with him, take some time to talk with him. I figured he was lonely. That's what's wrong with most people today—just plain lonely, just need somebody to talk to. Well, I've worked him up to a 50¢ tip! D'you know, he's a *shrink?* People pay to talk to *him,* and *he* comes in and talks to me for free! Ain't it funny?" The coffee fell a little over the brim of my full cup.

Noticing I was writing, and with my left hand, she exclaimed, "*I* was left-handed, too, growing up. But the nuns made me write with my right hand. I'm sure that's why I've been a nervous person ever since! When my kids were old enough to go to school, I went down and told those nuns that if any of them were left-handed, to leave 'em be. I wasn't gonna let the same thing happen to my kids as happened to me! Honestly, I think you got to be a genius to be left-handed in a right-handed world." With that she returned to her post behind the counter.

I was stunned. I believed she was speaking about much more than which hand I wrote with. I looked down at what I had written about others who had been forced "to write with their right hand" in a sense, the anxiety and suffering church and society's coercion had caused countless gay people. I believed the waitress intuited far more about me than I had disclosed. I felt deeply moved by her unqualified affirmation. I smiled in gratitude toward this minister who dispensed wisdom and insight as readily as coffee and sweet rolls. Her counter was at once pulpit and communion table, an integration of word and sacrament. The church needed ministers like her. The commonwealth of God had come near.

In August 1976 a brief visit home to Los Angeles before my final year at Yale contained exciting possibilities. The first was the possible continuation of my relationship with John, as my poem had deeply moved him, and his departure for Los Angeles had made us both realize the importance of one another to our lives. Regardless of the distance separating us when I returned to New Haven, the phone, letters, and visits would keep us emotionally bonded.

The second was my appointment to the Presbyterian Task Force to Study Homosexuality, mandated by the Baltimore Assembly. My experience as a gay man and as a minister within the lesbian/gay community uniquely qualified me to serve, so I was told, yet I wondered what being the only gay person on the nineteen-member committee would entail. The responsibility felt enormous, but I felt buoyed by the affirmation.

Third and finally, I received a phone call from Rev. Ross Greek, pastor of the West Hollywood Presbyterian Church, which eventually would mean a call to ministry. On previous occasions I had unsuccessfully tried to contact him when I was in town, because I'd heard he was doing ministry within the gay community. Now, because of my appointment to the task force, he had heard of my work and wanted to speak with me. I had but one day left in Los Angeles, so I suggested we meet the next morning.

Finding the small stucco buildings that housed the church on Sunset Boulevard, I walked into its office and met the lumbering polar bear of a man named Ross Greek. He introduced me to a parttime staff member who led a ministry with the gay community. Together they proceeded to ask me questions that could be summed up in this way: "How do you 'church' gays? How do you make them feel that this is their church, too, sharing equally in the ministry?" I confessed my ministries had not directly addressed these questions: the one at Yale had been directed toward those already in the church; the one at Penn was more a ministry of presence, counseling, and community organizing. I said, however, that when I moved back to the Los Angeles area, I would be happy to work on a volunteer basis to help them bring gay people into the church. Little did I know that this offer would become a fulltime, salaried position that I would hold for nearly ten years after graduation the following spring. The Lazarus Project, a ministry calling gay and nongay people alike out of tomblike closets of fear and separation, as Jesus had called Lazarus to full, abundant life and community, would become the first ministry supported by a major denomination intended to reconcile gay and nongay Christians. It would serve as a window for many across the nation when the church shut the door on ordination. It certainly was *my* open window into the church.

As we continued our conversation, and Ross proclaimed the many issues that the church needed to address in society, he punctuated each part of his litany with a favorite phrase, "This is reality," while poking his index finger in the air for sermonic emphasis. I felt cheered meeting a minister who made *me* feel conservative and old hat. And he was in his sixties! His very presence in the church served as a sacrament of hope for me and, as I would find, for many others who felt left out. He gave me his characteristic bear hug, and off I went the next morning to my final year of seminary.

Chapter 12

THE TASK FORCE TO STUDY HOMOSEXUALITY

OCTOBER 1976–FEBRUARY 1978

Excited yet apprehensive, I flew to Chicago for the first meeting of the Task Force to Study Homosexuality. Checking into my room at the O'Hare Hilton, I discovered I'd been given a single room, for which I was at once grateful and suspicious. Task force members had been informed we would have roommates to cut expenses, standard operating procedure for church committees. Clearly, I thought, they were afraid to put the homosexual member of the task force in the same room with anybody! But when the task force gathered for the first time, we learned we'd *all* been placed in single rooms. Gail Buchwalter, a spunky pastor from Pittsburgh, echoed the feelings of many of us when she said, "When I saw I got a single room, I wondered, 'What's wrong with *me?*'" Kathy Young, our staff assistant, explained, "We thought it would be unfair to assign you roommates before you knew each other."

Our first meeting began with informal socializing, not unlike a church coffee hour, before formally convening and identifying ourselves. As we did so, it became clear the unique niche that each of us was intended to fill in this broadly representative task force. Our expertise included biblical studies, church history, Christian ethics, and applied theology. The secular fields of sociology, psychology, and medicine were also represented. And experience counted, too, from the minister's spouse whose church shared its building with a gay congregation to the black man and black woman who knew about prejudice firsthand. As I listened to the self-introductions, it seemed to me that more task force members were opposed to homosexuality than in support, with the majority undecided. Ironically, one of the opponents, Richard Lovelace of Gordon Conwell Seminary, confessed he had been "led to the Lord" by a homosexual Christian at Yale.

Virginia West Davidson, an elder from Rochester, New York, served as chairperson of the task force. Confluent personal and church histories destined her for this role. A close minister friend who was homosexual had sensitized her to the subject, so that, as a candidate for moderator of the Baltimore General Assembly, she said she would vote to ordain a homosexual candidate for ordination if the candidate were qualified in every other respect. She knew this viewpoint could cost her the election, which it did. She was, however, later appointed to chair the task force. Her dignity, wisdom, compassion, and fairness made her eminently qualified for the task.

The task force had been mandated to *lead* the church in a study of homosexuality, particularly as it related to ordination. We were also to deliver a study paper with recommendations to the 1978 General Assembly in San Diego. We began by framing our discussion with a series of questions we believed we needed to address. What is homosexuality? What new light do the social and medical sciences shed on the subject? What is the historical occasion for this study? What does scripture say to illumine the issue and our handling of it? What are the historical, theological, and ethical perspectives regarding not only homosexuality, but ordination as well? What is ordination within our Reformed tradition? What should the church's ministry with homosexual persons be?

The Presbyterian Panel is the arm of the church responsible for conducting opinion polls of the membership. At our request, the panel developed a survey to ascertain the typical church member's view of homosexuality and the ordination of homosexual persons. I objected to the phrasing of some of the questions, claiming the connotations of some words would skew the results overwhelmingly on the negative side. For example, the survey asked the respondent's view of the ordination of "avowed, practicing homosexuals." I pointed out that respondents would probably answer negatively to a question regarding the ordination of "avowed, practicing *hetero*sexuals," because the word *avowed* suggested flagrant flaunting of one's sexuality, and *practicing* sounded like promiscuity. *Avowed* further implied an aggressive political choice (like being an "avowed Communist" or an "avowed atheist"), whereas most homosexual persons might better be described as "self-acknowledged." I suggested the panel find alternate wording or at least explain that the phrase could also refer to a homosexual in a monogamous relationship or seeking same.

The panel refused to make any changes or explanations. To no one's surprise, then, the panel's results were overwhelmingly negative. It would have been a complete waste of money had it not been for one significant revelation from the poll: most who responded felt *they themselves* would be more accepting of an "avowed, practicing homosexual" pastor than the congregations to which they belonged.

Both to diffuse the controversy surrounding our study and to gain the insights of church members on our subject matter, we held four regional hearings, which proved more revealing than the survey had been. Yet many of us on the task force found the hearings frustrating: we had already learned so much that we found ourselves astounded and exasperated by the ignorance of the majority of those who testified. We felt insulted more than once as those who spoke decried the forty thousand dollars spent on the study (as if lesbians and gays themselves didn't give many times that amount to the church in a single year!). Many attacked us for *being* on the task force, questioning our own morals, character, and judgment. One woman declared the task force itself was an "abomination before the Lord"! Our faith and our intelligence were offended as person after person used their time (and ours) to read from a dusty Bible its handful of verses presumed to be about homosexuality—as if we hadn't heard them before, as if we couldn't recite them verbatim! As I watched yet one more leather-bound, gilt-edged Bible flap open, I often wished the testifier would read us other, more uplifting portions of scripture.

Our frustration surfaced most clearly during the question-and-answer period following individual testimony. We found ourselves making long, prefatory comments so that the testifier could understand the question. Or we presented them with new information and either asked them to respond to it or asked if the new knowledge would change their opinion. We confused and puzzled many witnesses, people who had never before questioned their view of homosexuality. Our long questions were brought to our attention by one task force member who had started timing them and found some ran as long as several minutes. Eventually we refrained from asking many questions, realizing that the hearings were not the best opportunity for educating others.

Despite the plethora of uninformed, poorly-informed, and misinformed persons testifying before the task force, there were moments of revelation. In St. Louis, for example, after one pastor testified proudly that he had broken up a lesbian relationship of many years' duration, another testified that homosexuals shouldn't be accepted because "they can't maintain long-term relationships." And in San Francisco, even those opposed to ordination of homosexuals got angry with the fourteen consecutive testifiers from a single congregation, all of whom presented the same point of view and quoted identical scriptural passages. At the same hearing a Japanese pastor spoke empathetically as a member of a once "undesirable" segment of American society, humbly asking for compassionate inclusion of homosexual Christians. In Philadelphia, where our task force scheduled a hearing in conjunction with the 1977 General Assembly so we might hear a broader representation of Presbyterians, a minister pointed out that the American ideal of the nuclear family was not biblical: "In the Old Testament, polygamy was the rule," he said, "And in the New Testament, Jesus proclaimed the family of faith superseded the claims of the biological family." Each hearing had its redeeming moments, but perhaps most significant of all was in Cleveland, our first hearing.

In the middle of the second day of the hearing, a pale, frightened woman testified, clutching her purse, glancing guardedly to the left, then to the right. As she spoke she fixed her eyes on a point somewhere above and behind our heads, causing several task force members to turn their heads to see what she was looking at. Apparently she was trying to focus on heavenly things rather than on the earthly bodies of the task force before her. The woman informed us she'd come to speak at the instruction of certain "voices." She wanted us to know she vehemently opposed the ordination of homosexuals and oh, by the way, weren't we familiar with the biblical admonitions against it? She then proceeded to recite all of them. We had only heard them twenty-two times that day from others.

As she chanted her homophobic litany, I daydreamed about a production of George Bernard Shaw's classic play, *Saint Joan,* which I'd seen earlier in the week. I thought of the voices Saint Joan heard that led to much applauded military victories. Subsequently, her voices displeased the church and the state. Because her voices disagreed with established customs and mores, she was tried for heresy, convicted, and burned at the stake.

As the woman testifying moved from the eighteenth to the twentieth chapter of Leviticus, I reflected on the fact that it was many years later before the church realized and admitted its mistake in executing Joan of Arc. The church finally decided her guidance came from God, and, feeling communal guilt, penitently canonized her. In death, she became Saint Joan, eternally sentenced to pray for the church that took away her life. In Shaw's play, she takes this as a sign she might return to earth, but the church suggests she stay in the heavenly realms, as it would be difficult to live with a saint.

The fearful woman before us proceeded from Old to New Testament, specifically to the apostle Paul—ironic, since his writings oppose women teaching men. My reverie continued. In Joan of Arc's time, heresy trials were a common way of determining what was and was not acceptable within the church. It occurred to me that heresy trials, uncommon in today's church, had been replaced by trials for ordination! We discover what is and what is not acceptable in belief and behavior in the church by observing whom the church ordains, rather than whom the church excommunicates. And so it was not until an openly gay candidate for ordination to the professional clergy came forward that the Presbyterian Church seriously began to grapple with homosexual Christians already in its midst.

The witness continued, listing all those sinners Paul believed would not enter the kingdom of heaven, oblivious to the red light that had clicked on some minutes before, signaling the end of her allotted time. Ginny Davidson kindly and gently informed the woman who heard voices that her time to testify had expired. The task force members asked a few polite questions, feeling sorry for her. I asked questions, but I can't remember if I bothered to state them aloud or left them in my mind. Thinking of Saint Joan's voices, my own sense of God's call, and this woman's voices, the seemingly unanswerable questions came to me: How do you determine which voices come from God? How do you test the Spirit? How do you recognize the Spirit of God in someone?

The woman returned to her seat in the audience, still cautiously looking left and right, stepping carefully as if to avoid the lines between the tiles, as children sometimes do in play. Apparently she was paralyzed by fear. One could not help but feel for her. So many people still believe salvation depends on not stepping on the lines! "For by grace you have been saved through faith, and this is not your own doing, it is the gift of God—not because of works, lest any one should boast," Paul had also written.

My questions regarding the Spirit remained unanswered until that evening, when we heard from two gay men. They described their experience as gay Christians, as lovers, and as part of a Presbyterian congregation, as well as of an ecumenical gay Christian support group. The task force experienced firsthand their love, joy, peace, patience, kindness, goodness, faithfulness, gentleness, and self-control: what Paul called fruits of the Spirit. An embarrassed, pitying silence had followed the fearful woman's testimony. But a respectful silence followed the testimony of these gay men. I searched the faces of the task force and the audience, discovering appreciative smiles, awe-filled stares, and a few befuddled and perplexed countenances. Bobbi White, sitting to my right, whispered reverently, "They're so gentle." After a day of hearing testimony in opposition to lesbians and gays, words filled with enmity, strife, jealousy, anger, selfishness, dissension, party spirit, and the like (what Paul called in Galatians "works of the flesh"), it was refreshing to hear of the fruit of the Spirit in the lives of these two men. Perfect, mature love, I thought to myself, *does* cast out all fear.

An altogether different spirit haunted the Consultation on Homosexuality sponsored by Presbyterians United for Biblical Concerns and held in a stronghold of conservative Presbyterianism, Pittsburgh. I was one of five task force members selected to hear this side of our church. The unspoken and unpublicized premise of the gathering was that homosexuality was sin.

The week before the meeting, during an intimate vesper Eucharist in the Yale Divinity School prayer chapel, I found myself becoming angrier and angrier that no positive presentation on homosexuality was to be offered at the consultation, though it passed itself off as an open, educational event. I didn't know why my indignation hadn't been kindled earlier; perhaps the Spirit moved as we shared communion, perhaps Christ's passion became my own in taking his body and blood. I felt distress that my anger should come in this liturgical moment of reconciliation. But, when it was over, I walked straight home and phoned the consultation's organizers, demanding to be included in its program. I couldn't believe my own assertiveness! When I was told the program was set and could not be changed, I replied, "You can change it if you want to, and I'd hate to have to disrupt it myself." Caught off guard, the organizers told me a change in the program would have to be approved by the planning committee.

That weekend I'd been invited to make a presentation at a "Homosexuality Information Day" designed by Seattle Presbytery. This well-planned event became the model the task force distributed throughout the church for other educational forums. It had evolved from what conservatives initially intended as a debate between me and a local gay man who had rejected his homosexuality and had adopted a celibate lifestyle. But, by the time it was held, a planning committee had developed it into a sophisticated, experiential learning event. Creative exercises at the beginning broke down tension while aiding participants to see the wide spectrum of opinion among Christians on issues related to homosexuality, from biblical interpretation to ordination. Presentations from those with expertise in biblical studies, theology, and sexual ethics further informed those in attendance. My presentation focused on personal faith experience. What remained of the debate idea was a panel discussion following my speech, in which the local gay celibate and I did not disagree but affirmed one another for making a choice spiritually appropriate for the other, much to the chagrin of those who had hoped to witness a real battle.

I brought my speech with me the following week to the consultation in Pittsburgh, arriving in the midst of a blizzard, an appropriately chilly greeting. The representatives from the Task Force to Study Homosexuality gathered at one of a hundred round tables set up in a ballroom of the William Penn Hotel. I noticed a couple of photographers taking pictures of us and realized we were probably considered significant participants. That anyone would want photographs of us reminded me forcefully of the historic nature of our work. With so many eyes upon us, I had all the more reason, during even the worst presentations, to listen impassively and not reveal my feelings. Yet most of the task force members could not maintain a straight face when a "Christian psychologist" described with disproportionate horror a little girl he had counseled who exhibited minor "tomboy characteristics."

Pathos followed comedy. Guy Charles, who ran an evangelical Christian counseling center for homosexuals in Virginia, spoke of his "sick" and "perverted" life as a "gay activist" of many years in New York City, a life filled with alcohol, drugs, and orgies. I whispered to another task force member, "If *I* lived like that, I'd want to convert, too!" He told of "sacrificing" his homosexual lover when he became a Christian and began this center for other "unfortunates." In an exchange between him and me during the question-and-answer period, he pleaded personally with me to be willing to "sacrifice for Christ." I became annoyed, since I believed I *had* sacrificed for Christ by coming out of the closet and helping the church to understand the issue. "I, too," I told him, "gave up a lover to follow my call to ministry, a lover who could not afford to be identified as gay in the church." Not long after this consultation, Guy Charles was discredited when male counselees alleged he had sex with them! The Christian publications and organizations that proudly heralded his story and ministry did not bother to report its conclusion.

Pathos followed pathos. Jerry Kirk, who had made himself prominent at the Baltimore Assembly, described his "healing" ministry with homosexuals. He spoke of "counseling" gay clients, encouraging them to tell him *everything* about their sexual experiences. I felt embarrassed for him in this naive display of apparent voyeurism. With all my counseling experience, I've seldom needed to ask for details of a counselee's sexual encounters.

Eventually I was permitted to speak, after an ambivalent introduction from a conservative task force member, who basically told the audience I was a nice guy but misguided. I delivered the speech I had prepared for Seattle, "A Newly Revealed Christian Experience." I described the importance of the Spirit in the early development of Christianity. In the early church, Gentiles had been required to convert first to Judaism before becoming Christian. In the tenth and eleventh chapters of Acts, however, the church encountered Gentiles who had received the baptism of the Holy Spirit without benefit of first subscribing to the law of Moses, which included circumcision. The church realized it could not withhold the waters of baptism from un-Judaized Gentiles if God had baptized them with the gifts of the Spirit. So Gentiles were welcomed into the church through the waters of baptism without first becoming Jews.

I explained that I believed the present church experiences an analogous situation in reference to homosexual Christians. Though we might have thought it necessary for them to become heterosexual to become Christian, God's Spirit is leading us to a new inclusiveness that does not require conformity of sexual orientation. The gifts of the Spirit in the lives and ministries of lesbian and gay Christians evidence God's welcome and blessing, calling the church to welcome them through baptism and bless their gifts through ordination.

I had begun to realize the church's problem in accepting gay people was not so much a sexual problem as a spiritual one. The church's lack of inclusiveness revealed our inability to be inclusive in our prayer life—we still tend to pray for people like us and people we like. We forget, as the early church is reminded by Peter in Acts, that "God shows no partiality." The church grew enormously and its mission expanded worldwide when it became inclusive of Gentiles. I believe the Spirit multiplies the church's ministry when we follow her lead to be inclusive rather than exclusive. Like the child's loaves and fishes, the more Christ nourishes, the more his resources expand. And the church is the Body of Christ.

As the task force listened to the church, I realized how little the church was listening for the Spirit in gay and lesbian Christians, and I grieved for the spiritual health and vitality of the church. Yet the church is not only its present incarnation; we are, indeed, "surrounded by so great a cloud of witnesses," as the words of Hebrews and the sacrament of Communion remind us. We are forever linked to "people of faith from all times and places." One person uniquely linked us to the church in history.

Back in New Haven, several friends kept suggesting I meet a new professor in Yale's history department, one engaged in fascinating research on gays in church history. Finally, one of these friends invited us both to dinner, and I found myself enthralled by Dr. John Boswell and his work. During the next task force meeting, I urged the rest to hear from him, and, though our next meeting's agenda had been planned, the task force made the time to do so based sheerly on my enthusiasm.

No one awed the task force like John Boswell. We had heard from experts in their fields whose familiar and famous names suggested power and authority. But Boswell was relatively unknown at the time; his handwritten manuscript of *Christianity, Social Tolerance and Homosexuality* was not quite finished and had yet to find a publisher. He looked young, his manner was unpretentious, and he seemed sincerely interested in our work. We quickly recognized his genius: a command of languages, history, biblical interpretation, the church, and theology—all the more palatable alongside his wit, humor, and charm. We found it easy to talk with him, since he was as eager to listen as to offer insights. Yet we were often dumbfounded because his fresh perspectives of ecclesiastical and civil histories and their relationship freed us to re-view our understanding of the church's attitudes toward homosexuality.

We were surprised to learn that homosexuality had been more or less tolerated by Christian society during several periods of history from the early to the medieval church, whereas usury (lending money at interest) had been at all times and everywhere condemned and was punished by excommunication if not worse. We did not know that the early church Fathers never saw in I Corinthians a reference to homosexuality, which calls into question some of the current translations of chapter 5, verse 6. We were unaware that when church authorities legislated against homosexual practice, they were pressured by civil governments to do so. And, of course, we had not heard of gay contributions to Christendom, from saints of great spiritual stature to military heroes of the bloody Crusades.

Bill Silver, whose quest for ordination had prompted our study, had offered a valuable commentary on the string of experts the task force consulted: "Don't let them forget to consult the best experts on the subject—gays and lesbians themselves." John Boswell confirmed this. In an introductory quote in his book he suggests that after every biblical, theological, ecclesiastical, historical, psychological, and biological question has been answered, antigay feelings will still be present in church and society. "One can't use reason to argue someone out of a position not arrived at by reason," Boswell often reminds his audiences. Phobias, irrational fears, are not overcome by reason so much as by experience. I believe the church and society's phobia regarding homosexuality and homosexual persons will be overcome by experiencing us.

A white-haired, New England Yankee lady, commenting to me about two men hugging, gave a simple explanation for her discomfort: "It's just that we're not used to it yet." Opponents have frequently criticized my appeals to experience as I argue for the full acceptance of lesbians and gays in the church, but faith (and the faith needed for acceptance) grows out of experience (communal and individual) more than books, even one so filled with faithful experience as the Bible. God as the author of faith seldom *reasons* someone into faith; personal conversion experiences (note the plural) are necessary. The Bible reveals this conversion process, in the Old Testament for the Jews, in the New Testament for the Christians. The faithful acceptance of gay people requires a similar process.

Just as John's first epistle speaks of perfect (or mature) love, a mature faith "casts out all fear." A mature faith is less afraid to be receptive to lesbian women and gay men; both *their* experience and the experience *of* them is welcomed even at the risk of being converted toward acceptance. Insecure, an immature faith either openly rejects gay experience and avoids opportunities to experience lesbians and gays, or pretends to listen and interact while maintaining a heart as hard as Pharaoh's. By virtue of its ability to integrate broader experience, a mature faith enjoys greater integrity than is possible for a faith that self-righteously blinds itself to another's experience of God.

From the start the task force lived with tension. Handling of controversy becomes as controversial as controversy itself. Our task force was born of controversy, our existence and work were controversial, and our recommendations, whatever they would be, would cause yet more controversy. And the controversy we were called to cope with, most of us knew, would not soon leave the church, while those who could not cope *would* leave the church. Those of weaker faith, as the apostle Paul described them, would be hurt by the controversy, whether they found the acceptance of homosexuality unthinkable, or the rejection of homosexual persons unthinkable, or the *experience* of controversy within the church unthinkable. Lest those who remained in the church feel smugly superior, it might be added that many of us did so by engaging in some denial that everything we believed was at stake in this controversy. How we read the Bible, how we integrated current experience into our faith, particularly scientific experience, how we viewed the church, how we envisioned the future, how we experienced Jesus Christ and (more broadly) God's interaction with the cosmos—these were just some of the issues at stake.

At heart, we of the task force found ourselves faced with two mysteries: the nature of sexuality, of homosexuality in particular, and the nature of God's grace. Scripture, the church, science, experience, theology, and faith would all inform us, guide us, and correct us, yet all were mere signposts pointing to the ultimate mystery of our creation and redemption. Were there laws of creation, either natural or revealed, that legislated against homosexuality even among the statistical minority which acknowledged this orientation? (Clearly a universal experience of exclusive homosexuality would discontinue the species; God's charge to "be fruitful and multiply" must, however, be understood as a communal rather than an individual responsibility, lest those who are infertile or celibate or use contraceptive devices be viewed as disobedient.) If there were such laws, how were these to be understood in the light of our experience of God's gracious act of redemption in Jesus Christ? Were they not, as other laws, now mediated, transmuted, or set aside by this ultimate revelation of God's unearned, unmerited love? At the foundation of our questions was a debate that Jesus carried on with the Pharisees and that the Reformers carried on with the Roman church; the relationship of the Law and the Gospel of grace.

After nearly a year of working together, rumor came to me that a task force member had said he believed I had enough of the grace of God in me to enter the kingdom of heaven, but that I had this one blind spot in the area of my sexuality. Via rumor I returned a message that *I* believed *he* had enough of the grace of God in him to enter the kingdom of heaven, but that he had this one little blind spot in the area of *my* sexuality! Though an amusing exchange, the church should cringe in horror that this too-frequent misunderstanding—that God's grace can somehow be meted out or measured—has crept into our affirmation of God's grace. It is the Law trying to gain control again of our consciences as it wrests regulatory management of God's free grace. Jesus' parable of the laborers of the vineyard, in which those hired late in the day receive the same wage as those hired earlier, demonstrates that salvation may not be quantified or qualified anymore than it may be earned. The parable was not intended as an economic example, but as an illustration of how salvation works: like the hirelings' equal wages, one person can't be more "saved" than another, nor can one receive only a little salvation. Those whom we experience as filled with God's grace and therefore more gracious are simply those who recognize more clearly the extent of God's grace in their lives. There is no way they may be more likely to enter the kingdom of heaven than another, though they already reap more of that commonwealth's benefits than others.

The tension between law and the gospel of grace occasionally erupted in anger. During one significant discussion, Don

Williams (of Fuller Theological Seminary) and George Edwards (of Louisville Presbyterian Theological Seminary) were going for the jugular—of the issue or of each other, we couldn't be sure which. Exegeting Paul's letter to the Romans, Edwards commented, "Paul says here that 'God gave them up to dishonorable passions'. Is this, then, Paul's theology? Of course not! God never gave anybody up! What kind of theology would that be? Paul is here using a rhetorical device to get his legalistic reader all worked up in self-righteous frenzy before he hits him over the head with his own inadequacy and dependency on God's grace." Then Edwards, sensing the crux of the difference between those on the task force who would ultimately favor acceptance of gays and those who would oppose it, attacked with righteous anger: "I know your God, Don Williams. Your God will not be satiated, his anger will not be alleviated, until he has drunk every drop of blood falling from poor, puny Jesus on the cross! Your God is a vengeful God, full of wrath! But I tell you, God is a God of mercy and compassion; he *is* the one on that cross sacrificed to bloodthirsty concepts of God like yours!" I believed this was no longer Edwards speaking, but the Holy Spirit. An amazed and troubled silence followed in the room, just as other miraculous interventions of the Spirit reported in scripture brought amazement and fear. The gospel of grace had been proclaimed. But it did have its cutting edge. The sword Jesus brought cut both ways, with one edge defending the oppressed and the other defeating the self-righteous.

Despite sharp differences of opinion, the angry arguments, the perceived obstinacy of a few, and the diversity of our belief and experience, the Task Force to Study Homosexuality became a vehicle of God's grace for me during our nearly two years of meetings, serving as a kind of mini-congregation that contributed to the development of my faith and my understanding of what it means to belong to a community of believers. We worshiped together, began and ended every session with prayer, learned and debated, expressed feelings as well as ideas, believed and doubted, suffered and celebrated together. We wished the church as a whole could have had our experience, could have been brought along the same way, so that it could approach the subjects we did with less fear and greater hope. All of this is not to say the task force was an experience of heaven; it was also hell, like any human institution (no matter how divinely inspired), unperfected in faith. But, just as one can't choose relatives, yet all belong to a biological family, we recognized that, though we might not have chosen one another, God had chosen us to be one family of faith.

Chapter 13

THE TASK FORCE
RECOMMENDATIONS
AND THE
CONSERVATIVE BACKLASH

SUMMER, 1977–SPRING, 1978

The Lazarus Project had been approved by Pacific Presbytery in May. Though national funds would not be available until January, if then, the West Hollywood Presbyterian Church was eager to have me begin as project director in August. Since I was seeking ordination in neighboring San Fernando Presbytery, I needed that governing body's permission to "labor outside its bounds." My ordination committee seemed pleased for me to take the position, recommending in my favor. But San Fernando Presbytery, hostile to homosexuality and the intended outreach of the Lazarus Project, caught me by surprise by defeating the recommendation after a heated debate during an untypically well-attended summer meeting. A church leader remarked to me afterward that the Presbytery was so hostile to me, "They wouldn't let you clerk in a grocery store!" I was devastated. I had come to realize this presbytery would not ordain me, but I never anticipated they'd deny me an opportunity to work for the church in a nonordained position. I phoned John from the meeting, barely able to speak, embarrassed by my church family's treatment, crying that these who did not know me personally could be so angry with me. Stunned and hurting with me, John comforted me as best he could.

In this experience, I observed a phenomenon that would repeat itself over and over in my relationship with the church: the committee had recommended in favor of me, but the larger body to which it reported rejected its recommendation. The committee had the opportunity to know me as a person, but the larger group knew me principally as an issue. Beyond people's openness to change in small groups and the contrasting mob mentality in large ones, I believe personalizing the issue becomes the central factor in transforming opinions on homosexuality. Every advance in the gay movement has been preceded by someone's willingness to incarnate the issue; every retreat means the necessary ratio of those willing to personalize the issue to those whose opinions need changing has not been achieved.

I could not take the job as Lazarus Project director till another solution was found. My ordination committee called for a special meeting of the Presbytery to consider the transfer of my candidacy for ordination from San Fernando to Pacific. Again, attendance was better than most specially-called meetings. This time my lover, John, was present for moral support. Fears had been expressed that the Presbytery might defeat my transfer out of sheer vindictiveness. After an hour's debate in which hostile questions surfaced, such as whether I were repentant enough to be transferred, the vote was taken. Because of voting irregularities at the earlier meeting, a written ballot was requested. The stated clerk, appointing neutral people to count ballots, pointed at John (not knowing his relationship to me) as a potential volunteer. "And you—who are you?" the clerk asked. John, caught off guard, stuttered, "I'm not a member of this church!" "Then you ought to be fair," came the clerk's mischievous rejoinder, breaking the gathering's tension with laughter. Later, John told me, in tabulating the ballots, he seemed to open all the negative ones! Nonetheless, thanks be to God, I "won" the vote, in time to take the position as Lazarus director. I had been granted permission to transfer my ordination process out of San Fernando Presbytery; whether Pacific Presbytery would receive me would be another matter.

The special presbytery meeting in August took place on Monday; on Tuesday I flew to Chicago for the decisive meeting of the Task Force to Study Homosexuality. I felt abused. Beleaguered and weary, I now faced a four-day meeting that Chair Ginny Davidson had described as our watershed. Tensely I would listen to each member of the task force reveal his or her position on the ordination of what we now referred to as "self-affirming, practicing homosexual persons." To me it felt like listening to jurors one by one rendering verdicts that meant prison or freedom. My heart was anxious.

When the burden has felt too heavy, God has often sent an angel of mercy to lift my spirits. As I boarded the flight to Chicago, an airline steward and I exchanged glances of recognition, smiling. It is a wondrous gift of God that we gay people are often able to recognize our own, even without stereotypes of behavior or look. It's like belonging to a secret club whose members are able to cheer one another with a simple exchange of looks and smiles. It's a shame I'd not been aware of this secret society growing up; I would have felt less alone. Facing the judgment of friends on the task force, I felt reassured of God's grace through this stranger's smile. He gave me complimentary drinks and talked with me. Upon arrival in Chicago, we had dinner together before he drove me to the Chicago Center for Continuing Education, site of the task force meeting scheduled to begin the next morning. The hospitality of this stranger eased whatever inhospitality I expected or experienced from the church. His interest in my efforts reminded me of the broader hope that gave perspective to whatever pain its actualization brought: the hope of the church's hospitality toward gay people like him.

The next day, we on the task force put ourselves through the identical regimen of the regional hearings. By this time I felt close to the other members of the task force, and even those I had anticipated voting negatively did not do so without affecting me. What hurt more were the votes against ordination by people who I had thought would support it, like the good-natured former missionary and the compassionate medical ethicist. It also hurt to find that one or two people whose unqualified support I had expected nevertheless voted for ordination "with reservations."

Not surprisingly, during my testimony, I devoted my time to the recent events regarding my call to ministry as director of the Lazarus Project and my candidacy for ordination. "As of the day before yesterday," I read in my prepared statement, "I am no longer a candidate for ordination under the care of the Presbytery of San Fernando." After describing the process, I illustrated my feelings by calling to memory lesbian women and gay men who had already stood before us, telling of their experience. I said, "I think you can guess my feelings at this point. Many of you feel them with me. I do not need to demonstrate them before you; you have seen my anger in a Joan Abrams, you have seen my tears and anxiety in an Ellen Sue Findley, you have seen my bitterness in a Bill Silver. But you have also seen my patience in a David Sindt. I am one with all these, and we are one with all 300,000 gay Presbyterians. To reject any of us because of our sexual orientation is to reject all of us."

Rather dramatically, perhaps, I concluded my testimony with: "Like a cloud the Presbytery of San Fernando has come between me and the dream of ordination, between me and the unfading light of God's grace in Jesus Christ, between me and the inbreaking kingdom. It is basically a cloud of ignorance bringing further darkness rather than light. We need yet more light. Remembering as Christians we are to be 'the salt of the earth,' this task force must salt the clouds of ignorance. There will be a brief storm, and rain will fall on the just and the unjust. But then the sun will shine again." Then I added, "Thank you for these past ten minutes and these past ten months," referring to the months lapsed since our first meeting.

My testimony had an effect. Though not changing anyone's vote, everyone was more aware of how his or her decision had personal ramifications for the many like me who now served or hoped someday to serve in ordained office. As one said, my very presence had "kept them honest," that is, mindful of the personal dimensions of the issue.

My testimony had a particular effect on one task force member. Willard Heckel, whose career of volunteer service to the church had led him to its highest elected office, moderator of the General Assembly, began his remarks by saying, "I'm going to do something no lawyer in his right mind would do, that is, say something I had not carefully planned to say. But Chris's testimony has moved me so deeply that I've got to say this." Then Willard eloquently came out to the rest of the task force as a gay man. This elder church leader, who had repeatedly served the church out of devotion to it and from a deep reservoir of faith, now spoke as one whose gifts might be denied. An emotionally-charged silence followed Willard's statement, and Chairperson Davidson, correctly sensing the mood of the others, asked for a brief recess during which individuals gave Willard hugs. I noted a few of our opponents on the task force sat frozen in place, surely appreciating the risk Willard had taken, yet unable to provide a gesture of assurance.

Early in our deliberations I had judged that Bob Simpson would serve as a litmus test of how education and exposure would affect someone open to it. Conservative in background (he had taken his undergraduate degree at Wheaton), his career as a pastor had sensitized him and opened his thinking to other than conservative positions. Now, as he testified, he informed us that when he began work on the task force, he opposed homosexuality and the ordination of homosexuals. But the ensuing months had taught him much, he said, not only about homosexuality but also about the kind of people gays and lesbians were. Now he was led to the conclusion that no, homosexuality was not a sin, though he added that his was a "soft 'no.'" He did not feel as confident as others, but he would stand with those who claimed homosexuality was not per se a bar to ordination.

Finally our testimonies were completed. Fourteen did not view homosexuality either as sin or as preventing ordination; five did. I had believed the task force would come to this conclusion, but I was considerably moved and uplifted to know it had done so with such a large majority. Lesbian women and gay men in the church would feel affirmed.

Now a new task began: listing areas of agreement between those holding the majority and minority positions, such as decriminalization of state sodomy laws, civil rights for gays and lesbians, welcoming lesbians and gays as church members and developing ministries for and with them, working against stereotyping in the media, counseling anyone affected by the church's decision, and identifying homophobia as a· sin of which the church needed to repent. Additionally we would take time to review and modify our background study paper, for which Rev. Byron Shafer, a professor at Fordham University, had been selected as principal writer, and in which we provided the distillation of our own education on the·subject. Finally, we would turn to our different positions on homosexuality, each group writing a proposed General Assembly policy statement on homosexuality and the church. The majority report would affirm that homosexuality was not a sin and no bar to ordination; the minority report would affirm that homosexuality was a sin and a bar to ordination.

The next and final meeting of the task force prior to the San Diego Assembly would be held in early January at the beginning of the Christian season of Epiphany. Epiphany is the celebration of the fulfillment of Isaiah's prophecy, "Arise, shine, for your light has come." For Christians, God's light has come into the world, God's glory has been revealed, in Jesus Christ. It felt fitting to me that our study document and conclusions would be released to the church and the public during this season of light, for we believed it would shed more light on whether God's glory manifested itself in the faithful experience of lesbian and gay Christians.

In January, a representative group from the task force was selected officially to present the results of our work to the church's Advisory Council on Church and Society. We met at Krisheim Retreat Center outside Philadelphia. This council was to receive our report, ask whatever questions were necessary, make what changes it felt were needed, and transmit it to the commissioners each presbytery would elect to serve as the 188th General Assembly, scheduled to meet in San Diego the following May. Representatives of church constituency groups, from official agencies to self-organized groups, had been invited to attend.

Members of the Task Force to Study Homosexuality who were present found ourselves duly humbled and our work placed in proper perspective as we introduced ourselves as members of "the task force," only to have Advisory Council members query, "Which one?" Suddenly we were aware we'd fallen into the same narrow focus on our work that much of the denomination had experienced. The Task Force on the Small Family Farm also reported to the Advisory Council that meeting. But our work had grabbed the headlines and the attention largely due to homophobia which enraged its victims at the thought someone might value homosexual persons enough to consider welcoming them as church members, let alone ordaining them to church leadership. Had those who suffered such homophobia been reared to hate and fear small family farmers, the Small Family Farm Task Force would have received similar attention.

The Advisory Council on Church and Society accepted our report, asking few questions and making but a handful of stylistic changes. The background paper was received as a study document for the church, and the council endorsed the recommendations of the majority report. The majority believed "self affirming, practicing homosexuals" *should* be ordained if qualified, yet refrained from asking the church at large to confirm our view. Rather, we simply asked the church to affirm that homosexuality per se is no bar to ordination. This would leave the governing bodies (the presbytery in the case of ordaining clergy, the congregation in the case of ordaining elders and deacons) the right to determine ordination on a case-by-case basis. We did not seek either a change or an interpretation of our church constitution that would *require* presbyteries and congregations to ordain homosexual persons. We recommended that the next General Assembly offer our conclusion as guideline rather than law. The authors of the minority report, those opposed to ordination, also did not wish to limit either the power of the presbytery nor the rights of the local congregation in selecting and ordaining leaders, while asking the General Assembly to offer opposite guidance.

Bill Silver was at this meeting representing Presbyterians for Gay Concerns. The previous year he and I had been elected to the leading posts of PGC, he as moderator and I as coordinator/treasurer, and later editor of the PGC newsletter, which I named *More Light.* Since my appointment to the task force, I had found myself increasingly uncomfortable around Bill. He seemed antagonistic and angry. When I first began attending task force meetings, I'd phone him from Kennedy airport on my return trip home before going on to New Haven. Eagerly I'd describe our latest proceedings. I could not understand why, toward the end of our conversations, he would become argumentative, saying things like "Why didn't you do this?" or "Why didn't you say that" or "When is the task force going to hear from *other* gay people?" Finally I realized how left out of the process he felt: the task force was determining his future, and he wasn't there to offer his viewpoint. I had been chosen to serve and not he, yet it was the question of his ordination that had surfaced the issue in the church. Was I an "Uncle Tom," taken with the affirmation and perceived glamour of serving on a national church committee, not militant, demanding, or worthy enough to represent either a Bill Silver or the broader gay community? Was I too compromising and accommodating, I wondered?

Bill and I had an opportunity to talk alone very late one evening in the basement canteen at Krisheim. What began as a casual conversation ended in a serious debate delineating a basic, ideological difference of approach between us. I held that what I did for the gay cause had to be on behalf of others, that I was not there to represent myself or a narrow segment, but the many who were closeted and had no voice. If I were there for myself, I told Bill, I'd rather be doing something else. I believed I had to be there for others who could not speak up for themselves; therefore, I presented a moderate viewpoint.

Essentially Bill's response to my position was "Let the dead bury the dead." He claimed I didn't and couldn't represent those other people. "Let them represent themselves," he advised, "we can't speak for them. We can and should only speak for ourselves. Our primary responsibility is to ourselves." "But," I countered, "knowing I'm doing this for others gives me strength and stamina." Bill responded, "You should have the same strength and stamina for yourself. Give yourself permission to be yourself. Give yourself permission to be angry. We have a right to be angry!"

Bill and I represented two views that would serve as an ongoing dialectic in what later became Presbyterians for Lesbian/Gay Concerns. Were we in this for ourselves, or on behalf of others, or both? Should we play the "good fruit" or represent the radical dimension of our existence within the church, questioning more broadly the church's exclusiveness and conformity, questioning more extensively the church's attitudes toward sexuality? Still wanting to be the "best little Christians in the world," some of us hesitated unleashing the Pandora's box of the broader issues of sexuality that the church needed to address. I campaigned on the acceptance of homosexuality within the same narrow confines most Christians accepted heterosexuality, expressed in covenant relationship. I knew the church needed to address other issues for heterosexual and homosexual alike: singleness without celibacy, sexual intimacy outside covenant relationships, bisexuality. But I did not want to confuse the issue for which I was fighting.

Though less well than I am able to do in retrospect, even then I understood the wisdom in Bill's argument. If, as Bill suggested, I had viewed myself as doing what I did solely for myself, later I would not have been wounded by the ingratitude I experienced at the hands of those for whom I fought, who distrusted, forgot, ignored, or were ignorant of my contributions to their liberation and well-being. I should have learned this from my ministry at Yale in which those for whom I became open criticized me for doing so and failed to offer adequate support. On the other hand, acting on behalf of others contributed to my protection against taking the attacks of our opposition personally, no matter how brutal or cruel. That stance may also have distanced me from the intense anger required to turn over the tables of those I perceived profaning God's temple, but the anger I did express seemed purer to me because it was on behalf of others rather than myself.

Having agreed on strategy as completely as we had at the Baltimore General Assembly, it pained Bill and me to disagree so heartily now. And yet the passion of our difference grew from recognizing how much was at stake in our confrontation with the church.

Backlash to the Task Force to Study Homosexuality itself began as early as its formation. The 1977 Philadelphia General Assembly rejected overtures from presbyteries which sought to abolish the task force or redirect our efforts toward finding "cures" to homosexuality. Reaction to our unannounced conclusions came as early as November 1977, when seventeen pastors of "high-steepled" (large, wealthy, and influential) churches met to strategize about how to counter the effect of our work. They issued a statement opposing the presumed liberal outcome of our work, and set the foundation for a gathering of several hundred Presbyterian clergy and lay leaders from around the country to make further plans to defeat the task force.

The task force's report and recommendations were made public on Monday, January 23, 1978, after the Advisory Council on Church and Society had acted and after the Presbyterian division of communications had distributed a summary of our findings to all Presbyterian pastors. This would allow Presbyterians to hear our findings from their pulpits on Sunday before learning it from the press on Monday. The media, of course, gave it wide coverage. It was exciting to see our work described in *Time* magazine and on the front page of the *Los Angeles Times,* as well as in numerous other public forums. Church work seldom gets this kind of attention.

Meanwhile, the meeting of several hundred church leaders was called to take place Monday, February 13th, at the O'Hare

Hilton in Chicago, the very place the task force had begun its deliberations. The largely white male gathering decided to support "the Chicago plan," a political strategy to defeat the task force majority report by pressuring presbyteries to take positions and elect General Assembly commissioners opposed to it. Even William P. Thompson, the Stated Clerk of the General Assembly, who had already and inappropriately (the task force believed) publicly stated his opposition to the ordination of homosexuals, felt compelled to remind presbyteries that assembly commissioners were not elected as representatives of a presbytery's point of view, but rather were *commissioned* to listen for the guidance of the Holy Spirit in General Assembly deliberations and to vote as that Spirit led them.

Supporters of the Chicago plan lost no time injecting their venom into my own Pacific Presbytery. Over two hundred presbyters representing the Presbytery's fifty-plus churches gathered at Bel Air Presbyterian Church for our regular February meeting, coincidentally scheduled on Valentine's Day. On the floor of the presbytery, Rev. Don Buteyn introduced the Chicago plan blueprint resolution freshly arrived from Chicago, opposing homosexual ordination. Buteyn was on staff of the First Presbyterian Church of Hollywood, a conservative high-steepled church with a noteworthy contingent of closeted homosexuals whom the staff avoids acknowledging, lest they lose members and money. At an earlier meeting the presbytery had determined not to receive me as a transfer candidate for ordination until the report of the Task Force to Study Homosexuality had come out and was studied and finally judged at the next General Assembly. Now, contradictorily, the Presbytery would consider a resolution opposing the conclusions of a report not yet available for study!

It was as if these clergy and lay leaders feared education on the subject, frightened that information in the task force's study paper would be persuasive and change votes. Astounded to witness them act immaturely, I sought permission to address them, both as a task force member and someone who led a ministry they supported. After discussion and the required two-thirds vote to permit me to do so, I expressed dismay that the Presbytery would pass judgment on a document they hadn't read. This was not my view of our Presbyterian heritage. I had chosen the Presbyterian Church as my church partly because of its valuing of education as well as due process. To pass this resolution would be to preempt any serious study of the task force report when published.

But homophobia had panicked them. The progressives in the meeting attempted to table the motion, but instead the question was called, and the resolution passed. Immediately the Presbytery turned to electing its commissioners to the General Assembly that would deal with the task force report. The same inhospitable and ungracious feelings that influenced the vote on the Chicago plan resolution influenced their selection of commissioners. I felt weak and sick to my stomach, disgusted by these leaders' insensitivity. I wondered if the church were worthy of my or anyone else's attention. What they had done was evil; I could not believe God looked down on the presbytery that day with anything but disdain. "Truly, it will be better in the endtime for Sodom, than for those [church councils] that do not receive you," Jesus might have told his gay disciples.

This scene would be replayed in a number of presbyteries throughout the county, so embedded and widespread was the homophobia. Presbyterians usually take pride in their scholarship. Generally they trust God to work through a committee process to illumine truth. Usually Presbyterians do things "decently and in order." What the Chicago plan illustrated again and again was how unnaturally homophobia made many Presbyterians behave. They feared current scholarship, distrusted our task force, and behaved indecently in their efforts to coerce defeat for the majority report's recommendation. No other committee or task force pronouncement could have engendered the same dread and irrational response.

In the debate that followed release of the task force report, I heard comments like, "If there had been more lay people on that task force, it would have come out the other way." In truth, the lay people on the task force *all* voted with the majority. It was five heterosexual, white, male clergy who took the minority position. The majority of fourteen consisted of lay and clergy, women and men, black and white, old and young. Another comment I often heard that needed correction was, "That liberal national staff in New York City led the task force to this conclusion." Quite the opposite! The "liberal staff" tried to dissuade us from taking as strong a stand as we did.

With opera, "it's not over till the fat lady sings." With politics and sports, "it's not over till it's over." With Presbyterians, it's not over till the next presbytery meeting. Recently, going through some mementoes of this period, I ran across the minutes of the Valentine's Day meeting and the one that followed in April. The latter reminded me of a protest filed in the April minutes, taking exception to the February action on homosexual ordination. In part it declared, "We have not taken the time to listen, only to speak. . . . The compulsion to render a fast verdict on this issue has denied Christ the right to teach his Church through his Spirit's full operation in our Church courts." As I read the list of sixty-five church leaders who had signed the protest—an honor role of hospitality, justice, and authentic Christianity—I realized why, despite the pain the Presbytery of the Pacific had caused and was yet to cause me, I continue to this day to serve within it. If God were willing to forgive Sodom its gross inhospitality if ten righteous persons could be found, then surely God must forgive an inhospitable presbytery in which sixty-five righteous persons were clearly evident.

Despite the Chicago plan's intent to shut out study and discussion of the report of the Task Force to Study Homosexuality, presbyteries and congregations throughout the country used it, along with two earlier study packets we had produced, to explore the issue of homosexuality and the church. Though of course many avoided study, by the end of our process, Presbyterians as a whole, I believe, became the denomination most informed on homosexuality at the grass roots level. Media coverage of the report and our debate was extensive, given its controversial and societal implications. If Calvinist, middle- to upper-middle-class and generally conservative (particularly in the area of personal morals) *Presbyterians* may talk about homosexuality, then *anyone* may do so! I heard many stories of non-Presbyterians seeking out the local Presbyterian pastor or church for counsel or comfort simply because they'd heard our denomination was actively learning about the subject and therefore might be more open to hearing their experience as gay or lesbian, or as a parent, spouse, sibling, child, or friend of someone who was homosexual.

Since the time of our appointment to the task force, many of us as individuals had been interpreting our work in various speaking engagements all over the United States. Now that our conclusions had been made public and our study paper and recommendations were being distributed, demands for interpretation intensified. As the task force's token gay member, I was among the busiest, speaking in urban, suburban, and rural areas in diverse sections of the country, frequently making two major trips per month. Luckily for my schedule, church people also drew on the resources of local members of Presbyterians for Gay Concerns, the Metropolitan Community Churches, and other denominational gay support groups for the personal dimensions of the issue.

Listeners to my presentations often thanked me for raising the level of the discussion by reflecting on spirituality, faith experience, and scripture (not simply those biblical passages related to homosexuality). The bottom line (so to speak) of the opposition was genital sexuality, whereas I spoke of general spirituality, that is, spirituality common to heterosexual and homosexual alike. The opposition seemed hung up on legalism and form rather than faith and content. Indeed, one of the opposition's arguments was that form *determined* content, therefore, homosexual relationship was inherently distorted in content because it followed neither biological nor scriptural form (the latter as "spelled out" in the Genesis creation stories). I believed this emphasis on form over content contradicted the spirit of Jesus' own declaration that external ritual ("not what goes into a man or woman") was superseded by internal response ("but what comes out of a man or woman's heart"). Genital expression is not as spiritually significant as the reasons that prompt it, whether lust or love. Except in obvious cases such as rape, prostitution, or exploitation, I believe motivation is as hidden as the heart and must be left for the lovers and God to judge.

Ironically, I tended to be more conservative than my opposition in interpreting the Genesis narratives of the creation of humankind. Adam, Eve, Cain, and Abel could hardly serve as the model of the ideal family, else we would expect all husbands to be disobedient, all wives to be treated as scapegoats, and all siblings to kill one another. The two creation stories in the first and second chapters of Genesis are simply intended to say that God created the world and humanity (the latter specially in God's image), that God created sexuality for mutual companionship and procreation, that humanity's purpose was communion with God and care for the creation, and that human sin interfered with that plan. To derive from these simple points that homosexuality is somehow precluded or a result of the fall, as my opposition did, is to be far too liberal with the text. That homosexual relationships may not procreate children (though perhaps "procreation" should not be limited to flesh and blood) does not exclude them from mutuality in relationship. Protestants hold that mutuality in relationship is adequate alone to validate covenants of marriage. Similar covenants between same-gender couples find fulfillment in mutual companionship as well as alternative forms of procreation: creating together a home, an extended family (of biological family and others), and possibly other worthwhile achievements.

The emphasis on faith and spirituality in my presentations clearly arose from two realizations. Witnessing Henri Nouwen's response to Troy Perry's presentation at Yale helped me discover the need to let my spirituality come out of the closet along with my sexuality and to suggest universal applications of my unique faith experience. The other realization was that it was this faith experience I chose to interpret rather than simply my sexual orientation and behavior. In my experience, sexual orientation was a given, like race or gender. How I responded in faith to that given was what was spiritually significant to me and therefore of interest to audiences. The opposition attacks what it believes about that "given," not the actual condition. In a way, then, they attack themselves. Therefore, I felt called less to defend the fact of my sexuality than to defend the faithfulness of my Christian response.

This distinction reveals how differently I view my sexuality and my faith. Sexuality is a matter of fact, my Christianity is a matter of faith. Though I believe God's creative, redemptive, and sustaining love is available to unbeliever and believer alike and is not self-chosen, yet I also believe I have *chosen* to respond to God's "irresistible grace" *as a Christian.* I have chosen to be Christian in a way I never chose to be homosexual. If someone attacks my Christianity, he or she attacks a very personal, intimate choice I have made. Since this is a belief-choice possible for anyone (I reject the notion of "the elect"), another's belief may question the worthiness of my choice in a way that someone else's belief about homosexuality does not threaten an unchosen sexual orientation.

The contrast is like water on rock versus water on earth. The rock, virtually unchangeable, sloughs off the water. In this analogy, the rock is sexual orientation. Earth, quite differently, soaks up the water and softens. Earth is faith. Water is other experience, other belief systems, other faiths. Some would say my faith should be like rock rather than like earth. But how then could it be fertile, how could it receive the seed of the gospel, how would it provide a fruitful harvest, as Jesus describes faith? My faith must be firm but openly receptive to the nutrients of experience, my own or the experience of faithful people throughout time and cultures.

Earth is more vulnerable to sticks and stones, as it were. Walking all over it makes an impression, unfortunately compacting it and making it more rigid and less receptive. Earth may become poisoned with toxic elements. It may dry up or it may wash away. Even so with faith. Faith, like earth, must be protected in its vulnerability. It must be defended against the sticks and stones that can disrupt or smother. It must not be taken for granted or treated "like dirt." We must preserve it from the bitterness that may seep in. We must save it from drying out from lack of experience and from washing away by too liberal exposure to competing beliefs.

So I have felt the need to defend, protect, preserve, and save my faith in a way I have not felt compelled to defend, protect, preserve, and save my sexual orientation. And I protect my faith for reasons far more personal, because, being a belief-choice rather than a given, my faith reflects more intimately who I am than my homosexual orientation. When someone attacks Christian faith per se, *I* am attacked personally. When someone attacks the Church per se, *I* am attacked, since I *am* the church in Christian theology, a part of the Body of Christ. This is not to say I do not welcome reform in both faith and church; it is to say those who would offer me the greatest hospitality will welcome my faith and church, immature ("unperfected") as each may be, as part of my ongoing process toward integrity.

There are people of faith who take reform as attack, feeling protective of faith and church. To return to my analogy, their earth of faith may have dried and hardened and become unreceptive to new waters of experience. Or their earth may be washing away and unable to tolerate one more drop of water. Aside from their fear of homosexuality and sexuality, these people may also fear new experience, in this case the experience of gay and lesbian Christians. They fear—irrationally, I believe—that this new experience will wash their faith away if they open the floodgates now closed against homosexuality or the broader issue of sexuality. For the same reasons I feel attacked when Christian faith per se is attacked, they similarly feel personally under attack and may become rabidly defensive. Other people whose earth of faith is soft enough to be receptive yet firm enough to take in more waters of experience regard the acceptance of lesbian and gay Christians as one more reform, rather than as an attack on their faith.

Ultimately and personally, I would be less concerned with how people judged my sexuality than with how they received my faith experience. In the story of Jesus speaking to the woman at the well, if the other Samaritans had preoccupied themselves with deliberations on the woman's sexuality, they would never have learned from her faith experience that Jesus was the Messiah in time to meet him themselves. Although I felt hurt by those who viewed my sexuality as anomaly in an otherwise good soul, what hurt more were those who couldn't get past my sexuality to my spirituality.

Yet, in my strong identification with other gay men and lesbian women, what hurt *most* was to witness their suffering at the hands of a church that treated them at best as tragically flawed and at worst as demonic heretics. Though such identification kept me from taking the attacks of our opposition personally, it yet enabled me to suffer with my lesbian sisters and gay brothers in their pain. That "suffering with," that compassion, fueled my passion for justice for gays, lesbians, their families, and friends. It was in the midst of that compassion that Christ communed with us. It was in that compassion that Christ commissioned us with the gospel that true worship lay not in a particular sexual form anymore than in a single ritual model. True worshipers worship "in Spirit and truth," Samaritan and Jew, homosexual, heterosexual, and bisexual alike.

The very thing that softened the blow for me personally when facing those who attacked homosexuality—that is, facing them on behalf of others who could not speak up for themselves—was paradoxically the same thing that drew me into an identification with other gays and lesbians that *was* intensely personal. The individual-personal was transcended by the collective-personal. I felt their hurts, their pain, their anger. I was buoyed by their courage, compassion, and love. Receiving a blow on their behalf was rendered less hurtful because the weight of its impact was distributed among many. Enjoying a victory on their behalf was rendered less prideful because the worthiness was similarly shared. "Bearing one another's burdens" is not idealism, but practical spirituality.

"If one member suffers, all suffer together. If one member is honored, all are honored together." That's the nature of the Body of Christ. I felt called to serve as a spokesperson for the many who were honored for their church work, but secretly suffered because of the church's attitudes toward homosexuality. I do not believe it coincidence that the first inkling of that call came when I would have liked to have spoken up for the gifted and giving homosexual youth worker expelled from the Baptist church in which I had been baptized into the Body of Christ.

In denying me permission to labor outside its bounds to serve as Lazarus Project director, the Presbytery of San Fernando had not simply attacked homosexuality in general or mine in particular. That I had anticipated; that I did not take personally. What did hurt personally was their denial of my faith experience and my call to ministry. Similarly, the five members of the Task Force to Study Homosexuality who opposed ordination of lesbians and gays did not hurt me personally in opposing homosexuality. What did hurt was their denial of my faith experience and my call to ministry that grew from my faith experience. I believed both the presbytery and the task force minority had not really *heard* my side of the story, reminiscent of the childhood Sunday school experience in which I was spanked for reaching out the window to retrieve crayons that another child had tossed out. I had believed I was doing good, but an adult interpretation determined otherwise, and I was devastated at being misunderstood. Now, responding to God's call within the context of my God-given sexuality, I believed I was doing good, but authorities' interpretation determined otherwise. The hurt and devastation I felt grew from being misunderstood by those whose respect I wanted.

Flying home to Los Angeles from one of my many trips, I caught a spectacular glimpse of the Grand Canyon, a beautiful sanctuary carved in the wilderness by a solitary river over a timespan of one to two million years. I thought of the church and of its attitudes toward gays and lesbians—attitudes that we were trying to shape, so that the church too could prove a sanctuary for yet more weary travelers on the way to the Promised Land. Unlike the river, we have had little time to resculpt the church. Though we find ourselves in a church that feels like a desert, we believe the movement in which we are involved as lesbian women and gay men will work on the church's faith and help carve a sanctuary of inviting beauty. Those who accuse us of eroding societal values are at least partly right—we are eroding superficial values to get at deeper values. We have an abiding faith in God's presence in earth and pray that the Spirit will use us as an instrument for stripping away the artificial icons, idols, and church walls between us and the depths of God's grandeur, beauty, and love.

The church too finds itself in a desert—that is, in the world, where the thirst for some deeper reality is great. The church has only begun to scratch the surface in overcoming the survival mentality so common in the desert, so common in our relationships between individuals, groups, and nations. The church has only begun to overcome its *own* survival mentality that inhibits its inclusiveness and relationships. Both civilization and the church are young and must be given time. Think of the one to two million years needed to create the Grand Canyon! We who have an abiding faith in God's incarnation in Christ's Body, the church, believe it will yet strip away injustice, mercilessness, prejudice, and hate, creating a sanctuary wherein the hidden depths of beauty and love within a humanity created in God's image might be revealed. And it *will* prove open to the waters of experience that the Spirit brings, because not even the church can resist God. The gay Christian experience is yet another stream that feeds into the river of the church's experience, as that river carves and sculpts the earth of faith.

A young man who had served as a Youth Advisory delegate to the Philadelphia General Assembly had been corresponding with me for counsel about telling his parents he was gay. He lived with them on a farm in the Midwest. When he described them as fairly conservative, I cautioned him about coming out to them, suggesting he wait till he went to college. Ignoring my advice, he went ahead and told them on New Year's Day. He wrote me of their surprisingly supportive response: his mother had "cried a little"; his father had been "joyously supportive." I believe their loving acceptance reflected our church's discussion on the matter. Regardless of the final outcome in San Diego, ministry had already been accomplished.

And ministry was happening for me without benefit of ordination in the West Hollywood Presbyterian Church through the work of the Lazarus Project. The resurrection image of Lazarus from which the ministry took its name would be justified by the congregation's growth, self-sustenance, and developing ministries in the decade to follow. If only other struggling urban churches would open their doors to nearby gay ghettos, they would have the spiritual resources to fulfill their ministries.

Yet West Hollywood Presbyterian Church was only beginning to serve as a spiritual community for me, and indeed its needs were as draining as its gifts were rejuvenating. I needed something more to sustain me in my hectic schedule of interpreting both a controversial document and the need for ministry within the gay community. I found myself relying on the energy of the gay community itself; it became my most significant spiritual community during this troubled time. Before and after task force meetings or speaking engagements, I was drawn to gay bars, not looking for a messianic lover as I had done when I first came out, but simply to be with others like myself, to soak up the collective energy of gay crowds, and to enjoy our existence in music and dancing. I was looking to keep alive a part of myself I had grown to appreciate: being gay. I felt, in a sense, that I was coming up for air in the lesbian/gay milieu before plunging again into the treacherous depths of mainstream society represented by the task force and the broader church.

I also experienced a joyful exuberance in the sensual dance of the disco on Saturday night—an exuberance that I wanted to experience in the spiritual dance of the church on Sunday mornings. Zorba and Jesus had danced on the shores of my experience in college. When I met Bill Johnson, the gay Christian minister who harmonized all the aspects of life I wished to harmonize, I had danced like Miriam after the Israelites' deliverance from Egyptian bondage and like David after the return of the Ark of the Covenant to Jerusalem, expressing my own deliverance from the closet and return to the "covenants of promise." My first visit to a gay bar in San Francisco had revealed to me that eleven o'clock Saturday night provides a form of communion for gays, just as eleven o'clock Sunday morning provides Communion for most Christians. Now, in West Hollywood discos, I often offered my dancing as prayer to God, expressing hurt, anger, grief, hope, love, and joy in the rapid motions of dancing.

The movie *Saturday Night Fever* was released about this time, and offered a parable of my Saturday night experience. When I was preparing a sermon about my efforts to integrate the experience of Saturday night with what happened in church on Sunday mornings, a student in a class at Colgate Rochester Divinity School gave me a title for the sermon. She commented, "It sounds like Saturday night fever versus Sunday morning fervor."

I gave this sermon to the West Hollywood congregation on the Sunday prior to the San Diego General Assembly. I distinguished between the fever of the character Tony in the film and the fervor of Miriam and David in our scriptures. "Fever" is temporary, artificially stimulated, an unhealthy rise in temperature. "Fervor" is ongoing, steadfast, genuinely inspired, a healthy lift of spirit. Yet I wanted the fervor we experienced with Miriam in liberation and with David in restoration to the covenant to infuse, instruct, and inform our own dance in the disco. And I wanted the enthusiasm, exuberant joy, and self-forgetfulness we experience in dancing to fuel, fill, and fulfill our worship in church. Our spirituality and our sensuality/sexuality need to know one another and find each other friends rather than strangers. We need to teach them to dance together in complementarity, inspiring and fulfilling one another as lovers, rather than pushing one another away. Spirituality should not be a wallflower at the disco on Saturday night anymore than sexuality and sensuality should be wallflowers in worship on Sunday morning.

Chapter 14

THE PRESBYTERIAN
GENERAL ASSEMBLY

SAN DIEGO
MAY, 1978

I am unable to offer a detailed, objective description of the United Presbyterian Church's General Assembly convened on May 16, 1978, in San Diego. It would be like recalling the plants and rocks I passed when I tumbled down that hill in junior high, or recounting the makes and models of cars whizzing past my spinning Volkswagen on that rain-slicked highway en route to seminary. Recollections of both my own action and that of others at the General Assembly are fragmentary, as was my memory of how I counseled the young man after his mother's devastating retort, "We should have let you die then." Involuntary tears come to my eyes even as I write these words. My stomach churns as I type the final draft. For what happened during the ensuing nine days of the assembly became not simply an attack on me and my people, but a refutation of all I believed and hoped for the church.

If the Task Force to Study Homosexuality thought it gathered under a cloud of controversy in its first meeting, we assembled now under a full-blown hurricane, a hurricane whose winds swirled around as well as within us. Many of us felt betrayed by three members of the minority who had fanned the flames of the Chicago plan. Two members of the minority had managed to capitalize on the controversy by writing books on the subject, one published prior to the assembly with the inflammatory title, *The Bond That Breaks: Will Homosexuality Split the Church?* The graphic on its cover was two ropes in the form of a cross, frayed in the center. The single thread that held it together suggested how the fragile unity of the church could easily be torn apart by this issue.

A member of the minority had allegedly divulged the homosexuality of Willard Heckel, breaking promised confidentiality. The resulting increased tension may have been a factor in the massive heart attack Heckel suffered that prevented his presence in San Diego. Furious, I wrote to the person who had revealed Willard's secret. Now, in our gathering, he claimed he had not done so. Still wanting to trust him, I apologized. Within days we obtained a copy of an article written by the individual in question which *did* reveal the self-disclosure of a gay member of the task force. Though Heckel was not specifically named in the article, the revelation itself was a breach of confidentiality. Our chairperson Ginny Davidson later remarked, "In a group of our size, you've got to imagine there's going to be a Judas *some*place." Disagreement and dissension within the task force had grown into distrust, suspicion, betrayal, and anger.

Our report was assigned to a special assembly committee to deal solely with our efforts. Committee membership was vigorously campaigned for by archconservatives. Once the special committee was convened, task force chairperson Davidson briefed them on the background study document. She was followed by representatives from the majority and minority positions, who outlined their respective viewpoints and recommendations. Beyond this, task force members were rarely consulted by this special committee. Most of us only addressed the committee if we signed up for time in the public hearings that followed the initial presentation of our report.

The open hearings contained a few memorable moments. A campus pastor from Long Island Presbytery came out of the closet as a gay man during his testimony. One of the "healed" homosexuals being touted about the assembly by our opposition testified that yes, indeed, he occasionally "fell from grace" and committed homosexual acts, confessing to one as recently as "last night on the beach." ("Changed" homosexuals often have a more active sex life than unchanged ones.) None of the "former" homosexuals who testified were Presbyterian; they were members of stricter, more authoritarian fundamentalist sects. A leader of Presbyterians United for Biblical Concerns began his comments with, "Let's tell it like it is!" A journalist wryly observed to me that no one wearing contact lenses, a toupee, and elevator shoes was about to "tell it like it is"! A member of the task force minority, who already had the ear of the special issues committee and hardly needed another forum to present his views, confessed to his own difficulty keeping sexuality within its proper framework: "We all, I guess, leak around the edges." A task force member, a touch of mockery in her voice, whispered to me, "I hope *I'm* not around when he starts leaking!"

When the committee closed its public hearings and began deliberations, it was decided early that if the committee attempted to tamper with the background study paper of the task force, which ran over one hundred pages, it would be meeting from May to Christmas. Since both majority and minority members of the task force worked together on the study document and both recommended its distribution, the committee concurred and moved to offer it for study. Those who voiced opposition to this action correctly charged that reading the paper might "change people's minds." Though the decision was made largely on procedural grounds, we who favored acceptance of gays and lesbians viewed it as a victory, convinced that education could foster more acceptance.

Then the committee debated whether to adopt the majority or minority opinions, a foregone conclusion given the makeup of both the committee and the entire Assembly. However, they dutifully discussed the matter, more or less at the insistence of the more progressive committee members, as well as some self-styled, antigay demagogues, who didn't want to miss opportunities to pontificate not only on homosexuality but on what had misled the denomination even to discuss it.

As I listened, I thought of a comment made to me in the process of setting up the Lazarus Project. A pastor asked me how I was going to survive the constant rejections I would face in the church. Perhaps too self-assured, I replied, "These people don't really know me. If they were friends and rejected me, then I would feel greater hurt." "Yes," he responded, "but it's the strangers in our lives who often make decisions which most vitally affect us." His wisdom grew from witnessing his wife's struggle for acceptance as a clergywoman. At the time I realized how truthfully he spoke: from strangers in Washington who decide where soldiers will offer their lives, to the strangers in city councils who determine how much police protection will be offered a community, life itself is often in the hands of those who do not know us or care about us. Certainly this was now the case as the fifty members of this special committee on the church and homosexuality, mostly strangers, prepared to vote on my future participation in the church. I did not believe they were "listening for the Spirit," the One who enables strangers to view one another as compassionately as we might the misjudged Christ.

Providentially, they did face the stranger whose future they were deciding and whose life they were judging. An increasingly outspoken young seminary advisory delegate confronted them as they voted on the ordination of "self-affirming, practicing homosexual persons." Before the committee voted, Sandy Brawders made a very personal plea: "I want you to know that as you vote, you are determining my future. For I am a lesbian woman as well as a candidate for ordination." A shock wave went through the committee. She was the only self-acknowledged homosexual member of the committee. But she was enough for them to know their "principled" action had personal ramifications. Of course this did not prevent the committee from voting against ordination. One member of the committee, another "high-steepled" pastor, sought absolution from me immediately following the vote. Extending his hand to shake mine during the break that followed, he said, "I hope you don't take this personally." How could he deny my faith experience, my call to ministry, my loving gift, and not expect me to take it personally? I refused his hand and walked past him without speaking. How could

I forgive someone who was unrepentant in zealous persecution of my people?

I chose to skip portions of the committee's deliberations after that. I chose rather to be with Presbyterians for Gay Concerns more and more as we gathered for prayer vigils, candlelight demonstrations, and daily opportunities for worship. When I did return to the committee I learned it had dispensed with both the majority and minority position papers and was writing its own comparatively theologically-impoverished statement, using a member of the task force minority as its main resource. As the committee approved the sentence, "Therefore, it appears that what is really important is not what homosexuality is, but what we believe about it," I thought to myself, "How self-revealing. Don't confuse them with reality." It confirmed what I had believed all along: homophobic people can't attack homosexuality; they can only attack their confused notions of what it is, and so they really attack themselves. Homosexuality would not be condemned in the document, only what these people *thought* of it. I think Jesus referred to this dynamic when he said, "Judge not, that you be not judged. For with the judgment you pronounce you will be judged, and the measure you give will be the measure you get." Believing they were judging gays and lesbians, they actually judged themselves and their own vast ignorance.

The committee had determined that homosexuality was not a conscious choice, but a result of humanity's fall from grace. A clever way, I reflected sarcastically, to get around the fact that most gay people never make a conscious (and thereby moral or immoral) choice to be gay or lesbian. As they voted to remove the name of "Jesus Christ" from a paragraph in the document, a pastor from Sacramento turned to me and commented drily on the deletion: "I knew we'd get to it sooner or later."

As is true of most general assemblies, the conversations in the hallways were as significant as, or perhaps more so than, the discussions in the committee rooms or on the floor of the whole Assembly. A gay commissioner agonized, "I'm going to have to vote against ordination because the rest of my presbytery's contingent will be watching to keep everyone in line. I wouldn't survive a minute back home if I voted otherwise." The mother of a gay son described her pain on hearing the nasty comments about gays from fellow commissioners. "I'll probably be the only one in my section voting for ordination," she said. "Personally, I'm for ordination," one minister confessed, "but I think it'll split the church." "How can you expect to be ordained when you are promiscuous?" one man complained, "You should be working on marriage first." What an irony: the task force *had* considered recommending that the church develop a liturgical ceremony for gay coupling, but we found this idea more controversial than ordination. Audible gasps would arise among churchfolk to whom we mentioned the possibility, even in the midst of discussing ordination of gay people. Marriage seemed more sacred to them than ordination. Little did any of us know the church's first such ceremonies were performed for same gender couples in "spiritual friendships" in the ninth century, and that the first heterosexual marriages performed in the church did not occur till the eleventh century.

There were moments of grace, too. *The Advocate,* the national gay news magazine, coincidentally ran an article about me and my ministry in an issue available in vending machines near the convention center. That, plus media attention focused on the Assembly, contributed to an extraordinary bit of hospitality I experienced in a gay bar en route to my hotel after a particularly harrowing day at the Assembly. Dropping in for a quick beer and an opportunity to be with other gay people who were not Presbyterian, I soon found the bartender lining up several more beers behind the one I originally ordered. He explained they were anonymous gifts from other bar patrons who wished to express their appreciation for what I and others were doing on their behalf. The unconditional expressions of gratitude brought tears to my eyes.

Another moment of grace occurred in a humorous exchange at the annual Assembly dance hosted by the Witherspoon Society, a progressive social justice lobbying network within our denomination that had been very helpful to Presbyterians for Gay Concerns. An outspoken opponent of ordination of gays from the task force minority compared his conservative friends with the people at this gathering: "I must say you people do seem to have more fun." A member of the task force majority responded, "Have you ever considered there may be a *theological* reason for that?"

The most profound comfort I received came from Dr. Thelma Adair, who just two years before had been the first black woman elected General Assembly Moderator. I was standing behind her in line for the women's breakfast the day before the crucial vote on ordination within the full Assembly. She turned to me and simply reflected, "When I first started coming to general assemblies more than twenty years ago, blacks could not stay in the same hotels with white commissioners. We had to stay in private homes in outlying areas." That was all she said, but in those few words she placed the gay struggle within an appropriate perspective.

Finally the day of the full floor debate and vote on the issue of the ordination of lesbians and gays arrived on Monday, May 22. On the steps of the convention hall, where earlier Presbyterians for Gay Concerns had led a prayer vigil, lifting the name of each commissioner in prayer, fundamentalists with bullhorns and picket signs now swore Bible verses at incoming commissioners. The media scrambled for advantageous spots inside, while thousands of visitors poured into the limited seating at the rear of the hall and into the adjacent and larger civic hall, where three thousand people would watch the proceedings via closed circuit television.

Arrangements had been made for task force members to have seats scattered throughout the Assembly floor, reassigned from church leaders who had completed their tasks and departed. When I walked to my seat, however, another man was sitting in it. I explained I had been assigned the seat, but the man tried to ignore me, looking straight ahead and pretending not to see or hear me. I repeated my statement tensely, thinking this was no way to begin an afternoon that I already knew would be difficult. Still without looking at me, he replied belligerently, "The guy who was sitting here told me I could have this seat." I explained, "Well, that's not how it's being handled." As he yet tried to ignore both me and my dilemma, I looked about, searching for the staff person who had arranged the seating, hoping she might offer a solution. From that location I could not see her. "I'm on the task force whose report is coming up," I explained, "I'd like to have my seat." "I know who you are!" he mocked, gruff and hostile. "Well then, may I have my seat?" I pursued. "Oh, all right," he said, disgusted, "Now I know why you were so much trouble to the task force!" With that he stormed off. A surge of blood went to my head, again the boy reaching for crayons through the Sunday school classroom window: I was taken aback that I could be perceived as giving trouble to the task force. A part of me still wanted to give credibility to this middle-aged, well-dressed Presbyterian elder or minister and question my own behavior. But perhaps this man's arrogance prepared me for the inhospitality yet to be endured on the floor of this Assembly. It was bad enough that I had to sit alone, isolated from other task force members, separated from friends both in Presbyterians for Gay Concerns and in the West Hollywood Presbyterian Church contingent who had come for the day.

There had been a move to gain access to the floor so that I might address the commissioners, as if anything I might say could dissuade them from their certain judgment. As the request progressed through the bureaucracy, it was transformed into an invitation for me to lead the General Assembly in prayer—*after* the vote. For "balance," a leader of the opposition would follow me. As what was to become a four-hour floor debate began, I set about the task of writing what I thought might be the most important prayer of my life.

The position of the task force minority report, that homosexuals could not be ordained, had become the majority opinion of the General Assembly Committee on Homosexuality and the Church. But it was now supported by a new, hastily and poorly-written position paper. The task force majority report, that homosexuality was not per se a bar to ordination, became the committee's minority report. That would be presented by Sandra Brawders, the student from Princeton Theological Seminary. Another minority report that fell somewhere in between the two would also be presented. All recommended distribution and study of the original task force's background paper. All contained a list of recommendations on which everyone agreed, from gay civil rights to the need to reject the sin of homophobia. An important variation of the new majority's recommendations included encouraging "the development of support communities of homosexual Christians seeking sexual reorientation or meaningful, joyous, and productive celibate lifestyles."

A moment of light pierced the dreary ignorance that shrouded the Assembly that afternoon. It beamed from an individual who had not come to the Assembly with the intention of fulfilling any high calling, let alone risking career and life partner to do so. As Sandra Brawders stood to present the former task force majority report as the minority position of the special assembly committee, God's grace broke forth. It was something more than the harsh camera lights of the three networks covering her presentation. In her I witnessed a sacred presence, a sacred trust, a grace about her bearing that told me she had been born for this very moment. Saint Joan had returned to discern the spirits, to speak where the Spirit would lead the church, to rebuke the spirits of condemnation and exclusion. True, I looked upon her with eyes of faith. Yet wasn't that closer to the reality than those who looked with scorn, malice, and fear? And when she forcefully concluded with the revelation that her future as a lesbian Christian seeking ordination hung on their vote, the same shock pulsed through the Assembly as it had earlier through the committee. The immense surge of Spirit that washed over us left tears in my eyes. Unprovidentially, their vote would be her cross.

The Assembly defeated the two minority reports and proceeded to discuss the committee's majority opinion opposed to ordination of self-affirming, practicing homosexuals. The Reverend John Conner, who had served as General Assembly

Moderator during the preceding year of controversy, achieved an amendment. He had kept quiet during the debate to use all of his political clout for a fourteenth recommendation: that this decision "shall not be used to affect negatively the ordination rights of any United Presbyterian deacon, elder, or minister who has been ordained prior to this date." It was a "grandparent" clause to prevent "witch hunts," looking for homosexuals behind every pulpit. When it was accepted, the Assembly thought it had acted pastorally. But—again, this is a view from faith—I believe God moved the Assembly unintentionally to act prophetically. As God used their enemy Cyrus to return the Israelites to their homeland according to the prophet Isaiah, so God made use of this General Assembly. For why would it be permissible to God that gays and lesbians be ordained prior to May 22, 1978, and not permissible afterwards? The tension in which this position keeps the church ultimately has to be resolved, and I believe it will be resolved in God's favor with the full inclusion of God's lesbian and gay children in the membership and leadership of the church. I believe John Conner knew what God was doing.

Before the final vote on the committee's majority opinion, the Assembly adjourned for dinner. Presbyterians for Gay Concerns gathered in another room of the hall for an *agape* feast, sharing the bread and wine not of communion, but of loving solidarity. Since communion is a sacrament requiring ordination of its celebrant, it felt appropriate to employ its traditional counterpart that requires no ordained leadership. We gathered as mourners, for we knew it was just a matter of time before the judgment was rendered. Tears and sorrowful faces encircled the bread and wine. This was not a time for anger, only grief. We grieved for our lesbian sisters and our gay brothers, we grieved for those who loved us: parents, spouses, siblings, children, friends; we grieved for our church. On no one's face was the sorrow more evident than John Conner's, who had tried to help Presbyterians approach this issue compassionately and who himself had counseled numerous parents and gays and lesbians during his tenure as moderator. Preaching in the opening service of this Assembly, he had spoken of it as a family reunion in which no family member can be denied or rejected. Now the grief of family disruption and denial made him profoundly silent, while others expressed feelings, offered prayers, read scriptures, sang hymns, hugged one another. David Sindt, founder of Presbyterians for Gay Concerns, led us in the love feast. Yet it *was* communion. For, in those moments, within those believers, Christ's Spirit fed us with his body and his blood, offering us a communion in which Christ's own rejection and sacrifice were felt more keenly, while Christ's commonwealth was hoped and prayed for more dearly, a commonwealth in which all of God's children share equally the wealth of God's grace.

After the dinner break, more debate, and a prayer, the Assembly voted decisively its opposition to the ordination of homosexuals by concurring with the committee's majority opinion by a 90 percent to 10 percent vote. The judgment of the church was that gays and lesbians should be welcomed into the church, but not ordained to any church leadership position. The Assembly turned to prayer again. Having already been escorted to the dais, I for the first time faced my "accusers." They were overwhelmingly male, white, and middle-aged. Briefly it occurred to me that though these were the ones in power, most Presbyterians are women. And if women, people of color, lesbians, gays, and other minorities ever shared the power, our denomination would better reflect God's intended commonwealth. I smiled at the memory of Maggie Kuhn, founder of the Gray Panthers, a senior citizen's advocacy group, saying to a gathering of Presbyterians for Gay Concerns at a previous General Assembly: "Just think—in a hundred years there'll be all new commissioners!" I held that vision as I came to the microphone.

I prayed, thanking God for what had been accomplished in terms of study and acceptance, but also praying: "God of Grace, may we see the vision of the Kingdom, the vision that led Jesus to look beyond the religious councils of his day. May the Spirit enable us to look beyond this General Assembly, humbly remembering no General Assembly speaks fully of your truth or your future. Amen." As I read my longish, rather preachy prayer, I noticed my opponent out of the corner of my eye jotting notes for what I guessed would be a rebuttal prayer. Indeed, when he followed me with his own prayer, he addressed many of the same areas of concern I had, but from his own perspective.

I overhead an exchange between two commissioners opposed to ordination. "When do you think they'll vote to ordain homosexuals?" one asked as he yawned and stretched after the vote and our prayers. The other replied, "Probably within ten years, but I'll be retired by then." Even among those who voted against ordination, the question was not if but when.

The San Diego Assembly believed it had refrained from making their "definitive guidance" legally binding on presbyteries and congregations, which would still retain full power to ordain their leadership. But, during the ensuing summer, Stated Clerk William P. Thompson, who refused to offer an interpretation of the Assembly's action prior to the vote, chose to offer one afterward that claimed the action *was* legally binding. Though several presbyteries would question this interpretation at the following assembly, no action would be taken that contradicted Thompson's interpretation. Congregations opposing both the advice of the Assembly and its subsequent interpretation as law began passing resolutions welcoming persons into full membership, with rights of ordination, "regardless of sexual orientation." Thus would begin the "More Light" movement in the Presbyterian Church, so named because the 1976 General Assembly had declared God had "yet more light to break forth from [God's] word." I had already used the phrase *More Light* for the name of the newsletter published by Presbyterians for Gay Concerns.

In 1979, when the Presbyterian Church in the United States felt compelled because of impending reunion with our United Presbyterian Church to approve the same policy statement and recommendations, a black ecumenical delegate, a Methodist minister, gained the floor to offer a significant observation in the debate. "I notice that in this policy statement," he said, "both homosexuality and homophobia are condemned

as sin. The policy goes on to refuse ordination to unrepentant, homosexual persons. What of unrepentant, *homophobic*
candidates for the ministry?" The discussion continued as if
he had not spoken. The speck in the brother's eye was easier
to see.

A General Assembly was not asked again to vote on the
question until 1982, when a commissioner pointed out to his
committee and then to the full Assembly that one church in
his presbytery could not constitute either a board of elders or
of deacons if it could not ordain gays. The presbytery was
Pacific, the congregation West Hollywood. Partly in fear of a
hitch in the reunion of southern and northern Presbyterians
scheduled the following year, a committee motion recommending that ordination of homosexuals be left to presbyteries and congregations failed on the Assembly floor by an 80
percent to 20 percent vote, only slightly better than in 1978.
Ironically, the southern Presbyterians whom the assembly
wished to avoid offending apparently already had a policy
which left such a decision to the ordaining body, but this fact
was obscured by the opposition's strategy. I heard a commissioner mutter, exasperated, "Why does this issue keep coming
up?!" I wanted to reply, "It'll keep coming up till you get it
right!"

Believing that our cause was unfinished business, the task
force majority, Presbyterians for Gay Concerns, Witherspoon-
ers and other friends celebrated a wake following the San
Diego Assembly's vote. We gathered in someone's hotel suite
directly after the vote, realizing we had lost a battle but not
the war. It was as if we had left our grief at the *agape* meal
observed earlier; now it was time to balance our tears with
laughter. Wine, cheese, soda, and chips accompanied anec-
dotes and parodies of the Assembly debate. Bill Silver had
handcrafted funny awards for many of us that he presented
with dramatic flair. We even laughed at our own optimism,
which had led us to believe that the vote would be closer.

We had one bitter disappointment yet to come at this Assembly. Despite Monday's vote urging church members to
"reject in their own lives, and challenge in others, the sin of

homophobia, which drives homosexual persons away from Christ and his church," and the affirmation that "contact and dialogue should be encouraged among groups and persons of all persuasions on the issue of homosexuality," the Assembly on Wednesday voted not to receive the annual report of Presbyterians for Gay Concerns. This meant we were not to be included in the ongoing "dialogue." The homophobia yet rampant in this Assembly made the commissioners react angrily to "the homosexuals trying to raise the issue again" rather than rationally understand their own process that brought them our report at this time, a report I had submitted months earlier. It would not be till the following year that our presence would be accepted, though each year since we have had vociferous opponents demanding the rejection of our report.

Sandy Brawders spent an extra day in her San Diego hotel to recuperate from the ordeal of coming out as lesbian both at the Assembly and in the national media. Her seminary, church, and closeted lover back home in New Jersey were all stirred up by her doing so. She had been threatened with the loss of a seminary scholarship, and she feared the loss of her church job, as well as the loss of her lover, who disliked publicity. Sandy therefore took a day's respite before returning home to controversy. As she checked out of her hotel, she explained to the desk clerk that the General Assembly housing would not cover the extra day, and she would do so herself. The woman asked, "Aren't you the one that was on television?" In recounting the story later, Sandy said she had reluctantly replied "Yes," expecting the worst. "In that case, your room is free!" the woman beamed, "You were wonderful!"

Upon my return home to West Hollywood, I received encouraging letters from strangers. One, an author frequently on the bestseller list, commented on how well our side came across on television and in newspapers: "In defeat you and your colleagues won far more than you realize."

The week following the Assembly, there was a "Gay Night" at Disneyland. Disney officials had contracted for a private party with a tavern guild, not knowing the guild consisted of gay bars. Disney could not break the contract, so the event was held, the first (and for nearly ten years, the *only*) such evening at Disneyland. I had purchased tickets for several of us from Presbyterians for Gay Concerns. We needed this boost in spirits. Gay people streamed into the park, exchanging gleeful looks and comments. Never have I witnessed Disneyland so thoroughly enjoyed! Surely Disney himself intended such enthusiasm and participation in the magic of "the happiest place on earth." What a joyful contrast to the sad and depressing day I'd spent there as a youth upon learning of the church worker's homosexuality.

But even here there were signs of our oppression as gay people. Chairs and tables had been set up on the Tomorrowland dance floor to prevent same-gender couples from dancing. Yet gay people still moved to the live band music, ignoring the attempted blockade. I was so angry I wanted to jump onto the dance floor and turn over the tables so gay people could dance.

That Sunday I reflected on this experience and that of the General Assembly in a sermon entitled "Lord of the Dance." I described Jesus' anger at finding the moneychangers occupying the space in the temple set aside to enable women and foreigners to draw close to Yahweh, the God of Israel. The temple was divided into three sections. Only a high priest could enter the inner one, and only priests and the men of Israel could enter the middle one. The outer courtyard was for the women of Israel and the Gentile converts, and it was this area Jesus angrily cleared, overturning the tables of the vendors and money changers, reminding them of the inclusive theme of Isaiah, through whom God had declared the temple as "a house of prayer for all peoples." Jesus was making space for the disenfranchised and the stranger in this literal yet symbolic way. Sharing this anger at injustice and inhospitality, I too wanted to overturn the tables on the Disneyland dance floor, creating space for gay dancers. I too wanted to turn over the tables of the General Assembly commissioners to make room for gays and lesbians to dance out our faith, our love, our lives.

One of our opponents at the Assembly had described God as a kind of cosmic "choreographer" who dislikes any variation of the dance Adam and Eve were given to dance. But what then of our creation as co-creators in which improvisation is encouraged? What then of Jesus Christ who took leaps of faith outside conventional modes of religious expression? And what of the Spirit inspiring us to yet new forms of dance and consecrating still other forms? During the task force regional hearings, we had felt embarrassed for the troubled woman fearful of stepping on the lines dividing the floor tiles. Why then don't Christians feel similarly embarrassed for those troubled people fearful of variations of the Christian dance? Just as the temple of Jerusalem was to provide space for the stranger and the disenfranchised to "dance" close to God, the church must clear a place for the stranger and the disenfranchised to find sanctuary for our own dance of faith.

The following month the Presbytery of the Pacific met at the First Presbyterian Church of San Pedro. Now that the General Assembly had spoken, the Presbytery would decide whether to receive my transfer as a candidate for ordination. The candidates' committee had recommended in favor of me, distinguishing my reception as a candidate from actual ordination. After addressing the presbytery about my faith experience, I was excused to an office next to the chancel. The minister moderating the meeting, sympathetic to my cause, had privately suggested I might keep the door ajar to listen in on the debate. After an hour's discussion, painful for me to hear, the presbytery voted not to receive the transfer of my candidacy for ordination, thus terminating seven years as a candidate. I could not see the vote from the office, but later I was told the vote appeared split 60 percent to 40 percent, better odds than at the General Assembly. Before I was called from the office, however, Don Buteyn, who had introduced the Chicago plan resolution and had now helped lead the fight against me, said to the presbytery, "I'm concerned for Chris. I wonder if there is some way the presbytery might maintain a pastoral relationship with him." The presbytery's stated clerk, apparently disgusted both with the action and Buteyn's saccharin sentiment, dismissed him with, "Sounds like you want to take him under care as a candidate again!" "Oh no!" exclaimed Buteyn, who had moved a long way from his social activist days in the sixties.

Then I was astounded, still from the office, to hear someone suggest, "Let's ask him to pray—he gave such a nice prayer at General Assembly." Perhaps this came from someone who voted in my favor, but the presbytery's agreement reflected both its ambivalence and guilt. I had felt deep hurt and disappointment at the summary dismissal of my years of faith experience, my call to ministry, and my careful preparation in education and training. Now the hurt was transformed to rage that, though I was not worthy in their eyes to join the straight white male fraternity they dubbed the clergy, I was adequate and even exploitable enough to lead them in prayer. And what did this say of their valuing of prayer? I almost refused to do so, but immediately recognized I should never surrender any God-given opportunity to pray or bear witness to God's grace. Neither the minutes of the meeting nor my memory preserved the contents of the prayer I offered. But I do remember beginning with the irony, "O God, here they will not recognize my call to ministry, and yet they ask me to pray . . . "

After the prayer I walked down the center aisle of the church to the narthex, followed by a few supporters, mostly women, who offered me tearful hugs outside the sanctuary. There my grateful eyes saw John. He had hurried from work to the evening meeting, hurried so fast he had been stopped for a speeding ticket, at which time, flustered by the delay, he had locked his keys in the car! But he'd arrived in time for much of the debate, and he was there for me. He gave me a hug, and we drove home. As we entered my apartment, the phone rang, an elder from a Baltimore church calling to hear how things had gone. I could hardly bear his sobs on the phone as I told him. Then came the task of informing my parents. I phoned them the news, and they too cried, hurt and angry that the church could reject me.

And then John offered me the love the church denied.

EPILOGUE

After reading the previous chapter, the reader might ask, "Why didn't you leave the church then?" With the protagonist in the film *Hospital,* I reply, "Somebody's got to be responsible." It's not only *their* church, it's mine too. I want to be part of the church's reformation. How can I abandon gays and lesbians already within the church? How can I leave gay young people of future generations in the hands of homophobic individuals in the church intent on wounding their self-esteem and denying them the fullness of life?

Yes, in the church's inability to integrate lesbian and gay Christians fully into its life, the church lacks integrity. But how can I reject the church for a lack of integrity, when I also struggle to more fully realize this goal? It took years for my sexuality and spirituality to view one another as lovers rather than strangers. I don't expect the church to make the same transformation overnight. I've abandoned perfectionism as a spiritually desirable goal; how can I then require perfection of the church?

Denied ordination, I yet continued to receive the church's support as I ministered to lesbians, gays, their families, and friends, and as I challenged the homophobia of the church. Why would the church deny me ordination and yet affirm my ministry? Providentially, Presbyterians are not afraid to be inconsistent.

To describe the ten years of ministry that have followed through the Lazarus Project, the joys and sorrows, pleasures and pains, would require another book. I cannot capture the ministry's pathos and glory in a few words, nor even a chapter. I had yet many more lessons awaiting me as I pursued the welcoming of gay men and lesbian women into the church, encouraged those already present, and battled homophobia in the church and churchphobia in the gay community.

The Lazarus Project served as a ministry of reconciliation between the church and the lesbian and gay community. For the broader church that meant providing education on gay and lesbian issues, interpretation of our experience as Christians, and supportive counsel of gays and lesbians in other congregations. We hosted conferences, lectures, and events that brought churchpeople into contact not only with scholars, but with lesbians and gays themselves. And we provided speakers and resources for religious and secular groups.

For the West Hollywood Presbyterian Church, the Lazarus Project brought new life to a dying congregation as it welcomed gays and lesbians into its worship and ministry. Worship, Bible study, and pastoral counseling led gays and lesbians who had been rejected by other churches to value themselves as God's children. Membership, leadership, and staff multiplied, the buildings were renovated, and new programs of ministry were established. Within our congregation, the Spirit transformed the hunger of street people into a lunch program, an anti-gay ballot initiative into an ecumenical service for human rights, a murder into weekly worship for gay inmates of the county jail, prostitution on our street corner into halfway homes for women choosing another life pattern, isolation of gay clergy into a church professionals support group, and the onset of AIDS into a Christian support group. We witnessed God's love to the gay community through our ministry.

Obviously my ministry did not end with denial of ordination. The struggle for ordination itself had proven to be ministry. The denial of ordination ironically empowered my ministry, adding to it the honor that accrues to those who suffer for a compassionate cause and instilling hope in all those who believe in the church's ongoing reformation. While not the perfect outcome, my nonordination enjoyed more integrity than many ordinations.

After nearly a decade, I have left my position as Lazarus Project director to reflect and write. After years of writing this book in my mind and within my heart, I have finished committing it to paper. I could not have written it earlier. I needed the intervening years to gain perspective and understanding of what transpired. During a Lazarus conference, a pastor told me, "I still cannot vote to ordain homosexuals, but you do have a ministry in the church." This response is still painful for me to hear, yet the pain causes more grief than anger. What is ordination but affirmation of ministry? The lack of full acceptance of the ministry of lesbians and gays in the church continues to cause much pain and suffering. Our grief at being rejected by our church family as full members is intensified by the current AIDS crisis. Faced with this life-threatening illness, many have no church to turn to for comfort, healing, and prayer.

I have received comfort and healing in my prayer life. It was not lost on me that each time I felt the most lonely, hurt, grieving, angry, or despairing, prayer offered sanctuary to those feelings and transformed them to ministry. Twice, once at the San Diego Assembly and again at the meeting of Pacific Presbytery that followed, I had been *required* to pray, whether I felt like it or not, and somehow God spoke to me as I tried to speak with God. Prayer is God's prerogative in which we are always welcomed to participate. Accepting God's welcome is the choice of the spiritual life.

Yet the spiritual life is more than the absence or presence of words in silent meditation or spoken prayer. Accepting God's welcome is sometimes a matter of channels other than auditory or mental. I didn't say the right words at my baptism, and yet my immersion in the water served as an experience of reconciliation with God and a sign of permanent belonging to Christ's family, the church. In the somberly prayerful atmosphere in which most churches observe communion, I'm often surprised by the burst of flavor of the bread and wine which symbolize Christ's broken body and spilled blood. Christ's sacrifice shouldn't taste so *good*, one might think. And yet his presence *is* worth savoring.

Christians could accept the orthodoxy of the above sensual interpretations of the sacraments by which we belong to Christ and are nourished by his presence, even if such thoughts never occurred to them in quite the same way.

And most Christians would not object to my earlier description of the shore as a sanctuary that meted out God's grace to me in a way the sanctuary of the church could not. Most have experienced God's beauty and awesomeness in nature.

Most Christians would understand when I wrote of the ministry of Pachelbel's Canon "restoring my soul," of the potential for ministry in van Gogh's passionate paintings, and of the integrating effect on me in writing a fictional story about a woman to whom two van Gogh paintings ministered. Human creativity may have the same healing effect as divine creations in nature.

Christians could quickly identify with my intuitive sense of God's presence in tumbling down the hill in junior high, spinning on the highway on my way to seminary, and confronting other crises, from coping with my homosexuality to facing hostile church councils. Feeling out of control may lead one to rely on God.

Almost every Christian can assent to a mystical identification and continuity with the faithful experience of biblical figures, as I identified with Miriam's dance following the Hebrews' liberation and with Lazarus' resurrection from an isolating tomb. As I learned to do, Christians value "so great a cloud of witnesses" of God's grace depicted in church tradition as well.

Fewer Christians, perhaps, will comprehend my experience of Christ in the Brooklyn subway stranger or my experience of the Philadelphia cafe waitress as minister, though most would seek to understand. A remnant of Christians might appreciate the fruits of the Spirit I witnessed in the life of the gay couple who testified at the task force's Cleveland hearing.

Most Christians would recognize God's love in my family's attempt to understand, accept, and embrace me. And, if John's gender were female rather than male, all Christians could applaud my understanding of God's grace in John's faithful love.

Christians have enjoyed God in these various ways: the words and silences of prayer, the sacraments of baptism and communion, and the sacramental potential of nature, art, crises, people of faith, strangers, and faithful love relationships.

Those other than Christian will recognize in this list many ways in which they too experience God. The unique confession of Christians is that our perceptions stem from or lead to an experience of God embodied in Jesus Christ, and that our growing intuition of God's presence in the world is a gift of the Holy Spirit. The gift of enjoying God in the various ways I've described in turn gives rise to our thanksgiving, worship, preaching, service, evangelizing, community, scripture, and other spiritual writings.

Yet there is another way we experience God that we Christians do not want to talk about. A lesbian attending a workshop I was co-leading on homosexuality and the church told us she had no religious background. When asked why she was there, she explained, "In my lovemaking with my lover, I became aware of a spiritual realm I have never before experienced. Since spirituality is associated with God, I came here to find out about God." Our sexuality itself may serve as a means of grace, a way in which we accept God's welcome, the choice of the spiritual life.

How far we are from this understanding may be illustrated simply. Think with what approbation Christians would hear the giving of thanks to God for a meal in the dining room. Now consider how most Christians would react to the mere idea of giving thanks to God for a sexual experience in the bedroom. The wince at the thought suggests how far removed our sexuality is from our spirituality. Yet it too is God's gift, and like all of God's gifts, a way of knowing God's gracious love.

I believe accepting another's sexual orientation may be dependent on first accepting one's own. Outside of societally-induced homophobia, I believe that most Christians have difficulty accepting homosexuality in the church because they are unable to accept *any* sexuality as a means of God's grace. Not just accept—embrace.

The integrity of body and spirit is soul. The estrangement of sense and spirit bifurcates the soul. Those of us who have come out of the closet know too well the damage this does to our spiritual and sexual lives. They become strangers to one another.

Transforming strangers to lovers is the mission of the spiritual life. If spirituality is the connectedness of all things, prayer enables the revelation of this intimacy. Jesus commanded his followers to pray even for enemies, which suggests to me that even those people or things from which we're most estranged may be brought close to our hearts in prayer. Whether welcoming enemies, external strangers, or the stranger within, prayer helps us understand our relatedness, our integrity, with them, helping us to overcome the enmity, the "dividing walls of hostility." Just as we accept God's welcome in prayer, we are thereby enabled to extend that welcome to others.

Remember my terrifying dream of the gay man tapping me on my shoulder? Only in prayer was I able to welcome him as part of who God created me to be. Only in prayer am I able to continue a process of integrity, integrating my sexuality and spirituality. Prayer offered sanctuary to this stranger or perceived enemy within, revealing our intimacy.

Welcoming the stranger of sexuality into their prayer life, Christians may better be able to bring the "enemy" of homosexuality and homosexual persons into their prayer life. Lesbian and gay Christians collectively may serve as both prompter and model of the struggle to reconcile spirituality and sexuality.

The intimacy of sexuality and spirituality, of sense and spirit, of body and spirit may be revealed in our souls as we introduce them to one another in prayer. Strangers may become lovers, inviting one another to dance out our faith together. This dance may mean stepping on or out of lines, beyond former boundaries of expected performance. Rather than being programmed by a legalism that worships the false god of perfection, the soul of integrity is informed and inspired by the harmony of the true God's own integrity as it strives to "be mature as God in heaven is mature."

The soul that dances according to the law is stiff and fearful, as if salvation depended on its performance. It may tend toward magical thinking, that which believes God may be manipulated by one's actions, that salvation is somehow earned. The soul striving for integrity within and with God is relaxed and faithful, as if salvation has already been granted. Such a soul seeks to let go of controls on God, inviting God instead to be the centering force of its dance, a dance let loose by God's grace. An experience of this grace is the conversion realization that God's own integrity will not allow the letting go of the soul's hand in the dance.

To heal, to bring integrity to our prayer life, the church must affirm God's gift of *sexuality* as a means of grace, a means of accepting God's welcome, a means of "enjoying God and glorifying God forever," which is, according to the Westminster Catechism, the chief end of human existence.

To heal, to bring integrity to our spiritual communion, the church must affirm God's gift of *homosexuality* as a means of grace, a means of accepting God's welcome, a means of "enjoying God and glorifying God forever."

The church's inability to accept the faithful experience of its gay and lesbian members is, at heart, a spiritual problem rather than a sexual one. Unable to be inclusive of gays and lesbians in our prayer life, we are unable to be inclusive of them in our life as community. Unable to dance with them in prayer, the church is unable to dance with them in spiritual communion.

Thanks be to God, the church is beginning to examine the beams in its own eye, its phobias related to sex and homosexuality as well as its sexism and heterosexism. As those beams are removed, beams of more light will enable the church to see God's grace in the eyes of lesbian and gay Christians. Dancing our faith together will be less awkward, more grace-full. No longer strangers, we will embrace one another as lovers of God.